Gramsci's Common Sense

Kate Crehan

Gramsci's Common Sense

INEQUALITY AND ITS NARRATIVES

Duke University Press / Durham and London / 2016

Printed in the United States of America on acid-free paper ∞
Designed by Courtney Leigh Baker
Typeset in Minion Pro by Copperline

Library of Congress Cataloging-in-Publication Data
Names: Crehan, Kate A. F., author.
Title: Gramsci's common sense : inequality and its narratives /
Kate Crehan.
Description: Durham : Duke University Press, 2016. |
Includes bibliographical references and index.
Identifiers: LCCN 2016020792 (print)
LCCN 2016022035 (ebook)
ISBN 9780822362197 (hardcover : alk. paper)
ISBN 9780822362395 (pbk. : alk. paper)
ISBN 9780822373742 (e-book)
Subjects: LCSH: Gramsci, Antonio, 1891–1937—Political
and social views. | Marxian historiography. | Communism—
Italy—History. | Philosophy, Marxist.
Classification: LCC HX288.C74 2016 (print)
LCC HX288 (ebook)
DDC 355.43092—dc23
LC record available at https://lccn.loc.gov/2016020792

COVER ART: (*top*) Occupy Wall Street signs, epa european
pressphoto agency b.v./Alamy; (*bottom*) Occupy Vancouver
signs, Mark Oun/Alamy.

Every social stratum has its own "Common Sense" and its own "Good Sense," which are basically the most widespread conception of life and of man. —ANTONIO GRAMSCI, *The Prison Notebooks*

CONTENTS

For intellectuals who like to think of themselves as progressive, the relation between the knowledge they produce as scholars and the world beyond the academy is an ever-present question. This is a book about a thinker for whom this question was central, the Italian Marxist and cofounder of the Italian communist party, Antonio Gramsci. Paradoxically, it was his arrest in 1926 by the fascist government of Benito Mussolini that led to his greatest legacy: the prison notebooks he wrote while incarcerated. Condemned to twenty years in prison, his life as a political activist cut short, Gramsci was determined to continue his political engagement in the only way left open to him: a rigorous program of study. Prior to his imprisonment, he had written a vast quantity of journalism, but this he considered ephemeral, "written for the day," as he put it in one of the letters he wrote from prison (*PLII*, 66). Tellingly, he rejected any attempts to publish his journalism in book form. Prison, he hoped, would provide him with the time necessary for more in-depth, scholarly analysis. As a scholar, he had exacting standards, but he also believed that the truly important knowledge is knowledge that travels beyond the academic ghetto. This is a very different attitude from that espoused by another celebrated theorist of power, Michel Foucault. By the end of his life, according to his biographer Didier Eribon, Foucault worried that his books were being circulated too widely: "[T]oo wide a circulation for scholarly books was disastrous for their reception, because it brought with it a multitude of misunderstandings. The moment a book went beyond the circle of those to whom it was really addressed, that is, those scholars who knew the problems with which it dealt and the theoretical traditions to which it referred, it no longer produced 'effects of knowledge' but 'effects of opinion,' as Foucault called them." (Eribon 1991, 292)

Gramsci has none of Foucault's disdain for the effects of opinion. Indeed, the shared "opinions" that inform so much of how people live their day-to-day lives, and the processes by which they come to be shared, are one of the major concerns of the prison notebooks. He saw such "opinions" as playing a crucial role in the shaping of the social order—a social order he sought to change. A key term here is *senso comune* (common sense), the term Gramsci uses for all those heterogeneous beliefs people arrive at not through critical reflection, but encounter as already existing, self-evident truths. It is important to note, however, that the Italian *senso comune* is a far more neutral term than the English *common sense*. The English term, with its overwhelmingly positive connotations, puts the emphasis, so to speak, on the "sense," *senso comune* on the held-in-common (*comune*) nature of the beliefs. In the notebooks, Gramsci reflects on the complicated roots of such collective knowledge, its shifting and often contradictory components, the ways it becomes accepted as beyond question—and by whom—and when, and how it changes. The collective here is important: "What matters is not the opinion of Tom, Dick, and Harry but the ensemble of opinions that have become collective and a powerful factor in society" (*PNIII*, 347). Ultimately, what interests this political activist is the knowledge that mobilizes political movements capable of bringing about radical transformation. Indeed, he questions whether "a philosophical movement" is "properly so called when it is devoted to creating a specialized culture among restricted intellectual groups" (*SPN*, 330). For him, unlike Foucault, the most important knowledge would seem to be precisely knowledge that has spread beyond "those scholars who knew the problems with which it dealt and the theoretical traditions to which it referred," knowledge that, when embodied in self-aware collectivities, has the potential to act in the world. And for him, the primary such collectivities are classes.

Gramsci is often thought of as one of the Marxist tradition's foremost theorists of culture. What is often overlooked, as I argued in an earlier book, *Gramsci, Culture, and Anthropology*, is that culture is central to the notebooks because culture, understood in its anthropological sense of ways of life, is for their author one of the major ways the inequalities of class are lived on a day-to-day basis. That argument is also at the heart of this book, but here, rather than focus on Gramsci's understanding of culture, I tease out his understanding of class. I suggest that it is because he saw the fundamental inequalities of class as woven through every aspect of life that he paid so much attention to the mapping of *senso comune*, or popular opinion, and why he approached this mapping as he did. Given that the concept of class nowadays is so often taken as referring only to relations of economic inequality, it is important to stress that for Gramsci class includes far more than this.

The notebooks, as I read them, are underpinned by a concept of class, but one that is broad and inclusive, and certainly not confined to the realm of the economic. This is a notion of class that names structural inequalities reproduced over time. But while this inequality may in the famous last analysis have its roots in fundamental economic relations, it is never a simple epiphenomenon of these: class can take many different forms. The relationship between the fundamental inequalities that shape the realities human beings confront and the ever-shifting flux of lived experience is always complex and nuanced, never crudely deterministic. In the notebooks, we see their author reflecting on the myriad ways inequality manifests itself, on the varied landscapes of power it produces, and the complex ways those landscapes are experienced by those inhabiting them. It is easy to miss the centrality of class to the notebooks, in part because nowhere in them is the concept of class defined in any precise way. This, however, is because the nature of class is, as it were, their ultimate topic. We might think here of Marx's *Capital*, which, as many have complained, also never provides a clear definition of class. The point, it seems to me, is that both *Capital* and the prison notebooks set out to explore the complex ways structural inequality manifests itself in the context of human history. There is no succinct definition of class because the protean forms it assumes in actual times and places cannot be reduced to some simple essence.

One of the forms class assumes is particular worldviews. As human beings, we make sense of our lives through the narratives our particular time and place have made available to us—accounts of "how things are" with deep but never simple roots in the fundamental social relations of the worlds we inhabit. We may challenge or even reject those narratives, but the webs of intelligibility in which our socialization wraps us from the day of our birth are a reality from which we all begin; we are all, to some degree, creatures of popular opinion. And yet, at certain historical moments, there is radical social transformation. When and why does this happen? Running through the notebooks is the question: What is the relation between popular opinion and social transformation?

To map Gramsci's multifaceted understanding of class, I focus on three of his central concepts: subalternity, intellectuals, and common sense. I explore how, taken together, these constitute an approach to the terrain of class inequality as lived reality, one that opens up the diverse and shifting forms it can assume. Approaching inequality in this way allows us to trace out the complex relationship between the actuality of the circumstances in which people live and their explanations of those circumstances, the narratives they use to make sense of the world they encounter.

One reason why the passage from knowledge to opinion is such a complex question for Gramsci is that, on the one hand, he has enormous respect for those termed in the language of the day "the masses." Indeed, as we shall see, he believes that political narratives capable of mounting an effective challenge to the dominant hegemony have their roots in the experience of those masses. On the other hand, he is not a populist; intellectuals, for him, have a crucial role to play in elaborating and rendering coherent the incoherent knowledge possessed by those who are subordinated, those he terms subalterns. It is equally crucial, however, that the coherent philosophy developed by intellectuals find expression as a new common sense that resonates with those subalterns, and that the masses recognize as *their* knowledge. Only then does the sophisticated philosophy of intellectuals have the potential to become "a powerful factor in society" (*PNIII*: 347). In sum, the relationship between subalterns and intellectuals is, for Gramsci, profoundly dialogical; tracing out the complicated dialogue between the knowledge of the intellectuals and popular opinion is one of the notebooks' central concerns.

Complicating the relationship between knowledge and opinion still further, Gramsci sees the intellectuals who build on subaltern common sense to create a new philosophy as themselves produced by that subaltern group. One way this happens is through the political party: "The political party for some social groups is nothing other than their specific way of elaborating their own category of organic intellectuals directly in the political and philosophical field" (*SPN*: 15). The intellectuals produced organically by a group or class as it rises to power need to be distinguished from traditional intellectuals. This distinction, and the web of relationships linking intellectuals, subalterns, and common sense is at the heart of Gramsci's approach to inequality as lived reality, an approach that sees class as a complex knotting together of economic, social, and political realities with narratives of those realities.

This book is organized in two parts. The first four chapters map out the broad contours of subalternity, intellectuals, and common sense as laid out in the notebooks: chapter 1 focuses on subalternity; chapter 2 on intellectuals; and chapter 3 on common sense. Chapter 4 argues that, taken together, these three concepts constitute a theorization of the complex, dialogical relationship between the experience of inequality, exploitation, and oppression, and the political narratives that articulate that experience.

The three chapters of part 2 address the question of the notebooks' relevance for contemporary analysts. Given that they were written some eighty years ago, can the reflections of this twentieth-century, Italian Marxist, nonetheless provide a useful starting point for those interested in understanding twenty-first-century inequality and its historical roots? To suggest the potential usefulness of Gramsci's linked concepts of subalternity, intellectuals, and common sense I have taken them to three different case studies, one historical and two contemporary. To help elucidate the often misunderstood concept of organic intellectuals, chapter 5 takes us back to eighteenth-century Scotland and a moment when a new bourgeois order, based on industrial capitalism, was beginning to emerge. The chapter focuses on Adam Smith, a thinker who would come to be seen as one of the first theorists of capitalism. What does this luminary of the Scottish Enlightenment look like if we go beyond his popular image and locate him in his historical context? Can we see him as a bourgeois, organic intellectual? I have chosen a historical rather than a contemporary figure as an example of an organic intellectual because it is only with the benefit of hindsight that we can definitively identify an emerging class's organic intellectuals. Within the flux of the contemporary moment, it is never certain which of the many existing currents of thought genuinely represent a new hegemony in gestation.

The case studies in chapters 6 and 7 take us from the eighteenth century to the present day, and from the concept of organic intellectuals to that of common sense. Each chapter looks at a political movement that could be seen as having attempted to popularize, or create, a particular common sense: chapter 6 focuses on the Tea Party, a movement from the political right, chapter 7 on Occupy Wall Street, an upswelling of discontent that brought together a range of activists from the left. The chapters explore the two movements' different forms of common sense. In the case of the Tea Party, this is a common sense with roots in a far-from-new capitalist narrative, one often seen as originating with Adam Smith. Occupy Wall Street, by contrast, was perhaps struggling toward a new configuration of common sense—one capable of capturing in a visceral way the feeling of many in twenty-first-century America that they are living in an economic system that benefits only the wealthy. The concluding chapter reflects on what the approach to class we find in Gramsci's notebooks has to offer readers in the twenty-first century, particularly those interested in addressing the gross inequalities of our contemporary, globalized world.

In the course of writing this book, I have benefited from discussions of Gramsci with many colleagues and friends. Joseph Buttigieg, Alessandro Carlucci, Marcus Green, Aisha Khan, Shirley Lindenbaum, Maureen Mackintosh, Mauro Pala, Frank Rosengarten, Steve Striffler, and Cosimo Zene all helped me think through the issues raised by the notebooks, and the value to be gained from reading them today. Two workshops at which I presented preliminary versions of some of my arguments helped me refine and sometimes rethink those arguments: the 2010 workshop organized by Cosimo Zene at SOAS, which brought together Gramsci's theorization of subalternity with that of B. R. Ambedkar's of Dalits, and the 2013 workshop, "Antonio Gramsci: In the World," organized by Roberto Dainotto and Fredric Jameson at Duke University. The two anonymous reviewers for Duke University Press provided extremely insightful and helpful comments.

Mark Porter-Webb's help with finding and formatting the images of the "We are the 99 Percent" Tumblr posts and the Occupy slogans was invaluable. I am also enormously grateful to my editor at Duke, Gisela Fosado, for her support for my project and for her exemplary efficiency.

FSPN   *Further Selections from the Prison Notebooks/Antonio Gramsci.*
       Translated and edited by Derek Boothman. Minneapolis: University of Minnesota Press, 1995.

PLI   *Letters from Prison: Antonio Gramsci*, vol. I. Edited by Frank
       Rosengarten. Translated by Ray Rosenthal. New York: Columbia
       University Press, 1994.

PLII   *Letters from Prison: Antonio Gramsci*, vol. II. Edited by Frank
       Rosengarten. Translated by Ray Rosenthal. New York: Columbia
       University Press, 1994.

PNI   *Antonio Gramsci: Prison Notebooks*, vol. I. Edited by Joseph A.
       Buttigieg. Translated by Joseph A. Buttigieg and Antonio Callari.
       New York: Columbia University Press, 1992.

PNII   *Antonio Gramsci: Prison Notebooks*, vol. II. Translated and edited
       by Joseph A. Buttigieg. New York: Columbia University Press,
       1996.

PNIII *Antonio Gramsci: Prison Notebooks*, vol. III. Translated and
       edited by Joseph A. Buttigieg. New York: Columbia University
       Press, 2007.

SCW   *Antonio Gramsci: Selections from Cultural Writings.* Edited
       by David Forgacs and Geoffrey Nowell-Smith. Translated by
       William Boelhower. London: Lawrence and Wishart, 1985.

SPN   *Selections from the Prison Notebooks of Antonio Gramsci.* Edited
       and translated by Quintin Hoare and Geoffrey Nowell Smith.
       London: Lawrence and Wishart, 1971.

PART I. *Subalternity, Intellectuals, and Common Sense*

Subalternity

It really must be stressed that it is precisely the first elements, the most elementary things, which are the first to be forgotten. . . . The first element is that there really do exist rulers and ruled, leaders and led.
—SELECTIONS FROM THE PRISON NOTEBOOKS, 144

This is a book about narratives of inequality. In his history of modern capitalism, *Capital in the Twenty-First Century*, Thomas Piketty observes, "The history of inequality is shaped by the way economic, social, and political actors view what is just and what is not, as well as by the relative power of those actors and the collective choices that result" (Piketty 2014, 20). As an economist, Piketty's focus, however, is on the quantitative measurement of inequality, and the policy reforms that might lessen it, rather than on the processes by which "economic, social, and political actors" arrive at their understandings of "what is just and what is not." It is those processes that this book explores. What are the origins of the narratives that explain why specific inequalities are inevitable, necessary, indeed beneficial, or conversely unjust, harmful, and far from inevitable? And how do certain of those narratives establish themselves as self-evident truths, the kind of "truths" that the Italian Marxist, Antonio Gramsci, refers to as *senso comune* (common sense)?

Inequality was once commonly theorized using a Marxist concept of class. In recent years, however, class has fallen from favor in both academic and popular circles. But if we want to understand inequality, how it is lived, and why people see it as just or conversely unjust, perhaps we have been too quick to write off the usefulness of a Marxist notion of class. One reason this approach to inequality has fallen into disfavor is that all too often nowadays the Marxist concept of class is understood as confined to the realm of the economic, as when Richard Wolin writes of "orthodox Marxism's stress on the universalizing framework of 'class,' which reduced social conflict unilaterally to the opposition between wage labor and capital" (2010, 358). Understood in this reductive way, class is indeed easy to dismiss as overly simplistic. The Marxist tradition, however, contains far richer and more interesting versions of class that encompass the many other ways structural inequality manifests itself, and that pay attention to the different ways people in different social locations understand "what is just and what is not." A particularly rich and nuanced approach to inequality is to be found in the now celebrated notebooks Gramsci wrote during his years of imprisonment by the fascist regime of Benito Mussolini. At the heart of this approach is a concern with the complex passage from lived experience, itself always mediated by the existing explanations of that experience, to political narratives and political movements capable of bringing about radical change.

Class, as long as it is not defined in narrowly economic terms, is fundamental to Gramsci's thought. I approach his nuanced and multifaceted understanding of class through three concepts that I see as central to his theorization of power: subalternity, intellectuals, and common sense. Tracing his use of these concepts and their interlinkages provides something like a map of his approach to the complex relationship between the particular economic and political vantage points from which people view the world, and their conceptions of that world.

This chapter introduces the concept of subalternity we find in the notebooks. First, however, it is necessary to say something about the nature of those notebooks as a text. Unfinished, never prepared for publication by Gramsci, and consisting as they do of a series of separate notes that range over very disparate topics, they present the reader with a challenge. And unless we understand the conditions under which they were written, and the basic questions they address, it is difficult to grasp the creative and open Marxism that informs the overall project, a Marxism that is always attentive to the multiple forms in which the inequality between "rulers and ruled, leaders and led" manifests itself.

Reading Gramsci

In November 1926, even though as an elected parliamentary deputy he should have had immunity from prosecution, Gramsci was arrested by the fascist authorities. He and twenty-one other leaders of the Italian communist party were then subjected to a show trial in June 1928. Conviction was never in doubt, and one of the longest sentences was handed down to the future author of the prison notebooks: twenty years, four months, and five days. Referring to this physically diminutive but intellectually imposing prisoner, the prosecutor famously declared: "We must prevent this brain from functioning for twenty years." For his part, Gramsci was determined to keep his brain functioning. He petitioned for a single cell and permission to write. The petition was granted in January 1929, and on the 8th of February he would make his first entry in the first notebook. He continued to work on the notebooks until 1935, when his deteriorating health made further work impossible. He would die in 1937, a patient in the Quisisana clinic still under surveillance, a few days after the expiration of his now reduced sentence.

After their publication in Italy in the late 1940s, the notebooks soon began to acquire an international readership. A key moment in the Anglophone world was the publication of Quintin Hoare and Geoffrey Nowell Smith's *Selections from the Prison Notebooks of Antonio Gramsci* (1971), which includes a substantial number of the notes, organized thematically. The volume was rapidly taken up by social scientists across a wide range of disciplines and has never gone out of print. Raymond Williams's *Marxism and Literature*, published in 1977, further popularized Gramsci's concepts among those unable to read Italian, as did the work of Stuart Hall and other members of University of Birmingham's Centre for Cultural Studies. As yet, however, there is no complete English translation of the notebooks, although the first three volumes of a planned five-volume edition, edited by Joseph Buttigieg, have appeared.

As a text, the thirty-three notebooks resist succinct summary. While there are certain recurrent themes, their richness lies in the ways their author explores and expands on these themes; grasping the argument requires close reading. In part this is because Gramsci gives us not polished summations of his reflections but rather tracks left by a mind continually on the move. We accompany Gramsci on his journeys through a thickly wooded intellectual terrain. Sometimes he sticks to the paths already marked out, but often he veers off, carving out his own path as he challenges conventional categories and established thinking. This is particularly true of his writings on intellectuals and the production of knowledge. Keeping up with this thinker requires that we pay careful attention to the twists and turns of his ever-active mind.

The very form of the notebooks confronts us with a problem. Each one consists of series of separate notes, varying in length from a sentence or two to many pages. Together they "possess all the intricacies and perplexities of a textual labyrinth," as Buttigieg has written (*PNI*, ix). If we are to find our way through this labyrinth, it is helpful to begin by considering the conditions in which Gramsci was writing, and how he approached the task of recording his reflections.

Two people who were crucial for Gramsci's physical and intellectual survival during his incarceration were Tatiana Schucht, a sister of his wife Julia, and Piero Sraffa, a left-leaning Italian economist and long-standing friend. Tatiana was an unfailing source of practical and emotional support. Remaining in Italy until his death, largely so that she would be in a position to provide this support, Tatiana did everything she could to ease the many hardships of prison life. Keeping him supplied with writing materials was one of her tasks. The prisoner was very clear as to what he wanted. She was, he wrote to her, to provide him with "notebooks of a normal format like those used in school, and not with too many pages, at most forty to fifty, so they are not inevitably transformed into increasingly jumbled miscellaneous tomes" (*PLII*, 141). Maintaining order was not easy, however. Gramsci would work on a number of different notebooks simultaneously. His intention was to keep different ones for different topics, but this was not always possible. For one thing, his mind worked in such a way that he was continually seeing connections between apparently separate topics. Another problem was that the prison authorities insisted that the notebooks be kept in storage. At any one time he was only allowed to have a limited number of them with him in his cell. Consequently, he would sometimes use whichever was at hand. To add to the reader's difficulty, the notes themselves can be fragmentary and elliptical, leaving them open to a wide range of interpretations. The openness of his thought is in fact one of his strengths as a theorist, but it does mean that if we are to find our way through Gramsci's labyrinth, we need to read him with extreme care.

Although living in Britain by the time of Gramsci's arrest, Sraffa made regular trips to Italy, during which he would visit Gramsci in prison. He was also in contact with a number of leading Italian communists living in exile, and he spearheaded a campaign in the international media for the release of this major political figure. This helped ensure that Mussolini's prisoner was not forgotten by the wider world. Most important, as regards the notebooks, Sraffa opened an account with a Milan bookstore in Gramsci's name (paid for by the independently wealthy Sraffa) that allowed him to obtain books and other publications. Although he was limited in his ordering by what the prison authorities would allow, the account still enabled him to obtain a wide range of books and periodicals. Without Tatiana and Sraffa, it is unlikely that we would have the notebooks: it was their support that enabled them to be written, and after their author's death it was they who ensured the notebooks' survival.

In addition to the notebooks, we also have many of his letters written from prison, available in English in Frank Rosengarten's superb edition. The largest number were written to Tatiana. Once sentenced, prisoners were only allowed to write to relatives. Although he wrote to various members of his family, Tatiana became his main correspondent. In part this was because he often found it hard to write to his wife. She was living in Moscow throughout his imprisonment but had various emotional and physical problems and wrote only intermittently.

The bookstore account was a particularly crucial resource given the dialogic character of Gramsci's thought. Most commonly a note will begin with his engaging with another author. In one of his letters to Tatiana, written in December 1930, he explains his need as an intellectual to feel himself engaged in a dialogue: "Perhaps it is because my entire intellectual formation has been of a polemical order; even thinking 'disinterestedly' is difficult for me, that is, studying for study's sake. Only occasionally, but rarely, does it happen that I lose myself in a specific order of reflections and find, so to speak, in the things themselves enough interest to devote myself to their analysis. Ordinarily, I need to set out from a dialogical or dialectical standpoint, otherwise I don't experience any intellectual stimulation. As I once told you, I don't like to cast stones into the darkness; I want to feel a concrete interlocutor or adversary" (*PLI*, 369).

The reluctance to focus simply on "the things themselves," however, is not only about wanting to "feel a concrete interlocutor." It also speaks to a concern with ideas as living realities rather than pure thought, abstracted from the messy flux of day-to-day life. The books he requested included not only serious academic scholarship but popular history, sociology, politics, and writings on cultural topics. And his orders included a range of newspapers and periodicals, from as wide a political spectrum as the prison authorities would allow. One reason he insisted on reading so much popular, ephemeral stuff is because, for him, what is important are not debates confined to a few intellectuals, but the ideas and beliefs that inform and shape the lives lived by the mass of the population.

Gramsci was especially interested in ideas and beliefs which had established themselves as "common sense" (senso comune). As he writes in one note (part of which I quoted in the preface): "[I]s a philosophical movement properly so called when it is devoted to creating a specialised culture among restricted intellectual groups, or rather when, and only when, in the process of elaborating a form of thought superior to 'common sense' and coherent on a scientific plane, it never forgets to remain in contact with the simple[1] [common people] and indeed finds in this contact the source of the problems it sets out to study and to resolve? (*SPN*, 330). Were he alive today and writing in the United States, Gramsci would certainly be an avid follower of the whole spectrum of media, from WBAI to Fox, from *The Nation* to Rupert Murdoch's tabloids, not to mention the ever-expanding media landscape, including social media, of the internet. For the contemporary Anglophone reader, the dialogical character of the prison notebooks can present problems. Reading Gramsci's reflections on what he is reading is often like hearing a single participant in an ongoing conversation. Those other participants range from major thinkers to long-forgotten journalists, and for those unfamiliar with these interlocutors and the relevant debates, the argument can be hard to follow.

The sometimes fragmentary form of the notes is not, however, merely the result of Gramsci's need to engage in debate and his concern with ideas as they are lived. There is also the problem of what he referred to as his "methodological scruples." He had to overcome enormous obstacles to achieve his education: poor schools with inadequate teachers in his impoverished homeland of Sardinia, a lack of family resources, and his own ill health. Thanks to hard work and extraordinary persistence, he eventually won a highly competitive, although far from lucrative, scholarship to Turin University. For several years in Turin, despite the extreme poverty to which his meagerly funded scholarship condemned him, he studied language and philology with ferocious intensity, before finally dropping out to become a full-time political activist and journalist. In later life, he would continue to hold scholarship to the highest standards, writing in one letter to Tatiana: "You must also keep in mind that the habit of rigorous philological discipline that I acquired during my university studies has given me perhaps an excessive supply of methodological scru-

---

1. Gramsci uses the term *semplici*. Given the pejorative connotations of the literal English translation "the simple," it is important to note that, as Marcus Green explains in his entry on *semplici* in the *Dizionario Gramsciano* (Liguori and Voza 2009), Gramsci uses this term "to refer to the Catholic Church's paternalistic view of common people and peasants as 'simple and sincere souls' in contrast to the Church's superior view of cultured intellectuals."

ples" (*PLII*, 52). In the notebooks he repeatedly stresses the provisional, unfinished character of his notes, writing, for instance, "These notes often consist of assertions that have not been verified, that may be called 'rough first drafts'; after further study, some of them may be discarded, and it might even be the case that the opposite of what they assert will be shown to be true" (*PNIII*, 231).

The conditions under which the prison notebooks were composed made scholarship worthy of the name impossible in their author's eyes. For such a dialogic thinker, access to books and periodicals was crucial, and yet before ordering any publication from his bookstore account he had to apply for permission to the prison authorities, permission that might well be denied. Moreover, as the official prison stamp to be found on each page of every notebook testifies, every word he wrote was subject to the oversight of the prison censors. Over the years the degree of censorship varied, but it was a constant presence, although, as Marcus Green argues, its role in shaping the notebooks has been much exaggerated (Green 2011a). His lack of access to adequate library resources was, for Gramsci, a far greater obstacle to serious scholarship. Earlier in the same letter in which he notes his "methodological scruples," he also explains: "One might say that right now I no longer have a true program of studies and work and of course this was bound to happen. I had set myself the aim of reflecting on a particular set of problems, but it was inevitable that at a certain stage these reflections would of necessity move into a phase of documentation and then to a phase of work and elaboration that requires great libraries" (*PLII*, 51–52).

The notebooks document a thought process in which Gramsci is continually torn between the creativity of his ever-active mind, forever throwing off ideas and suggesting new avenues of research to pursue, and his methodological scruples. The emotional force of those scruples is suggested by this sentence at the end of one note: "In general, remember that all these notes are provisional and written as they flow from the pen: they must be reviewed and checked in detail because they undoubtedly contain many imprecisions, anachronisms, wrong approaches, etc., *that do not imply wrongdoing* because the notes have solely the function of quick memoranda" (*PNII*, 158; emphasis mine). The phrase "that do not imply wrongdoing" is surely very revealing. If we want to understand the notebooks' often fragmentary and allusive style we need to remember not only the very real and physical censors omnipresent in his prison life, but also the equally inescapable academic policemen permanently lodged in his head. One way it seems he is able to quiet these internal judges is by continually reassuring himself that what he writes is no more than "rough first drafts." The question of what Gramsci actually achieved in the prison notebooks is, of course, another matter.

Something that can frustrate contemporary analysts interested in using this Marxist's concepts in their own work is the notebooks' apparent lack of fixed and precise definitions of basic terms such as *subalternity*, *intellectuals*, and *common sense*. Also, the notebooks were written at a particular, and now somewhat distant, historical moment; their reflections are responses to specific events and interlocutors viewed in the context of that historical moment. Nonetheless, underlying the notes as a whole it is possible to trace out the contours of an analytical approach that we can take to times and places quite remote from Italy in the mid-twentieth century. As an anthropologist, I have attempted to take this approach and combine it with the detailed ethnography that is a strength of my discipline.[2] The case studies in part II of this book, while based on secondary literature rather than my own fieldwork, represent concrete examples of how contemporary analysts might use Gramsci's concepts in their own studies.

The notebooks certainly challenge the reader. Their note form and their dialogic character make it hard sometimes to follow Gramsci's thought as he debates with absent adversaries and pursues ideas as they lead him down new and sometimes unexpected paths. He himself, however, gives us some useful guidance. How should one proceed, he asks, and he clearly has Marx in mind here, if one's goal is "to understand the birth of a conception of the world which has never been systematically expounded by its founder"? (*SPN*, 382). We should, he tells us, look for the spirit or leitmotif in the body of thought as a whole: "Search for the *Leitmotiv*, for the rhythm of the thought as it develops, should be more important than that for single casual affirmations and isolated aphorisms" (*SPN*, 383–84). It is this rhythm and this leitmotif (or leitmotifs) that I have sought to hear in my reading of the notebooks.

Subaltern Voices

In the last thirty years, Gramsci's concept of subalternity has been taken up by many analysts, particularly scholars of the Global South. A much debated question is the degree to which subalterns are able to understand and articulate their own subalternity. This is a central question in the notebooks, and, indeed, this book. Two contemporary theorists with diametrically opposed positions on this issue are Gayatri Spivak, feminist literary critic and coeditor of the first *Subaltern Studies Reader*; and James Scott, author of the much cited

2. See, for instance, Crehan 1997, 2011a, and 2014.

Weapons of the Weak: Everyday Forms of Peasant Resistance; Domination and the Arts of Resistance; and other works celebrating the agency of the subordinated. Teasing out something of Spivak's and Scott's opposed positions can help clarify the epistemological claims at stake here and, before turning to Gramsci himself, I want to look briefly at their respective arguments.

In a celebrated article, Spivak took as her title the question: "Can the Subaltern Speak?"[3] She has acknowledged Gramsci as a significant influence, this influence coming primarily via the early work of the historian Ranajit Guha and the Subaltern Studies Group (Spivak 2010b, 232–33). She was, she tells us, "so overwhelmed" by Guha's "On Some Aspects of the Historiography of Colonial India" (1988), essentially the manifesto of the Subaltern Studies Group, that she withdrew an earlier version of "Can the Subaltern Speak?," then called "Power and Desire," in order to rethink and rewrite it radically. Later, however, she would come to reject what she saw as Guha's transformation of the Gramscian notion of subalternity, explaining: "I did not then understand that Guha's understanding of the subaltern world would subsequently take on board a much broader transformation of the Gramscian idea insofar as the subaltern, according to Guha, would call out in a collective voice. I never went that way at all" (Spivak 2010b, 233). But how much of a transformation is this? As I read the notebooks, Gramsci's primary interest is very much the collective voice. Remember his insistence in one of the passages I quoted in the preface that what is important is "the ensemble of opinions that have become collective and a powerful factor in society" (*PNIII*, 347). I shall come back to the question of individual and collective subaltern voices, and to the role the Subaltern Studies Group played in popularizing the term subaltern. For the moment, I want to concentrate on the central argument of Spivak's essay: her rejection of the claims of theorists of the Global North to "know" and speak for subalterns of the Global South.

Two theorists with whom she engages at length are Michel Foucault and Gilles Deleuze, focusing particularly on the published exchange between them, "Intellectuals and Power: A Conversation between Michel Foucault and Gilles Deleuze" (Foucault 1977). She notes that the two French theorists assume, indeed assert, that "the oppressed, if given the chance . . . *can speak*

---

3. The most widely known version of "Can the Subaltern Speak?" is probably the one first published in Nelson and Grossberg (1988, 271–313). An earlier version, "Can the Subaltern Speak? Speculations on Widow Sacrifice," had appeared in *Wedge* (Spivak 1985, 120–30). Spivak (1999, 244–311) is an expanded version of the essay. Morris (2010) includes both the 1988 and the 1999 versions.

and know their conditions" (Spivak 2010a, 252). She quotes Foucault's insistence that "the masses *know* perfectly well, clearly . . . they know far better than [the intellectual] and they certainly say it very well" (quoted in Spivak 2010a, 241, Foucault's emphasis). Spivak points out that the "masses" Foucault and Deleuze have in mind here are those of the Global North.[4] In other words, subalterns who have long been subject to advanced capitalist regimes and their sophisticated mechanisms of social reproduction. Spivak's focus is, as she puts it, "on the other side of the international division of labour," that is, subalterns in the Global South. It is with reference to those subalterns that she poses her famous question: Can the subaltern speak? (Spivak 2010a, 252). Her primary concern, however, is not subalterns in the Global South in general, but the particular predicament of female subalterns, doubly silenced, first because of the subalternity they share with male subalterns, then because of the subalternity they experience as women.

Spivak goes on to explore the nature of this silencing through an examination of the debates around the British colonial authorities' abolition of *sati* (widow sacrifice) in India. What we see in these debates, according to Spivak, is the meanings of women's actions being argued over by men, with the individual women themselves rendered mute. As Spivak puts it, ending the practice whereby some Hindu widows would immolate themselves on their husband's funeral pyre, "has been generally understood as 'White men saving brown women from brown men.' White women . . . have not produced an alternative understanding. Against this is the Indian nativist argument, a parody of the nostalgia for lost origins: 'The women actually wanted to die'" (Spivak 2010a, 269). Spivak's point here is that we never hear the testimony of the women themselves, although she is quick to add, "Such a testimony would not be ideology-transcendent or 'fully' subjective, of course, but it would have constituted the ingredients for producing a countersentence" (Spivak 2010a, 269).

It would take us too far afield to follow Spivak's complex and nuanced arguments in any detail, but her basic argument that the condition of subalternity involves a particular kind of muting, is certainly central to Gramsci's under-

---

4. In fairness to Foucault, it should be noted that in the sentence quoted by Spivak, Foucault is specifically referring to the French masses of May 1968. Spivak omits the beginning of the sentence, which makes this clear. The full sentence in the original (a conversation recorded in 1973) reads: "In the most recent upheaval [May 1968, popularly known as the 'events of May'], the intellectual discovered that the masses no longer need him to gain knowledge: they *know* perfectly well, without illusion; they know far better than he and they are certainly capable of expressing themselves" (Foucault 1977, 207).

standing of subalternity. The position of Spivak (and Gramsci) here is very different from that of James Scott. For Scott, subalterns can and do speak. This is, indeed, at the heart of his argument in *Domination and the Arts of Resistance*. Scott accepts that subaltern speech may be muted in the presence of the powerful but insists that, nonetheless, "[e]very subordinate group creates, out of its ordeal, a 'hidden transcript' that represents a critique of power spoken behind the back of the dominant" (1990, xii). And as long as theorists are prepared to seek out the secluded spots where the exploited and oppressed feel free to speak, they can find these "hidden transcripts." It is, as he puts it, "outside the earshot of powerholders, where the hidden transcript is to be sought. The disparity between what we find here and what is said in the presence of power is a rough measure of what has been suppressed from power-laden political communication. The hidden transcript is, for this reason, the privileged site for nonhegemonic, contrapuntal, dissident, subversive discourse" (1990, 25).

Scott's insistence that all subordinate groups have their own "critique of power," and his general respect for such groups' ability to understand and articulate such critiques are shared by many anthropologists. One of the strengths of the anthropological tradition is precisely a stress on genuinely listening to those studied. As Malinowski so famously claimed in his introduction to *Argonauts of the Western Pacific*, the final goal of the anthropologist is "to grasp the native's point of view" (Malinowski 1984, 25). Gramsci's frequent disparagement of subaltern common sense, and his insistence that coherent and effective critiques of power require the intervention of intellectuals, albeit the organic intellectuals who have emerged out of subaltern experience, can strike anthropologists as patronizing. It is important to remember, however, that the Italian Marxist's goal was never simply to grasp the subaltern view, to see the world through subaltern eyes: his goal was social transformation. And this required not only the mapping of common sense and the identification of the good sense he saw as embedded within it, but its translation (within the context of the political party) into effective political narratives capable of mobilizing large masses.

Spivak does not specifically engage with Scott in "Can the Subaltern Speak?" It seems likely, however, that she would see his approach as falling under what she dismisses as "[t]he banality of leftist intellectuals' lists of self-knowing, politically canny subalterns" (Spivak 2012, 243). The key difference between Scott and Spivak here is that for Scott, subalterns understand and are fully able to articulate their subalternity; it is only their fear of the "powerholders" that keeps them silent, while for Spivak their muting is more radical. Subalterns, especially female subalterns, have neither the words nor the concepts to articulate their condition in a language their oppressors are capable of comprehending.

So where does Gramsci stand on this question? There is no easy answer. Discovering whether or not the subalterns of the notebooks can "speak," and to the extent they do, what forms this speech might take, requires a careful reading of those notebooks; it cannot be summed up in a single sound bite. Having laid out something of what is at issue, therefore, I shall leave the question hanging, letting it resonate through this and the next two chapters before returning to it in chapter 4. First, we need to ask, who are subalterns in the notebooks? This is the question on which I focus for the remainder of this chapter.

Who Are Subalterns?

Thanks in large part to the Subaltern Studies Group, the term *subaltern* has now entered the academic mainstream. In the course of its journey, however, it has lost much of the multilayered richness it has in the notebooks. Beginning in the 1980s, the Subaltern Studies Group (which included Spivak) produced numerous papers, published in a series of volumes entitled *Subaltern Studies*, that challenged and rethought the standard accounts of Indian history. Although they would later move away from Gramsci, for the first five years nearly all their work would be, as an editor's note to *Selected Subaltern Studies* puts it, "an expansion and enrichment of Antonio Gramsci's notion of the subaltern" (Guha and Spivak 1988, xii). These South Asian scholars drew new attention to the place of this term in the notebooks, and all those interested in navigating the notebooks' labyrinth owe them a debt of gratitude. Their belief that the notion of the subaltern was in need of "expansion and enrichment," however, derives from a particular reading of the notebooks, one that argues that much of Gramsci's innovative terminology, such as his use of the category subalterns, and his references to "philosophy of praxis" rather than Marxism, should be seen as self-censorship, an anxiety to avoid arousing the suspicions of the prison censors.[5] According to this reading—one that has been enormously influential—*subaltern* is simply a euphemism for *proletariat*.[6] Having

5. See Haug (2000) for a detailed argument that the term *philosophy of praxis* is not a euphemism for Marxism, used by Gramsci to deflect the attention of the prison censors, but rather a way of naming Marxism that captures Gramsci's own understanding of Marxism.

6. Spivak (1992, 324), Lloyd (1993, 126), Rogall (1998, 2), and Beverley (1999, 12), for example, all claim that *subaltern* is Gramsci's code word for *proletariat* (see Green 2011a).

decided that *subaltern* was no more than a codeword for *proletariat*, it is not surprising that these scholars ended up, as David Ludden (one of the group) has put it, "reinventing subalternity" (cited in Green 2011a, 387). In effect, as Marcus Green writes in his authoritative account of the meaning of *subalternity* in the notebooks, "subaltern studies opened Gramsci to a new reading that highlighted the importance of the subaltern in his work, but then closed off its own reading by misinterpreting the meaning of the 'subaltern' in his writings" (2011a, 388). It is true that Gramsci did at times avoid using terms and names too obviously linked to Marxism or the Soviet Union, but by no means always; the term *proletariat*, for example, appears over seventy times in the notebooks (2011a, 392). As for *subaltern*, "[a]nalysis of the complete *Prison Notebooks* reveals no indication that Gramsci devised and used the term 'subaltern' as a codeword or euphemism for the word 'proletariat'" (2011a, 392). The problem with attributing the unfamiliar terminology we find in the notebooks to self-censorship is that this suppresses the open and expansive quality of Gramsci's Marxism.

In the case of subalternity, as with so many of the theoretical concepts in the notebooks, Gramsci never provides us with a precise definition. This, however, is not due to any lack of precision in his thinking. Rather, it speaks to a fundamental characteristic of his concepts. For Gramsci, as for Marx, while general abstract concepts have their place, they are often not particularly useful once the analysis moves to the specifics of a particular time and place. In the *Grundrisse*, for example, Marx writes of *production*: "[T]here is no production in general, . . . Production is always a *particular* branch of production— e.g. agriculture, cattle-raising, manufactures etc.—or it is a *totality*" (Marx 1973, 86). As a totality, the condition of subalternity is broadly inclusive, encompassing all those who are oppressed rather than oppressing, ruled rather than ruling. Green notes that at different points in Notebook 25 (the notebook devoted to subaltern social groups) Gramsci "identifies slaves, peasants, religious groups, women, different races, and the proletariat as subaltern social groups" (2011b, 69). The diffuse and general character of subalternity in general is captured in a passage in which Gramsci explains why what he terms an unfortunate "deterministic, fatalistic and mechanistic element has been a direct ideological 'aroma' emanating from the philosophy of praxis." For him, this "has been made necessary and justified historically by the 'subaltern' character of certain social strata" (*SPN*, 336) and their need to endure repeated defeat: "When you don't have the initiative in the struggle and the struggle itself comes eventually to be identified with a series of defeats, mechanical determinism becomes a tremendous force of moral resistance, of cohesion and of patient and obstinate perseverance. 'I have been defeated for the moment, but the tide of history is working for me in the long term'" (*SPN*, 336).

Once, however, we are talking about a specific time and place, subalterns, for Gramsci, are always particular kinds of subaltern. Tellingly, as Buttigieg has pointed out, the notebooks never speak of the subaltern in the singular; they talk of subaltern classes or subaltern social groups, as in the title given to Notebook 25: "On the Margins of History (The History of Subaltern Social Groups)." It is a mistake, Buttigieg stresses, to seek "a precise definition of 'subaltern' or 'subaltern social groups/classes' as conceived by Gramsci: he does not regard them as a single, much less a homogeneous, entity. It is precisely why he always refers to them in the plural" (Buttigieg 2013, 36). The point is that if we want to define *subalternity* precisely, then we need to know which particular subalterns, at which particular historical moment, we are talking about. What defines their specific form of subalternity? And here it is important to remember, as Peter Thomas has stressed, in a talk in which he too draws attention to the fact that "the term subaltern in the singular does not appear in Gramsci's work" (Thomas 2015), that subalterns do not exist in isolation from the state. Indeed, the nature of their subalternity is in large part defined by the specific ways they are incorporated into the state—the state here being understood in the wide sense of "the entire complex of practical and theoretical activities with which the ruling class not only justifies and maintains its dominance, but manages to win over the active consent of those over whom it rules" (*SPN*, 244).

It is precisely subalternity's lack of specificity as a general term that makes it a useful concept for those interested in analyzing inequality but resistant to the rigidities of simplistic, overly economistic versions of Marxism. It is useful because it is not limited to a specific type of oppression, such as economic exploitation, but includes the many different ways inequality and subordination can manifest themselves. Inequality can, for instance, burrow deep into the mind. A letter Gramsci wrote to his wife toward the end of his life, when he and his wife resumed contact after a long hiatus, provides an example of subalternity as internalized "mind-forged manacles," to quote William Blake: "In general, however, it seems to me that you put yourself (and not only in this connection) in a subaltern rather than a dominant position. That is, you assume the position of someone incapable of historically criticizing ideologies by dominating them, explaining and justifying them as a historical necessity of the past; of someone who, brought into contact with a specific world of emotions, feels attracted or repulsed by it, remaining always within the sphere of emotion and immediate passion" (*PLII*, 318). More generally, to borrow the words of Aimé Césaire used by Frantz Fanon in the epigraph to *Black Skin, White Masks*, we could say of subalterns who are subordinated mentally that they "have been skillfully injected with fear, inferiority complexes, trepidation, servility, despair, abasement" (Fanon 1967, 7). The psychological dimension of subalternity is another of the notebooks' leitmotifs.

In sum, Gramsci's concept of subalternity encompasses subordination in all its many forms, including internalized subordination. If we want to go beyond this general level and map the specific and highly variable forms it assumes in any given time and place, we need to undertake careful empirical analysis of that time and place. The next chapter moves from the concept of subalternity to that of intellectuals, the second of the three major concepts I see as central to Gramsci's approach to class.

2

Intellectuals

That all members of a political party should be regarded as intellectuals is an affirmation that can easily lend itself to mockery and caricature. But if one thinks about it nothing could be more exact. There are of course distinctions of level to be made. A party might have a greater or lesser proportion of members in the higher grades or in the lower, but this is not the point. What matters is the function, which is directive and organisational, i.e., educative, i.e., intellectual.
— SELECTIONS FROM THE PRISON NOTEBOOKS, 16

Gramsci stresses the importance of searching for a thinker's leitmotif (*SPN*, 383). This chapter focuses on three leitmotifs that resonate through the note-books: the nature and role of intellectuals, the processes through which "knowledge" is produced and reproduced, and the relationship between the "knowledge" of intellectuals and the "feeling" of subalterns. These leitmotifs appear as early as the first formulation of the study project that would become the prison notebooks, sketched out in a letter to Tatiana written a few months after his arrest.

His fascist prosecutors may have been determined to prevent Gramsci's brain from functioning, but he was equally determined that while they might lock up his body, they would not confine his brain. At the same time, he was acutely aware of prison's power to destroy a prisoner mentally. To combat this, he proposed to commit himself to a programme of focused study: "I would like," he writes to Tatiana, "to concentrate intensely and systematically on some subject that would absorb and provide a center to my inner life" (*PLI*, 83). He goes on to list four topics he plans to study. The first is "the formation of the public spirit in Italy during the past century; in other words, a study of Italian intellectuals, their origins, their groupings in accordance with cultural currents, and their various ways of thinking, etc. etc." (*PLI*, 83). The other three are comparative linguistics (the focus of his studies at Turin University), Pirandello, and the serial novel and popular taste in literature. For him, the four topics are linked: "At bottom, if you examine them thoroughly, there is a certain homogeneity among these four subjects: the creative spirit of the people in its diverse stages and degrees of development is in equal measure at their base" (*PLI*, 84). Over the years, as he worked on his notebooks, Gramsci would cover many more subjects than these four, and neither Pirandello nor comparative linguistics would be a major focus. But the theme of "the creative spirit of the people in its diverse stages and degrees of development," the ways "the people" understand and explain their world, would be a major leitmotif in the notebooks. The fact that he saw the history of this "creative spirit" "at the base" of his study of Italian intellectuals provides an important clue as to why he saw the topic of intellectuals as so central.

For Gramsci, the knowledge produced by intellectuals is never the result of some "head birth": pure thought springing fully formed from an individual mind as Athena sprang from the head of Zeus. Rather, the intellectuals' "knowledge" is always, and in fundamental ways, shaped by the beliefs, assumptions, and attitudes of the wider worlds in which those intellectuals live. Intellectuals are inextricably bound into existing power structures; to a significant degree they are products of their time and place. It is surely in part because this is his starting point that he finds it so hard, as he explained to Tatiana in the letter quoted in chapter 1, to focus on beliefs and ideas considered in isolation from their historical context.

Gramsci's description of his prison studies as having at their base "the creative spirit of the people in its diverse stages and degrees of development" also directs us to the question of the relationship between the knowledge of intellectuals and what it is this knowledge "knows." But this is to jump ahead. Before we can move on to that question, we need to understand how he approaches the production of knowledge in general. And to understand that we need first to spend a little time teasing out the meaning of one of Gramsci's central concepts, the organic.

The Organic and the Conjunctural

Underlying the rhythm of Gramsci's thought in the notebooks are certain basic oppositions. Three such oppositions central to his understanding of the nature and role of intellectuals are organic/conjunctural; coherent/incoherent; and reason/feeling. I begin with the opposition of the organic and the conjunctural.

To understand what *organic* signifies in the notebooks, it is helpful to remember the author's training in philology. According to the *Oxford English Dictionary* (OED), within philology, *organic* means "belonging to the etymological structure of a word; not secondary or fortuitous." The organic is inherent, structural. The conjunctural, while certainly real, could always be other than it is without changing the basic structural realities. To appreciate why the distinction between the organic and the conjunctural is so important to Gramsci, we need to remember that even if his thinking is not that of an economic determinist, it is rooted in the Marxist tradition. Since Marx himself is so frequently misunderstood on this point, let me explain what I mean by this.

For Gramsci, as for Marx, people's understanding of the world in which they live derives ultimately from that world's economic realities, but only ultimately. A comment in one note helps clarify his position. Referring to a famous letter Engels wrote to Joseph Bloch after Marx's death, Gramsci writes: "Engels's statement too should be recalled, that the economy is only the mainspring of history 'in the last analysis'" (*SPN*, 162). Given the frequency with which Marx and Marxism are accused of economic determinism, it is worth quoting the relevant passage from Engels's letter: "According to the materialist conception of history, the *ultimately* determining factor in history is the production and reproduction of real life. Neither Marx nor I have ever asserted more than this. Hence if somebody twists this into saying that the economic factor is the *only* determining one, he transforms the proposition into a meaningless, abstract, absurd phrase" (Marx and Engels 1975, 394; Engels's emphasis).

In sum, while Marx, Engels, and Gramsci all take it as axiomatic that "the production and reproduction of real life" shape ideas and beliefs, they never see that shaping as predetermined or unilinear. This is especially true of Gramsci; the stress, for him, always falls on Engels's "ultimately." In addition, for him, "the production and reproduction of real life" includes the internalized mental landscapes of those living that "real life." Ideas and beliefs, which exist not only in the minds of individuals but are embodied in institutions and social practices, need to be seen as an inherent part of the material realities of oppression and exploitation. It should not be forgotten, Gramsci insists, that one "proposition of the philosophy of praxis [Marxism]" is "that 'popular beliefs' and similar ideas are themselves material forces" (*SPN*, 165). While the language of superstructure and infrastructure is maintained throughout the notebooks, the careful attention to the always entwined realities of the material and the ideational transcends any simplistic infrastructure/superstructure dichotomy.[1]

In common with Marx and Engels, Gramsci sees human history as advancing over time, not that he thought of history as following an inexorable teleology, as he makes clear in his scathing critique of the position that objects "on principle" to any compromise: "For the conception upon which the aversion is based can only be the iron conviction that there exist objective laws of historical development similar in kind to natural laws, together with a belief in a predetermined teleology like that of a religion: since favourable conditions are inevitably going to appear, and since these, in a rather mysterious way, will bring about palingenetic events, it is evident that any deliberate initiative tending to predispose and plan these conditions is not only useless but even harmful" (*SPN*, 168). At the same time, he sees the emergence of the idea of progress as "a fundamental and epoch-making cultural event . . . The birth and the development of the idea of progress correspond to a widespread consciousness that a certain relationship has been reached between society and nature . . . such that as a result mankind as a whole is more sure of its future and can conceive "rationally" of plans through which to govern its entire life" (*SPN*, 357).

This Marxist may reject any predetermined historical endpoint, but he does believe that the material forces of production have the potential to move history forward: "The ensemble of the material forces of production is at the same time a crystallisation of all past history and the basis of present and future history: it is both a document and an active and actual propulsive force" (*SPN*, 466). It is the task of progressive political forces, such as the Italian communist party (of which he was a cofounder) to realize this potential. And a crucial element of this task is the dissemination of an advanced "conception of the world," one arrived at through critical thought: "When one's conception of the world is not critical and coherent but disjointed and episodic, one belongs simultaneously to a multiplicity of mass human groups. The personality is strangely composite: it contains Stone Age elements and principles of a more advanced science, prejudices from all past phases of history at the local level and intuitions of a future philosophy which will be that of a human race united

1. Thomas has a helpful and clarifying discussion of base and superstructure, superstructures and ideologies (2010, 95–102).

the world over. To criticise one's own conception of the world means therefore to make it a coherent unity and to raise it to the level reached by the most advanced thought in the world" (*SPN*, 324).

The distinction between the organic and the conjunctural derives from Gramsci's progressivism. The distinction allows him to separate out that which is shaped by fundamental economic forces from all the varied and unpredictable contingencies of history. While this neat distinction never maps the messy confusion of historical reality in any simple way, it can provide a helpful guide through that confusion. Understanding the history of a particular place, or particular events, requires us to look both at how that history unfolded in that place at that moment, and at the structural forces underpinning the surface flux. In the notebooks, Gramsci repeatedly stresses that there is no substitute for careful empirical analysis. Without this, Marxism easily degenerates into "economistic superstition." Such superstition, he writes, appeals to "second-rate intellectuals, who do not intend to overtax their brains but still wish to appear to know everything. As Engels wrote, many people find it very convenient to think that they can have the whole of history and all political and philosophical wisdom in their pockets at little cost and no trouble, concentrated into a few short formulae" (*SPN*, 164). This also applies to the concept of class. For Gramsci, neither the meaning of class as a theoretical category, nor its lived reality, can be "concentrated into a few short formulae." There is no substitute for the painstaking work of tracing out the particular forms structured inequalities—rooted in, but not determined by, economic relations—manifest themselves in any given time and place.

One of Gramsci's best known uses of the term *organic* is his distinction between organic and traditional intellectuals. Traditional intellectuals are essentially all those trained in the conceptual and philosophical elaboration of ideas, and shaped as intellectuals within the existing academic infrastructure and its knowledge producing practices (*SPN*, 334). All subaltern social groups or classes, as they begin their rise to dominance, confront this established body of intellectuals: "Every 'essential' social group which emerges into history out of the preceding economic structure, and as an expression of a development of this structure, has found (at least in all of history up to the present) categories of intellectuals already in existence and which seemed indeed to represent an historical continuity uninterrupted even by the most complicated and radical changes in political and social forms" (*SPN*, 6–7). In the course of its rise to power, such an essential social group creates its own organic intellectuals.

The distinction between traditional and organic intellectuals is central to

Gramsci's theorization of the role of intellectuals. Nonetheless it can be hard to grasp. Just how hard is indicated by the fact that even Eric Hobsbawm, a great admirer of the author of the notebooks, confesses himself somewhat puzzled as to why Gramsci insists so strongly on this distinction. In an essay published in 2011, Hobsbawm begins by describing the Italian thinker as "the most original [Marxist] thinker produced in the West since 1917" (2011, 316), but then goes on to write: "I think that [Gramsci's] distinction between the so-called 'traditional' intellectuals and the 'organic' intellectuals produced by a new class itself is, at least in some countries, less significant than he suggests." Hobsbawm, however, is quick to add something of a disclaimer: "It may be, of course, that I have not entirely grasped his difficult and complex thought here, and I ought certainly to stress that the question is of great importance to Gramsci himself, to judge by the amount of space he devoted to it" (2011, 325–26).

We can find an important clue as to why Gramsci thought it so important to distinguish between traditional and organic intellectuals in the letter to Tatiana laying out his plans for study in prison. The key is his claim that the study of Italian intellectuals and his other four topics are all at their base about "the creative spirit of the people in its diverse stages and degrees of development" (*PLI*, 84). Unraveling Gramsci's thought, however, requires teasing out what for him defines intellectuals, since the intellectuals of the notebooks are not intellectuals as conventionally defined.

To explain this Italian Marxist's radical rethinking of the nature and social role of intellectuals, it is helpful to begin with another influential thinker, the literary critic and sometime polemicist, Edward Said. Said, like Hobsbawm, was an admirer of Gramsci, and his account of intellectuals, *Representations of the Intellectual* (1994), draws heavily on the concept of organic intellectuals. But while Said may believe Gramsci to be "a brilliant political philosopher" (Said 1994, 3), he nonetheless fundamentally misreads the notebooks' theorization of knowledge production. The stark contrast between the organic intellectuals of *Representations* and those we find in the notebooks, precisely because it is so stark, will, I hope, clarify Gramsci's concept, as well as help the reader get beyond some deeply ingrained associations conjured up by the term *intellectual*.

The Universal Intellectual

Originally presented on BBC radio as the Reith Lectures in 1993, *Representations* is a plea for the importance of the independent intellectual, one not shackled to institutions or special interests, one who fearlessly speaks truth to power, as the popular phrase has it.[2] I focus here on two assumptions, central to Said's text, both explicitly rejected by Gramsci. The first is that the study of intellectuals means the study of individual intellectuals, the second that genuine intellectuals are independent of particular classes or other social groupings.

Gramsci is one of the two major theorists of the intellectual around whom Said constructs his argument in *Representations*. The other is Julien Benda, a thinker from the opposite end of the political spectrum. From Benda's *La trahison des clercs* (Treason of the intellectuals), Said takes the figure of the intellectual as one of a select priestly elite devoted to the pursuit of universal knowledge; from Gramsci he takes the concept of the organic intellectual. In Said's reading, organic intellectuals are the journeymen of knowledge production, available for hire by any group. This, however, is to misread the notebooks. The reason Said gets Gramsci so wrong is bound up with his commitment to the notion of the intellectual as an autonomous, independent individual, and his failure to recognize the notebooks' radical rejection of this model.

Said explains that he is primarily interested in intellectuals as individuals: "[In *Representations of the Intellectual*] the individual is my principal concern" (68).[3] And for him, such individuals have a very particular public role. In his introductory lecture he insists that "the intellectual is an *individual* with a specific public role in society" (11; emphasis mine). Later he elaborates on this point: throughout his lectures, he explains, he has been suggesting that the intellectual represents "an *individual* vocation, an energy, a stubborn force engaging as a committed and recognizable voice in language and in society with a whole slew of issues, all of them having to do in the end with a combination of enlightenment and emancipation or freedom" (73; emphasis mine).

Taking the individual as the starting point, and insisting on the intellectual's public role as a champion of enlightenment and emancipation, necessarily poses the question of individual intellectuals' relationship to their society. Is a genuinely independent intellectual possible? Said puts it like this: "[T]he question remains as to whether there is or can be anything like an independent, autonomously functioning intellectual, one who is not beholden to, and

2. The Reith Lectures began in 1948 with an inaugural series by Bertrand Russell. Every year since then, the BBC has invited a prominent thinker to deliver a series of lectures on a topic of his or her choice, designed for a general audience rather than a specialist academic one.

3. All quotations in this section are taken from Said 1994.

therefore constrained by, his or her affiliations with universities that pay salaries, political parties that demand loyalty to a party line, think tanks that while they may offer freedom to do research perhaps more subtly compromise judgement and restrain the critical voice" (67–68).

The intellectual who is genuinely committed to the intellectual "vocation," it would seem, must stand a little apart from society. And this is where Said turns to Benda. Benda, born some twenty-four years earlier than Gramsci, published his celebrated, and controversial, *La trahison des clercs* in 1927, a couple of years before Gramsci began the prison notebooks. *La trahison* is chiefly remembered today for Benda's denunciation of intellectuals who betray their calling, those who sell out for political or material rewards, but also central to the book, as Said notes, is a notion of the exemplary intellectual. Within "the combative rhetoric of Benda's basically very conservative work is to be found this figure of the intellectual as a being set apart, someone able to speak the truth to power, a crusty, eloquent, fantastically courageous and angry individual for whom no worldly power is too big or imposing to be criticized and pointedly taken to task" (8).

This portrait of the intellectual, while it assumes the vocational, almost religious character of the intellectual calling, also rejects the stereotype of intellectuals as "totally disengaged, other worldly, ivory-towered thinkers, intensely private and devoted to abstruse, perhaps even occult subjects" (5–6). On the contrary, Said argues, for Benda, "Real intellectuals are never more themselves than when, moved by metaphysical passion and disinterested principles of justice and truth, they denounce corruption, defend the weak, defy imperfect or oppressive authority" (6). These are intellectuals who are engaged with their societies, but always from a vantage point of universal and eternal values. Such intellectuals, if they are to fulfill their vocation, cannot be too closely linked with any specific interests; they must maintain their commitment to transcendent human values. It is this figure of the universal intellectual for which Said argues, and to which he counterposes the figure of the organic intellectual, a figure he claims to find in the notebooks.

As Said reads Gramsci, organic intellectuals are those "directly connected to classes or enterprises that used intellectuals to organize interests, gain more power, get more control. . . . Today's advertising or public relations expert, who devises techniques for winning a detergent or airline company a larger share of the market, would be considered an organic intellectual according to Gramsci, someone who in a democratic society tried to gain the consent of potential customers, win approval, marshal consumer or voter opinion" (4).

Given how far these supine servants of political and commercial interests are from the principled, independent intellectuals favored by Said, what is it that this Gramsci admirer finds so useful in the figure of the organic intellectual, an intellectual who is, as he writes, "always on the move, on the make?" (4). Above all, the Reith lecturer sees the Italian Marxist as having presciently identified the ever-increasing importance of intellectuals in the modern world. These intellectuals, these churners out of advertising copy and political spin, may not bear much resemblance to Benda's real intellectuals, but they run much of contemporary society. Indeed, Said goes so far as to claim that, for Gramsci, intellectuals have replaced classes, lauding "Gramsci's pioneering suggestions in *The Prison Notebooks* which almost for the first time saw intellectuals, and not social classes, as pivotal to the workings of modern society" (10). But this, too, is a serious misreading of Gramsci's understanding of both intellectuals and classes.

Producing and Reproducing Knowledge

Said's characterization of intellectuals is grounded in his assumption that intellectuals are defined by their possession of specific skills, and that the intellectual vocation demands that the intellectual remain "a being set apart, someone able to speak the truth to power." Gramsci begins from a quite different assumption: the starting-point for a study of intellectuals should not be individual knowledge-producers, but the whole process of knowledge production. In the notebooks he explicitly challenges the conventional definition of the intellectual, writing:

> What are the "maximum" limits of acceptance of the term "intellectual"? Can one find a unitary criterion to characterise equally all the diverse and disparate activities of intellectuals and to distinguish these at the same time and in an essential way from the activities of other social groupings? The most widespread error of method seems to me that of having looked for this criterion of distinction in the intrinsic nature of intellectual activities, rather than in the ensemble of the system of relations in which these activities (and therefore the intellectual groups who personify them) have their place within the general complex of social relations.

He then makes a key point: "Indeed the worker or proletarian, for example, is not specifically characterised by his manual or instrumental work, but by performing this work in specific conditions and in specific social relations." (*SPN*, 8)

In other words, what defines people as intellectuals is not a particular set of mental skills, but the role they have in society. Intellectuals are not simply those who think, or think in a particular way, but those whose thoughts and pronouncements are considered to have a certain weight and authority. In a certain sense, it could be said, as this same note goes on to argue, that everyone is an intellectual since every sentient being thinks: "There is no human activity from which every form of intellectual participation can be excluded: *homo faber* cannot be separated from *homo sapiens*" (*SPN*, 9). Gramsci would agree here with Coleridge that practice always has inherent within it some form of theory, "for the meanest of men has his Theory: and to think at all is to theorize" (Coleridge 1969, 189). But while everyone is an intellectual in this limited sense, "not all men have in society the function of intellectuals" (*SPN*, 9). To illustrate the point, Gramsci provides this footnote: "Thus, because it can happen that everyone at some time fries a couple of eggs or sews up a tear in a jacket, we do not necessarily say that everyone is a cook or a tailor" (*SPN*, 9).

The "intrinsic nature of intellectual activities" is not completely irrelevant, however. Within the broad category *intellectual* Gramsci recognizes the existence of important forms of differentiation: "Indeed, intellectual activity must also be distinguished in terms of its intrinsic characteristics . . . at the highest level would be the creators of the various sciences, philosophy, art, etc., at the lowest the most humble 'administrators' and divulgators of pre-existing, traditional, accumulated intellectual wealth" (*SPN*, 13). Nonetheless, from the heights of the great creative innovators to the most humble administrators and divulgators, all those laboring in the vineyards of knowledge production and distribution fall within Gramsci's definition of intellectuals. What defines them as such is the context within which their activity occurs: all those whose role is the production or distribution of knowledge are in some sense intellectuals. And while intellectuals may like to think of themselves as totally autonomous and independent, in reality they have been shaped by the social and intellectual worlds they inhabit; the knowledge they produce comes not just from them as individuals, but from the larger social forces they represent. This does not mean, however, that they are no more than the mouthpieces of such forces, the spineless functionaries identified as necessary to governments. Those always ready "to spew out propaganda against official enemies, euphemisms and, on a larger scale, whole systems of Orwellian Newspeak, which could disguise the truth of what was occurring in the name of institutional 'expediency' or 'national honor'" (Said 1994, 6). The linkages between intellectuals and social groupings we find in the notebooks are far more complex and mediated. At the level of the individual intellectual, Gramsci would undoubtedly agree with Said that intellectuals have a moral duty to pursue "truth." As someone who had lived through the rise of fascism in Italy, he was only too aware that individual intellectuals can, and often do, sell out to those in power. There were plenty of examples of turncoat intellectuals who had become loyal servants of Mussolini's regime, but this is essentially irrelevant to the more fundamental epistemological questions with which Gramsci is concerned.

In a footnote to a passage reflecting on the role of southern Italian intellectuals Gramsci again notes that the category *intellectuals* should be defined broadly; knowledge needs to be distributed as well as produced. Those who are part of the distribution mechanism, at however humble a level, also qualify as intellectuals: "By 'intellectuals' must be understood not those strata commonly described by this term, but in general the entire social stratum which exercises an organisational function in the wide sense—whether in the field of production, or in that of culture, or in that of political administration. They correspond to the NCOs and junior officers in the army, and also partly to the higher officers who have risen from the ranks" (*SPN*, 97). It is worth noting that Gramsci's unequivocal inclusion of this stratum, those we might term intellectual functionaries, within the category *intellectuals* has none of Said's moral condemnation. These are not intellectuals who are inherently "on the make," although some individuals among them may well be. His neutrality here can be explained by the fact that he is not measuring them against the model of Benda or Said's universal, autonomous intellectual, against which such humble functionaries cannot but fall woefully short. For him these functionaries are simply one element in the general process of knowledge production and distribution.

Organic Intellectuals

The concept of organic intellectuals is at the heart of the notebooks' theorization of knowledge production, but grasping the concept demands careful reading, since once again nowhere does Gramsci give us a nice, capsule definition. A good place to begin is with his apparently categorical rejection of the possibility of peasant intellectuals. The long note "The Formation of the Intellectuals" is unambiguous: "It is to be noted that the mass of the peasantry, although it performs an essential function in the world of production, does not elaborate its own 'organic' intellectuals" (*SPN*, 6). This unequivocal assertion can make contemporary readers uncomfortable, particularly perhaps anthropologists, but if we look at what lies behind it, at why this Sardinian sees peasants as incapable of producing their own organic intellectuals, the nature of the organicity of organic intellectuals begins to emerge.

The first point is that the note refers specifically to Italian peasants. We can see this if we look at the context of the assertion that "the mass of the peasantry . . . does not elaborate its own 'organic' intellectuals." The sentence continues, "nor does it 'assimilate' any stratum of 'traditional' intellectuals, although it is from the peasantry that other social groups draw many of their intellectuals and a high proportion of traditional intellectuals are of peasant origin" (*SPN*, 6). This makes it clear that the context is twentieth-century Italy, not some abstract category, peasant.

Second, it is not that Gramsci considers individual peasants as inherently less intellectually capable than individuals from other social groups, as he notes "a high proportion of traditional intellectuals are of peasant origin." The point is that peasants, as a collective social entity, are not positioned to generate the kind of radically alternative narrative necessary to supplant the existing hegemony. It is true that peasants can and do resist perceived injustices and oppression, but typically this takes the form of what Scott terms "low-profile forms of resistance that dare not speak in their own name" (Scott 1992, 19). When peasant resistance does take a collective form, as with the millenarian movement of the charismatic, nineteenth-century visionary Davide Lazzaretti (see *PNII*, 18–20), it tends to look backward rather than forward. Gramsci was a Marxist committed to a progressive view of history, one who had been shaped by early twentieth-century capitalism. For him, a political narrative with the genuine potential to challenge the dominant hegemony could only emerge out of subalternity as experienced by the industrial proletariat, the primary form of subalternity under the capitalism with which he was familiar. It was this capitalist subaltern location that he believed would give birth to organic intellectuals capable of articulating subaltern experience as new political narratives confident "to speak in their own name." He certainly recognizes that peasant experience generates its own knowledge, and he stresses that any successful progressive movement in a country like Italy, with a large peasant population, needs to reach out to peasants and incorporate peasant demands. This, however, did not change what he saw as a basic reality: in the Italy of his time the subalternity experienced by Italian peasants was not capable of creating its own independent, organic intellectuals.

The rejection of the possibility of organic, peasant intellectuals should alert us to the fact that the concept of organic intellectuals puts the emphasis on the organic rather than the intellectual. Organic intellectuals are not a particular kind of intellectual. They are the form in which the knowledge generated out of the lived experience of a social group with the potential to become hegemonic achieves coherence and authority. In other words, the Marxist notion of structure is not some kind of "hidden god." Provided it is understood historically, it is "the ensemble of social relations in which real people move and act, as an ensemble of objective conditions . . . The philosophy of praxis is bound up not only with immanentism but also with the subjective conception of reality in so far as it turns this latter upside down, explaining it as a historical fact, as the 'historical subjectivity of a social group,' as a real fact which presents itself as a phenomenon of philosophical 'speculation' while it is simply a practical act, the form assumed by a concrete social content and the way that the whole of society is led to fashion a moral unity for itself" (*FSPN*, 347–48).

If we want to understand why a given group sees the world as it does, we need to start with that "conception of reality" and its links to how those "real people move and act," rather than the particular, historical thinkers who first formulated this conception. This is what Gramsci means when he writes that the philosophy of praxis turns what seems to be the subjective conception of reality upside down. Rather than being the product of "speculation" on the part of individual intellectuals, conceptions of reality that represent "the historical subjectivity of a social group" are in fact "the form assumed by a concrete social content."

What Organic Intellectuals Do

The notebooks may not provide us with a neat, capsule definition of organic intellectuals, but a number of notes tell us what organic intellectuals do. A passage in one note, to which I shall return a number of times, is particularly clear: "Every social group, coming into existence on the original terrain of an essential function in the world of economic production, creates together with itself, organically, one or more strata of intellectuals which give it homogeneity and an awareness of its own function not only in the economic but also in the social and political fields" (*SPN*, 5). The point here is that the social group itself creates its intellectuals. It must create its own intellectuals because a group "coming into existence on the original terrain of an essential function in the world of economic production" remains entangled in the hegemonic worldview of the existing dominant class. Subalterns, as Scott argues, may have a "'hidden transcript' that represents a critique of power spoken behind the back of the dominant" (Scott 1992, xii), but this critique remains fragmentary and incoherent. Subalterns may reject certain aspects of the existing hegemonic narrative, but the very condition of subalternity makes them incapable of formulating a coherent alternative. Organic intellectuals are necessary if the incoherent experience of a social group or class is to be transformed into a coherent narrative, or set of narratives.

An opposition between coherence and incoherence, like that between the organic and the conjunctural, runs through the notebooks. For Gramsci, as I explore in the next two chapters, incoherence is a primary characteristic of the "ambiguous, contradictory and multiform" common sense (*senso comune*) (*SPN*, 423) subalterns use to make sense of their world. One of the tasks of the organic intellectuals that a social group or class emerging from subalternity "creates together with itself," is to turn that class's incoherent common sense into coherent political narratives.

It should be stressed that organic intellectuals are not necessarily progressive; all major classes have their own organic intellectuals. Moving from Gramsci's day to more recent times, we can find a number of narratives which provide a dominant class with "an awareness of its function." A good example is the argument, popular on the American right, that there is nothing wrong with the rich enjoying historically low levels of taxation since they are "job-creators." All taxing the rich does, it is claimed, is prevent them from creating jobs, thereby harming the less well-off who need these jobs. According to this reasoning, the growing disparity between rich and poor to be found in the United States and other advanced capitalist societies is a necessary price we have to pay if those who are not rich are to find jobs. Behind the simplistic, easily grasped narrative is a theory of economic growth deriving from the intellectual work of academic economists such as George Reisman (a student of the fiercely promarket Ludwig von Mises). We may reject the argument as a simple misrepresentation of economic reality, but it does provide a coherent, however inaccurate, explanation of why what might seem unjust is nonetheless necessary.

The institutions and practices that provide homogeneity, awareness, and so on change over time. The nature of organic intellectuals and the kind of knowledge they produce are not fixed: emerging classes bring into being new kinds of intellectuals, new forms of knowledge and new institutional structures. Specific kinds of intellectuals will emerge out of the particular conditions that define a given class; intellectuals capable of producing the forms of knowledge that class needs: "It can be observed that the 'organic' intellectuals which every new class creates alongside itself and elaborates in the course of its development, are for the most part 'specialisations' of partial aspects of the primitive activity of the new social type which the new class has brought into prominence" (*SPN*, 6). A little earlier in the same note, Gramsci provides examples of intellectuals specific to capitalism: "The capitalist entrepreneur creates alongside himself the industrial technician, the specialist in political economy, the organisers of a new culture, of a new legal system, etc." (*SPN*, 5). The shape a newly emerging class's forms of knowledge production will assume only becomes fully apparent, however, once that class has established its hegemony.

Reflecting on the effects of the Reformation, one note discusses the creation of intellectuals by major social groups or classes:

> In the history of cultural developments, it is important to pay special attention to the organisation of culture and the personnel through whom this organisation takes concrete form. G. De Ruggiero's volume on Renaissance and Reformation brings out the attitude of very many intellectuals, with Erasmus at their head: they gave way in the face of persecution and the stake. The bearer of the Reformation was therefore the German people itself in its totality, as undifferentiated mass, not the intellectuals. It is precisely this desertion of the intellectuals in the face of the enemy which explains the "sterility" of the Reformation in the immediate sphere of high culture, until, by a process of selection, the people, which remained faithful to the cause, produced a new group of intellectuals culminating in classical philosophy.
>
> Something similar has happened up to now with the philosophy of praxis. The great intellectuals formed on the terrain of this philosophy, besides being few in number, were not linked with the people, they did not emerge from the people, but were the expression of traditional intermediary classes, to which they returned at the great "turning points" of history. (*SPN*, 397)

Note here that it is "the people," those who "remained faithful to the cause," who "produced a new group of intellectuals culminating in classical philosophy."

It is important to emphasize that the organic character of intellectuals is not a question of the personal origins of individual intellectuals; it is determined, rather, by the role they play in the process of a given class's production of knowledge. Gramsci himself, for instance, was the son of a petty bureaucrat. He spent his early youth in a Sardinian village among peasants before leaving for the mainland and Turin University. His life in Sardinia and his student years undoubtedly helped shape him; as I have stressed, he never lost the profound respect for rigorous scholarship he acquired, and his formal studies in linguistics continued to inform his theoretical approach. As a progressive Marxist intellectual, however, what above all else formed him was his life as an activist within the Italian Left. It was as an organizer of workers in Turin and elsewhere, and as a political journalist and educator, first within the Socialist Party and then the Communist Party, that he acquired his "feeling" for working-class life. As an intellectual, he can be seen as an example of an organic, working-class intellectual who was, and saw himself to be, a part of a collective endeavor to provide that emerging working class with "homogeneity and an awareness of its own function not only in the economic but also in the social and political fields" (*SPN*, 5).

Intellectuals and Classes

Intellectuals in the notebooks play a crucial role in the transformation of a class's lived experience into coherent, shared narratives that explain and make sense of the world as viewed from the vantage point of that class. But this does not mean, as Said claims, that Gramsci "saw intellectuals, and not social classes, as pivotal to the workings of modern society" (1994, 10). A careful reading of the notebooks makes it clear that for their author, as for Marx, the primary actors in history are classes (see, for instance, the long note "Analysis of Situations. Relations of Force"; *SPN*, 175–85). For Gramsci, there is no free-floating group of autonomous intellectuals ready to be called into service by a new class. Intellectuals do not constitute a distinct class: there is no "independent class of intellectuals, but every social group has its own stratum of intellectuals, or tends to form one" (*SPN*, 60). He is not suggesting here that every component subclass within the major cleavages has its own intellectuals, only that the major, fundamental classes do. As a fundamental class emerges from subalternity, it creates, out of its particular conditions of existence, its own organic intellectuals, who provide it with a coherent understanding of itself as a class and with leadership. Gramsci's argument that "all members of a political party should be regarded as intellectuals" (*SPN*, 16, see this chapter's epigraph) helps clarify his understanding of what defines intellectuals, as long as we bear in mind that *party* in the notebooks refers not just to formal political parties, but to a wide range of organisations that bring those with common interests together. The complexity of the historical process by which classes create intellectuals, and by which those intellectuals enable a class to acquire a sense of itself as a class and, ultimately, to act in history is captured in this passage:

> A human mass does not "distinguish" itself, does not become independent in its own right without, in the widest sense, organising itself; and

there is no organisation without intellectuals, that is without organisers and leaders, in other words, without the theoretical aspect of the theory-practice nexus being distinguished concretely by the existence of a group of people "specialised" in conceptual and philosophical elaboration of ideas. But the process of creating intellectuals is long, difficult, full of contradictions, advances and retreats, dispersals and regroupings . . .

The process of development is tied to a dialectic between the intellectuals and the masses. The intellectual stratum develops both quantitatively and qualitatively, but every leap forward towards a new breadth and complexity of the intellectual stratum is tied to an analogous movement on the part of the mass of the "simple," who raise themselves to higher levels of culture and at the same time extend their circle of influence towards the stratum of specialised intellectuals, producing outstanding individuals and groups of greater or less importance. (*SPN*, 334–35)

The emergence of new kinds of intellectuals is an essential part of class formation. And since it is the particular nature of the social relations underpinning a given class that call into being particular forms of intellectuals, it is impossible to know in advance what form its organic intellectuals will take. The ecclesiastical scholars of the feudal age, for example, were very different from the scientists, technical experts, journalists and men (and sometimes women) of letters, who emerged together with capitalism. But once a class and its organic intellectuals has established dominance, its forms of knowledge production will coalesce into particular kinds of institutions with their own cultures of learning and ways of disseminating knowledge. Capitalism, for instance, is associated with the rise of the modern secular university. Over time, established institutions of learning develop their own bases of power and their own deeply entrenched cultures. To those who inhabit such venerable institutions — the intellectuals Gramsci terms "traditional" — their world of learning can seem remote from the power struggles of politicians beyond the walls of their ivory tower. They can, indeed, come to see themselves as genuinely autonomous. Such "traditional intellectuals . . . experience through an '*esprit de corps*' their uninterrupted historical continuity and their special qualifications, they thus put themselves forward as autonomous and independent of the dominant social group" (*SPN*, 7). It is this self-image of the autonomous intellectual that lies behind the model of the intellectual held up as ideal by Benda and Said, the universal intellectual who speaks from the vantage point of transcendent and eternal human values. But such pretensions are illusory; intellectuals who claim to be disinterested seekers of truth, above the hurly-burly of class struggle, are deluding themselves. Benedetto Croce, for instance, "thinks he is writing a history from which every element of class has been exorcised and he is, instead, producing a highly accurate and praiseworthy description of the political masterpiece whereby a particular class manages to present and have the conditions for its existence and development as a class accepted as a universal principle, as a world view, as a religion. In other words he is describing in the very act the development of a practical means of government and of domination" (*FSPN*, 353).

This does not, however, render the individual intellectual as no more than "a faceless professional, a competent member of a class just going about her/his business," to use Said's dismissive formulation (11). Said's insistence that "the purpose of the intellectual's activity is to advance human freedom and knowledge" (17) is certainly appealing, but Gramsci, as I read him, would counter that intellectuals, like everyone else, are always the product of a particular time and place. And while they may strive "to advance human freedom and knowledge," they do this in circumstances not of their own choosing, to paraphrase Marx's famous formulation in *The Eighteenth Brumaire of Louis Napoleon*. We need to be alert to the ways specific intellectuals are located within specific knowledge-producing institutions and practices, and to the links those institutions and practices have to particular classes. This, it should be noted, is a quite separate question from that of the individual intellectual's responsibility to remain intellectually honest, to refuse slavish adherence to the party line simply because it is the party line. Rather, Gramsci insists on the importance of the fundamental ontological and epistemological assumptions that intellectuals take as their starting-point in a given time and place, in other words, the assumptions intellectuals make as to the nature of reality and the means by which we can acquire knowledge about that reality. As a result, rather than focusing on individual intellectuals, he explores the institutions, practices, and shared knowledge-worlds within which specific intellectuals function.

In the notebooks, the focus is on the collective, shared narratives and assumptions that have their ultimate origin in the common experience of particular social groups and classes. It is important, however, to stress the "ultimate" here. This is not a case of simple causality: the process by which "the production and reproduction of real life" (to quote again Engels's letter to Bloch) find expression in specific narratives is always complex and highly mediated. Understanding that process requires a careful analysis of the nature and role of intellectuals in different historical periods. This is why, as Buttigieg puts it, "Gramsci never doubted the centrality of the study on the intellectuals to almost everything else he wanted to do" (*PNI*, 29).

In sum, Gramsci argues that new classes produce new kinds of intellectuals and new forms of knowledge production, organically linked to the lived realities of those classes. This is why he sees his study of Italian intellectuals as being at its base about "the creative spirit of the people in its diverse stages and degrees of development," as he wrote to Tatiana (*PLI*, 84). Organic intellectuals not only help to bring about fundamental social change through their ability to transform raw, inchoate experience into articulate, coherent narratives, as intellectuals, they themselves emerge out of that experience. What such knowledge producers embody is, indeed, "the creative spirit of the people." The new intellectuals and forms of knowledge production associated with the emergence of a formerly subaltern class to dominance will not be those of existing traditional intellectuals and systems of knowledge production. As a revolutionary activist and historical progressive, Gramsci was especially concerned with the role organic intellectuals play in a subaltern group's rise to hegemony, and to him it was clear that such intellectuals could not simply be traditional intellectuals with progressive aims; they would represent a new kind of knowledge producer. This is why the distinction between organic and traditional intellectuals—the distinction that puzzles Hobsbawm—is so central to his thought.

Feeling, Knowing, and Historical Blocs
The question of the relationship between intellectuals and those termed in different notes the common people, the popular masses or popular element, runs through the notebooks. Ultimately, the foundational content of new political narratives, narratives capable of becoming a social force with the power to inspire collective action and social transformation, comes from the practical activity of that popular element. Articulating and bringing coherence to that content is the task of the organic intellectuals brought into being by a rising class. For this to happen, however, there needs to be organic cohesion between intellectuals and masses. Gramsci is highly critical of what he refers to as "the so-called Popular Universities" (independent institutes of adult education that existed at the time in Italy) and their failure to provide "any organic quality either of philosophical thought or of organisational stability and central cultural direction . . . one could only have had cultural stability and an organic quality of thought if there had existed the same unity between the intellectuals

and the simple [common people] as there should be between theory and practice. That is, if the intellectuals had been organically the intellectuals of those masses, and if they had worked out and made coherent the principles and the problems raised by the masses in their practical activity, thus constituting a cultural and social bloc" (*SPN*, 330). Intellectuals, the note continues, need to maintain genuine links with the common people since ultimately it is the knowledge of the masses, rooted in their practical activity, which is "the source of the problems [the intellectuals' knowledge] sets out to study and to resolve." Only through such dialogue "does a philosophy become 'historical,' purify itself of intellectualistic elements of an individual character and become 'life'" (*SPN*, 330). For there to be a politically effective "cultural and social bloc," the "knowledge" of the intellectuals needs to be brought together with the "feeling" of the popular element. This opposition between reason and emotion runs through the notebooks in the same way as that between the organic and the conjunctural, or the coherent and incoherent. We can see it particularly clearly in a note reflecting on feeling and knowing:

> The popular element "feels" but does not always know or understand; the intellectual element "knows" but does not always understand and in particular does not always feel. . . . The intellectual's error consists in believing that one can know without understanding and even more without feeling and being impassioned (not only for knowledge in itself but also for the object of knowledge): in other words that the intellectual can be an intellectual (and not a pure pedant) if distinct and separate from the people-nation, that is, without feeling the elementary passions of the people, understanding them and therefore explaining and justifying them in the particular historical situation and connecting them dialectically to the laws of history and to a superior conception of the world, scientifically and coherently elaborated—i.e. knowledge. One cannot make politics-history without this passion, without this sentimental connection between intellectuals and people-nation. In the absence of such a nexus the relations between the intellectual and the people-nation are, or are reduced to, relationships of a purely bureaucratic and formal order; the intellectuals become a caste, or a priesthood . . .
>
> If the relationship between intellectuals and people-nation, between the leaders and the led, the rulers and the ruled, is provided by an organic cohesion in which feeling-passion becomes understanding and thence knowledge (not mechanically but in a way that is alive), then and only then is the relationship one of representation. Only then can

there take place an exchange of individual elements between the rulers and ruled, leaders [*dirigenti*] and led, and can the shared life be realised which alone is a social force—with the creation of the "historical bloc." (*SPN*, 418)

The term *historical bloc* in the notebooks has sometimes been understood as referring to an assemblage of class alliances, but, as David Forgacs and Derek Boothman have argued, this is a misreading (Boothman 2000, 125; Forgacs 1998, 424). In general, the term Gramsci uses when he speaks of alliances between classes or fractions of classes is *social bloc*, or *dominant social bloc* (see, for instance, *SPN*, 223). This usage in turn needs to be distinguished from "the cultural and social bloc," constituted by the masses and their organic intellectuals, to which he refers in his critical reflections on the Popular Universities. The term *historical bloc* refers to the relationship, always complicated and highly mediated in the notebooks, between material base and superstructures.[4] Gramsci defines *historical bloc* as follows, "Concept of 'historical bloc,' i.e., unity between nature and spirit (structure and superstructure)" (*SPN*, 137). Thomas provides this helpful gloss: "[Gramsci] views the superstructures not as mechanically derived from an originary 'base,' but as constituting a dialectical unity or 'historical bloc' with the dominant relations of production, the means by which they were organised, guaranteed, and made to endure (or, just as importantly, challenged and transformed)" (Thomas 2010, 100). Gramsci's always complex and nonreductive approach to the relation between base and superstructure is evident: "Another proposition of Marx is that a popular conviction often has the same energy as a material force or something of the kind, which is extremely significant. The analysis of these propositions [of Marx] tends, I think, to reinforce the conception of *historical bloc* in which precisely material forces are the content and ideologies are the form." Characteristically, he immediately adds, "though this distinction has purely didactic value, since the material forces would be inconceivable historically without form and the ideologies would be individual fancies without the material forces" (*SPN*, 377). We can see the same stress on such dichotomies as essentially heuristic in the note on feeling and knowing. On the one hand, there is a distinction between emotion and reason; on the other, only if there is "organic cohesion" between the intellectuals' knowing and the feeling of the "people-nation" can they constitute a "social force."

---

4. Boothman (2000) traces the genealogy of the term *historical bloc* as used in the notebooks.

At the same time, intellectuals and common people alike inhabit both the rational world of the intellect and the emotional world of feeling. Whatever we do for a living, we all engage in intellectual activity to some extent. Everyone "carries on some form of intellectual activity, that is, he is a 'philosopher', an artist, a man of taste, he participates in a particular conception of the world, has a conscious line of moral conduct, and therefore contributes to sustain a conception of the world or to modify it, that is, to bring into being new modes of thought" (*SPN*, 9). Similarly, even the most desiccated professional intellectual has some form of emotional life. Nonetheless, if we want to analyze the nature of different kinds of "knowledge" it is helpful to make a distinction between the knowledge-based reason of those who "have in society the function of intellectuals" (*SPN*, 9), and the emotional certainties of the popular element.

The "organic cohesion in which feeling-passion becomes understanding and thence knowledge" goes far beyond simply enabling progressive organizations to reach the "people-nation" more effectively. At the root of the notebooks' insistence on the need for organic cohesion between intellectuals and the subaltern group out of which they have emerged is a fundamental epistemological claim: the lived experience of subalternity provides intellectuals with the raw material to which they give coherent form. Gramsci, unlike some other Marxist intellectuals and activists, does not believe that intellectuals have all the answers. Marxism, for him, is a living body of thought, still in the process of coalescing into coherence. And because it is the product of a subaltern group, it is still in the process of formation: Marxism "is the conception of a subaltern social group, deprived of historical initiative, in continuous but disorganic expansion, unable to go beyond a certain qualitative level, which still remains below the level of the possession of the State and of the real exercise of hegemony over the whole of society which alone permits a certain organic equilibrium in the development of the intellectual group" (*SPN*, 396). Marx did not deliver a fully formed philosophy to the suffering masses, like some Moses descending from the mountain with his tablets of stone. Marxism is a philosophy still struggling to be born. Rooted in a condition of subalternity that has yet to be coherently articulated, it cannot but be somewhat rough and jagged. And yet within its rawness, Gramsci argues, lies the beginnings of a coherent philosophy with the potential to envisage a world without subalternity. The first formulations of this philosophy are necessarily crude: "Is it possible that a 'formally' new conception can present itself in a guise other than the crude, unsophisticated version of the populace? And yet the historian, with the benefit of all necessary perspective, manages to establish and understand the fact that the beginnings of a new world, rough and jagged though they always are, are better than the passing away of the world in its death-throes and the swan song it produces" (*SPN*, 342–43).

These new beginnings are rooted in the practical activity of subaltern groups. The collective experience of specific subaltern life-worlds give rise to new narratives that explain how the world is, and why it is as it is. The word *collective* here is key: sufficiently large numbers of people need to feel the truth of a new way of explaining their world, and how it might be transformed. The conceptions of the world that Gramsci has in mind are the broad, overarching ones that underpin a new epoch, such as the bourgeois worldview that with the rise of capitalism supplanted the previously dominant, feudal worldview. He is also interested in narrower, more parochial, even individual narratives, but in the main this is because of the linkages between such parochial understandings and more encompassing narratives. His primary concern is always with the processes by which large groups of people come to adopt new worldviews and thereby become capable of historical acts that bring about fundamental social change. Such acts are carried out by groups or classes, not individuals: "An historical act can only be performed by 'collective man,' and this presupposes the attainment of a 'cultural-social' unity through which a multiplicity of dispersed wills, with heterogeneous aims, are welded together with a single aim, on the basis of an equal and common conception of the world, both general and particular" (*SPN*, 349).

Achieving a cultural-social unity based on a common conception of the world requires considerable political work. New conceptions of the world may emerge out of economic realities, but they do not do so automatically. In no sense is Gramsci an economic determinist. Rather, he sees shifts in basic economic relations, such as those that occurred during the decline of feudalism, as creating possibilities for new narratives and new cultures to emerge — possibilities that may or may not be realized. These embryonic beginnings of new conceptions of the world emerging from subaltern vantage points challenge existing hegemonic narratives. They do not, however, emerge on their own or fully formed; they are born together with political movements rooted in specific material realities. While the mass of a class may know and understand their subalternity emotionally, they are unable to articulate it in a coherent form. But if there is genuine organic cohesion between the popular element and their intellectuals, organic intellectuals will emerge who can create coherent and persuasive narratives rooted in the specific experience of a given subaltern class.

Some readers may be made uncomfortable by Gramsci's apparently sharp distinction between intellectuals and masses, but we need to remember, first, the heuristic nature of such distinctions in the notebooks and, second, his insistence that working-class organic intellectuals are created by the class itself as it emerges from subalternity. An article written by the young Gramsci for the socialist weekly *Il Grido del Popolo* in 1918 gives us a glimpse of his vision of this process at work in political parties and other working-class organizations. The article is a response to a piece in the reformist *La Giustizia* by one Camillo Prampolini ridiculing *Il Grido* for using language that no proletarian could possibly understand. "So why Camillo Prampolini's cheap irony about the 'interpreters' of the proletariat who can't make themselves understood by the proletarians? Because Prampolini, with all his good sense and rule of thumb, thinks in abstractions. The proletariat is a practical construct: in reality there are individual proletarians, more or less educated, more or less equipped by the class struggle to understand the most refined socialist concepts." Proletarians, Gramsci goes on to explain, "have spontaneously formed an intellectual and cultural hierarchy, and reciprocal education is at work where the activity of the writers and propagandists cannot penetrate. In workers' circles and leagues, in conversations outside the factory, the word of socialist criticism is dissected, propagated, made ductile and malleable for every mind and every culture. In a complex and varied environment like that of a major industrial city the organs of capillary transmission of opinion, which the will of the leaders would never succeed in creating and setting up, arise spontaneously" (*SCW*, 32–34).

As is clear from this early journalistic piece, the distribution of knowledge is of as much concern to Gramsci as its production. He was one of the editors of *L'Ordine Nuovo*, a socialist journal launched in 1919, influential among workers during the heady days of the Turin factory occupations. In the notebooks, he would refer to the journal's editorial board's "collective discussion and criticism (made up of suggestions, advice, comments on method, and criticism which is constructive and aimed at mutual education) in which each individual functions as a specialist in his own field and helps to complete the expertise of the collectivity, the average level of the individual editors is in fact successfully raised so that it reaches the altitude or capacity of the most highly skilled" (*SPN*, 28).

The organic intellectual here, we might say, is not an individual but a collective. Political parties are another crucial site for this kind of collective intellectual work: parties are "the crucibles where the unification of theory and practice, understood as a real historical process, takes place" (*SPN*, 335). Throughout the notebooks, the focus is the social relations within which knowledge is produced, rather than individual knowledge producers. As Gramsci writes in the passage quoted above in which he challenges conventional understandings of the intellectual, it is "the ensemble of the system of relations" within which such production and distribution takes place, and the place of these particular relations "within the general complex of social relations" that defines the intellectual (*SPN*, 8). Intellectuals as living human beings are, as it were, personifications of these relations.

From this perspective, traditional intellectuals embody existing power relations rather than new ones struggling to be born. On their own, they cannot come up with the radically new conception of the world required for social transformation; the knowledge they produce is linked to the past rather than the future. This does not mean, however, that they are unimportant; they need to be won over to the side of the progressive forces: "One of the most important characteristics of any group that is developing towards dominance is its struggle to assimilate and to conquer 'ideologically' the traditional intellectuals, but this assimilation and conquest is made quicker and more efficacious the more the group in question succeeds in simultaneously elaborating its own organic intellectuals" (*SPN*, 10). That elaboration involves a collective transformation of inchoate subaltern knowledge into coherence. This fundamental assumption explains why Gramsci believed that his study of Italian intellectuals and their history has at its base, as he wrote to Tatiana, "the creative spirit of the people in its diverse stages and degrees of development." One of the sites where we can find inchoate fragments of "the spirit of the people" existing within the interstices of dominant hegemonic narratives is *senso comune*. Chapter 3 explores this terrain.

3

Common Sense

Common sense creates the folklore of the future, that is as a relatively rigid
phase of popular knowledge at a given time and place.
— SELECTIONS FROM THE PRISON NOTEBOOKS, 326

Senso comune, in the notebooks, is that accumulation of taken-for-granted
"knowledge" to be found in every human community. In any given time and
place, this accumulation provides a heterogeneous bundle of assumed certainties that structure the basic landscapes within which individuals are socialized
and chart their individual life courses. The problem for those who read the
notebooks in English, as I do, is that *senso comune* has no simple, English
equivalent. The standard translation, common sense, is a mistranslation. The
Anglophone reader who wants to grasp the meaning *common sense* has for
Gramsci needs to begin by recognizing the difference between the English
term *common sense* and *senso comune*.

The term *common sense* has a complex history, laid out in exemplary fashion in Sophia Rosenfeld's *Common Sense: A Political History*. It originated
as a technical term (*koinè aisthèsis*) in Aristotelian philosophy that named a
supposed extra sense, beyond the five basic ones (vision, hearing, taste, smell,
and touch). Possessed by all humans, this sense was thought of as enabling us
to organize the disparate impressions received from the other five. It was at
the beginning of the eighteenth century that this old philosophical term first
acquired its modern English meaning: "[T]hose plain, self-evident truths or

conventional wisdom that one needed no sophistication to grasp and no proof to accept precisely because they accorded so well with the basic (common sense) intellectual capacities and experiences of the whole social body" (Rosenfeld 2011, 23). For the English-speaker, common sense came to denote, in the words of the OED, "good sound practical sense; combined tact and readiness in dealing with the every-day affairs of life; general sagacity." *Senso comune*, by contrast, is a more neutral term that lacks these strong positive connotations, referring rather to the beliefs and opinions held in common, or thought to be held in common, by the mass of the population; all those heterogeneous narratives and accepted "facts" that structure so much of what we take to be no more than simple reality. Despite its being a mistranslation, I have nevertheless chosen to use the English term rather than leave *senso comune* untranslated.[1] Coupling *common sense* and Gramsci's radically different understanding of the taken-for-granted in everyday life will, I hope, help draw attention to some of the hidden baggage that comes with the English term, and in addition provide Anglophones with an alternative way of thinking about this apparently self-evident word and what it names. I begin with the English concept of common sense.

Plain Wisdom

As human beings, we have a basic need to feel we understand the world in which we live. All of us, whoever we are and wherever we live, are continually engaged in a process of making sense of the everyday reality we confront. Most of the time, we do not consciously think much about this: we feel we know the world (or worlds) we inhabit and are able, more or less unthinkingly, to fit what happens to us into our preexisting narratives of how things are. We may be happy, angry, or resigned to what we perceive as reality, but in general we tend to assume that we know how to navigate our way through it. Those of us who are English-speakers often refer to the knowledge we use in this scarcely conscious way as common sense, the meaning of which we take as self-evident. And as long as we do not think too hard about it, common sense can be defined easily enough along the lines of the OED definition, given above, or, to take another of the OED's definitions: "The endowment of natural intelligence possessed by rational beings; ordinary, normal or average understanding; the plain wisdom which is everyone's inheritance." The obviousness of common

---

1. For an argument for staying with the Italian term, see Thomas (2010, 16).

sense is the obviousness to which the Supreme Court Justice Potter Stewart appealed when, in 1964, he famously refused to define hard-core pornography, explaining, "[P]erhaps I could never succeed in intelligibly doing so. But I know it when I see it" (Jacobellis v. Ohio 378 US 184 [1964]). In other words, on being shown a possibly pornographic movie, all those with "ordinary, normal or average understanding" know whether it is indeed pornographic, even if they could not articulate why. Central to the notion of common sense is that its truths need, as Rosenfeld writes, "no sophistication to grasp and no proof to accept." Their truth is agreed to by "the whole social body," and immediately apparent to anyone of normal intelligence.

But is this plain wisdom supposedly possessed by all normal rational beings always so obvious, or shared by the whole social body? Take, for instance, the statement by one political commentator, Chris Matthews, in a full-page ad for the MSNBC cable channel in the *New York Times* (December 25, 2011). Alongside two giant photos of Matthews are three short sentences: "Rebuilding America creates jobs. It's not about politics. It's about common sense." This is an example of common sense as an appeal to an incontrovertible fact, something that any rational being cannot but recognize as true. But what does "rebuilding America" mean? How would it translate into actual policies? It seems unlikely that the common sense of a self-professed liberal like Matthews would seem similarly obvious to a libertarian like Ron Paul, or a Tea Party enthusiast. All too often one rational being's obvious fact is another's questionable, or flat out wrong, assertion. There is more than one common sense. And then these incontrovertible facts have a way of shifting over time. A film that might have seemed obviously pornographic in the 1950s, might by today's standards be judged as warranting no more than PG certification.

An additional complication is common sense's two distinct strands of meaning. "In modern parlance," as Rosenfeld writes, "we sometimes use common sense to mean the basic human faculty that lets us make elemental judgements about everyday matters based on everyday real-world experience . . . Other times we mean the widely shared and seemingly self-evident conclusions drawn from this faculty, the truisms about which all sensible people agree without argument or even discussion" (2011, 1). The slippage between these meanings is one source of common sense's persuasive force: no person with this assumed basic human faculty could deny the truth of commonsense facts.

Common Sense and Good Sense

It is the second of Rosenfeld's meanings that predominates in the notebooks: in general, common sense is the assemblage of truisms accepted within a particular social world, the popular knowledge referred to in the epigraph of this chapter, which, while always heterogeneous, also assumes relatively rigidified forms (*SPN*, 326). In this, Gramsci's common sense differs from another way of conceptualizing taken-for-granted knowledge that has been adopted by many social scientists. This is Pierre Bourdieu's concept of habitus. Habitus is defined by Bourdieu as "systems of durable, transposable dispositions, structured structures predisposed to function as structuring structures, . . principles which generate and organize practices and representations" (Bourdieu 1990, 53). In the course of their socialization, individuals internalize the particular dispositions of their time and place. Given how many social scientists have adopted habitus as a way of naming taken-for-granted knowledge, it is worthwhile noting the key difference that while *common sense* in the notebooks refers primarily to the content of popular knowledge, *habitus* refers to the cognitive structures or dispositions that generate that knowledge.[2]

In addition to focusing on popular knowledge rather than mental structures, the common sense of the notebooks, unlike habitus, is inherently unsystematic. Certain elements of these assemblages of truisms may exhibit shared characteristics (the extent to which they do can only be determined by empirical investigation), but as a whole these accumulations are too multiple and various to constitute a coherent system. This incoherence, for Gramsci always a negative quality, reflects the condition of subalternity itself. As he writes in one passage, "Common sense takes countless different forms. Its most fundamental characteristic is that it is a conception which, even in the brain of one individual, is fragmentary, incoherent and [inconsistent], in conformity with the social and cultural position of those masses whose philosophy it is" (*SPN*, 419).[3]

Common sense is not confined to the masses, however. In another note, for instance, after distinguishing between philosophy and common sense, Gramsci immediately adds, "But every philosophy has a tendency to become the common sense of a fairly limited environment (that of all the intellectuals)" (*SPN*,

2. Crehan (2011b) provides an in-depth exploration of the difference between Gramsci's *common sense* and Bourdieu's.

3. Where *inconsistent* appears, Gramsci writes *inconsequente*, which Hoare and Nowell Smith translate as *inconsequential*. In this context, *inconsistent* would be a more accurate translation. I am grateful to Frank Rosengarten for drawing my attention to this mistranslation.

330). To some degree, we all live in a commonsense world, just not the same one: "Every social class has its own 'common sense'" (*SCW*, 420). We all continually channel the stream of events that wash over us into familiar narratives, making sense of what would otherwise appear random. The knowledge we draw on to do this is derived both from the particular circles in which we move, and our own life experiences as these are mediated by the narratives available to us. Over time this knowledge comes to constitute a solid, emotionally persuasive core against which we test both what happens to us, and how others explain the world to us. In a sense, we all have our own particular stock of common sense. Much of this will be shared by others in our immediate environment, diverging as those others become more distant. At any historical moment, even within the same place, there will be multiple narratives, some closely connected and overlapping, some conflicting and contradictory, but all of which are, to some rational beings, self-evident truths. One way to think about this tangle of narratives, which seem in certain ways to resemble each other and yet may not share any single characteristic, is as sharing what Wittgenstein termed "family resemblances." When we look at the multitude of apparently self-evident truths defined as common sense, it is hard to identify any one constant feature. We see rather "a complicated network of similarities overlapping and criss-crossing: sometimes overall similarities, sometimes similarities of detail" that, as with "the various resemblances between members of a family: build, features, colour of eyes, gait, temperament, etc, etc. overlap and criss-cross" (Wittgenstein 1968, 32). Similarly, while there is no one characteristic that all instances of common sense share, they seem, nonetheless, related. And it is these seemingly obvious similarities that help persuade us that there is indeed a single entity, common sense.

Despite all his criticisms, Gramsci's attitude to common sense is far from wholly negative. Embedded within the chaotic confusion of common sense that is both home and prison, he identifies what he terms *buon senso* (good sense). For instance, taking the common expression "being philosophical about it," he notes that while this expression may contain "an implicit invitation to resignation and patience," it can also be seen as an "invitation to people to reflect and to realise fully that whatever happens is basically rational and must be confronted as such." This appeal to use reason rather than blind emotion constitutes "the healthy nucleus that exists in 'common sense,' the part of it which can be called 'good sense' and which deserves to be made more unitary and coherent" (*SPN*, 328). Note that this good sense still needs to be made "more unitary and coherent," work that is done by intellectuals. Reflecting on "the merit of what is normally termed 'common sense' or 'good sense," he concludes that this merit consists not simply "in the fact that, if only implicitly, common sense applies the principle of causality, but in the much more limited fact that in a whole range of judgments common sense identifies the exact cause, simple and to hand, and does not let itself be distracted by fancy quibbles and pseudo-profound, pseudoscientific metaphysical mumbo-jumbo" (*SPN*, 348).

For Gramsci, we could say, common sense is a multistranded, entwined knot of, on the one hand, clear sightedness (good sense), which is not fooled by the sophistry of spin doctors; but, on the other, blinkered shortsightedness clinging defensively to the comfortable and the familiar. Common sense is, as he puts it, "crudely neophobe and conservative" (*SPN*, 423). But common sense is more than this; its nuggets of good sense also reflect "the creative spirit of the people." Those in search of genuine social transformation need to begin with those nuggets. As he writes in a passage quoted in the previous chapter, "Is it possible that a 'formally' new conception can present itself in a guise other than the crude, unsophisticated version of the populace?" (*SPN*, 342).

The doubleness of the attitude to common sense we find in the notebooks is sometimes missed, as by Rosenfeld, when she claims that Gramsci advocates that revolutionaries simply incorporate the good sense to be found in common sense directly into their political narratives. She cites an anonymous publication, *La femme patriote, ou le gros bon sens* (The patriotic woman, or solid good sense), written at the time of the French Revolution, supposedly by a "simple woman." The "common sense political theory," advanced by this simple woman was one that, as paraphrased by Rosenfeld, "should be obvious even to the most humble in her audience: kings rule only because they take power by force; hereditary privileges are unjust; and everyone needs bread" (Rosenfeld, 189). This, Rosenfeld claims, "is precisely how Antonio Gramsci, writing in prison in the 1920s, imagined an effective revolutionary making his (or her) case. Rather than disdaining an often contradictory and *retardataire* common sense, . . . revolutionaries need to do as the woman of 'basic good sense': identify with the sentiments of ordinary people and build directly on those precepts of folk wisdom that are nascent and feel true but are currently obscured or immobilized by other basic conceptions embedded in the collective mind. In this manner, a new practical consciousness or common sense should come into being for a people as a whole (Rosenfeld 2011, 189–90). But this is to gloss over the complicated dialectical relationship between "precepts of folk wisdom" and developed and coherent political philosophies. Gramsci does make a fundamental epistemological claim that the "good sense" elements contained within common sense, which represent awareness born out of the concrete experience of subalternity, are the seeds from which new political narratives emerge. But these seeds, unlike plant seeds, do not contain within themselves all the genetic information they need to grow; they are no more than "rough and jagged" beginnings (*SPN*, 343). Only through dialogue between subalterns and their organic intellectuals can these beginnings develop into effective revolutionary narratives.

Gramsci's Antiromanticism

Gramsci takes common sense so seriously precisely because he discerns within its confusion the embryonic beginnings of new political narratives, narratives with the potential to challenge the existing hegemony in ways that go beyond mere defensive resistance. At the same time, he never romanticizes common sense. And here his dispassionate and clear-eyed attitude is in sharp contrast to that of a number of social theorists who have appealed to common sense as something like a touchstone of truth. A good example is the great theorist of totalitarianism, and near contemporary of Gramsci, Hannah Arendt, who would "build a political theory rooted in common sense" (Rosenfeld 2011, 248). At first sight, it might seem that what Arendt is talking about when she speaks of common sense is so different from the common sense to be found in the notebooks that it scarcely makes sense to compare them. But in fact this very difference can help reveal both the originality of Gramsci's concept and the particular character this protean entity assumes in the notebooks.

Over the years, Arendt's definition of common sense would shift back and forth between its two strands of meaning. Sometimes she wrote of it very much as "the basic human facility that lets us make elemental judgements about everyday matters," as when she argues that "common sense occupies such a high rank in the hierarchy of political qualities because it is the one sense that fits into reality as a whole our five strictly individual senses and the strictly particular data they perceive. It is by virtue of common sense that the other sense perceptions are known to disclose reality and are not merely felt as irritations or our nerves or resistance sensations of our bodies" (1998, 208–9). Sometimes, however, she broadens her definition to include a particular body of knowledge as well as a mental facility, as when she writes that totalitarianism has led to a "growth of meaninglessness and loss of common sense (and common sense is only that part of our mind and that portion of inherited wisdom which all men have in common in any given civilization)" (1994, 316–17). Her positive assessment of common sense, however, remains constant. The general "rightness" of common sense comes across strongly in her essay, "Understanding and Politics" (1954), in which she grapples with the problem of how it is possible for theorists to grasp the nature of totalitarian political systems. Common sense here becomes an Ariadne thread, securely guiding the scholar, who "must become very humble again and listen closely to popular language":

> True understanding always returns to the judgements and prejudices which preceded and guided the strictly scientific inquiry. The sciences can only illuminate, but neither prove nor disprove, the uncritical preliminary understanding from which they start. If the scientist, misguided by the very labor of his inquiry, begins to pose as an expert in politics and despise the popular understandings from which he started, he loses immediately the Ariadne thread of common sense which alone will guide him securely through the labyrinth of his own results. If, on the other hand, the scholar wants to transcend his own knowledge—and there is no other way to make knowledge meaningful except by transcending it—he must become very humble again and listen closely to the popular language, in which words like "totalitarianism" are daily used as political clichés and misused as catchwords, in order to reestablish contact between knowledge and understanding. (1994, 311)

A little later in the same essay, Arendt describes one of the sad realities of twentieth-century totalitarian societies as "the breakdown of our common inherited wisdom . . . we are living in a topsy-turvy world, a world where we cannot find our way by abiding by the rules of what was once common sense" (314).

Gramsci, too, insists that intellectuals must listen to "popular understandings," but he has none of Arendt's deference towards such understandings. While he stresses the importance of treating common sense seriously, he is anything but humble toward it. Indeed, he is scathing about intellectuals, such as Giovanni Gentile, who celebrate common sense. Gentile, a leading fascist intellectual and Minister for Public Education in Mussolini's government, had claimed that philosophy could be thought of "as a great effort accomplished by reflective thought to gain critical certainty of the truths of common sense and of the naive consciousness; of those truths of which it can be said that every man feels them naturally and which constitute the solid structure of the mentality he requires for everyday life" (quoted in *SPN*, 422). For Gramsci, this was simply "yet another example of the disordered crudity of Gentile's thought." Homing in on Gentile's formulation "the truths of common sense," Gramsci asks: "And what does a 'truth of common sense' mean? Gentile's philosophy, for example, is utterly contrary to common sense, whether one understands thereby the naïve philosophy of the people, which revolts against any form of subjectivist idealism, or whether one understands it to be good sense and a contemptuous attitude to the abstruseness, ingenuities and obscurity of certain forms of scientific and philosophical exposition" (*SPN*, 422–23). This does not mean, Gramsci continues, "that there are no truths in common sense. It means rather that common sense is an ambiguous, contradictory and multiform concept, and that to refer to common sense as a confirmation of truth is a nonsense" (*SPN*, 423). As he puts it a little earlier in the same note, "Common sense is a chaotic aggregate of disparate conceptions, and one can find there anything that one likes" (*SPN*, 422). The author of the notebooks, one feels, would have been equally dismissive of Arendt's notion of common sense as "the Ariadne thread" that guides the scholar "securely through the labyrinth of his own results."

For Arendt, it is the existence of a shared, common sense that enables human beings to live together. Common sense, as she writes in "Understanding and Politics," "presupposes a common world into which we all fit, where we can live together because we possess one sense which controls and adjusts all strictly particular sense data to those of all others" (Arendt 1994, 318). Here, as so often, she is drawing on Immanuel Kant, for whom a *sensus communis* (a common sense) "fits us into a community" (Arendt 1982, 70). The notion of a single common sense, "which all men have in common in any given civilization," is quite foreign to the spirit of the notebooks. For Gramsci, as for Marx, "any given civilization" is so fractured by inequality that understanding it requires us to begin with that inequality, those "most elementary things, which are the first to be forgotten," the fact that "there really do exist rulers and ruled, leaders and led" (*SPN*, 144). Common sense in all its multitudinous confusion is the product of a fractured world.

The common sense of the notebooks, unlike that of Arendt, is neither unitary, nor an unfailing source of truth. It may contain valuable good sense but it is inherently unreliable; we cannot use common sense as a touchstone of truth. Emerging out of a world structured by inequality, common sense's ever-shifting accumulations of disparate truisms are the precipitates of heterogeneous life worlds occupying quite different social and economic locations. The narratives that become hegemonic are those that reflect the world as seen from the vantage point of the rulers rather than the ruled. Those that emerge from less privileged locations are forced to exist within the interstices of the dominant explanations; an ability to impose commonsense truths, which assume that existing power relations are the only ones possible, is a crucial dimension of any power regime. Hegemony, it should be noted, does not require that those who are ruled, the subalterns, see their subjugation as justified, only that they see it as a fixed and unchangeable reality it would be futile to oppose. Only to the extent that we accept, whatever our actual social and economic location, the hegemonic narratives portraying the world as seen from the vantage point of those who hold power might we say that we inhabit a common, shared world.

Toward a New Common Sense and a New Culture

We find none of Arendt's romanticization in the notebooks. Here common sense is a confusion of unexamined truisms that must be continually questioned. We are all born into a particular time and place with its own ways of naming the world and the forces that shape it. But the knowledge we inherit is far from being any kind of plain wisdom. This may be the place we feel at home, but this home, with its known and well-worn furniture, can also be a prison. We need to recognize its confining walls, and refuse the embrace of its seductive familiarity. In a passage that reflects the Sardinian peasant milieu in which he spent his childhood, Gramsci describes our earliest "conception of the world" as being "mechanically imposed by the external environment, i.e. by one of the many social groups in which everyone is automatically involved from the moment of his entry into the conscious world (and this can be one's village or province; it can have its origins in the parish and the 'intellectual activity' of the local priest or ageing patriarch whose wisdom is law, or in the little old woman who has inherited the lore of the witches or the minor intellectual soured by his own stupidity and inability to act)" (*SPN*, 323). As the dismissive tone makes clear, Gramsci's argument is that while we may have no choice but to begin from the common sense into which we are born, we should not accept its comforting familiarities unthinkingly, but continually question them, dragging into the light of day all the implicit, taken-for-granted assumptions buried within that which presents itself as simple reality. We must subject everything we are told is just "the way things are" to careful and rigorous questioning. As an individual, one has an obligation "to work out consciously and critically one's own conception of the world and thus, in connection with the labours of one's own brain, choose one's sphere of activity, take an active part in the creation of the history of the world, be one's own guide, refusing to accept passively and supinely from outside the moulding of one's personality" (*SPN*, 323–24).

The reference here to taking "an active part in the creation of the history of the world" indicates that working out "consciously and critically one's own conception of the world" is not some solipsistic exercise, but part of the process by which the individual comes to make an active political choice. Whether we like it or not, we are all part of some collectivity: "We are all conformists of some conformism or other, always man-in-the-mass or collective man. The question is this: of what historical type is the conformism, the mass humanity to which one belongs?" (SPN, 324). The point is to examine critically the choices we have, and to make a conscious choice. Those who interrogate their "conception of the world . . . to make it a coherent unity," will raise their thought "to the level reached by the most advanced thought in the world" (SPN, 324). In other words, they will identify with the progressive forces propelling history forward. It is clear that the creation of the history of the world Gramsci has in mind is epochal social transformation. And for him, an essential element of such social transformation is the bringing into being of a new common sense and a new culture. Marx himself, he notes, makes many references to common sense in which we can see an implicit "assertion of the necessity for new popular beliefs, that is to say a new common sense and with it a new culture and a new philosophy which will be rooted in the popular consciousness with the same solidity and imperative quality as traditional beliefs" (SPN, 424).

Common sense in the notebooks, as in this passage, is treated as part of a broader concept of culture. And culture, the author argues, is central to twentieth-century Marxism, which "in its most recent stage of development . . . consists precisely in asserting the moment of hegemony as essential to its conception of the state and in attaching 'full weight' to the cultural factor, to cultural activity, to the necessity for a cultural front alongside the merely economic and merely political ones" (FSPN, 345). Elsewhere I have explored Gramsci's understanding of culture at length (Crehan 2002) and I shall not repeat that discussion here. Given the entanglement of common sense and culture in the notebooks, it is important, however, to say something about the place of culture in those reflections. Culture, for Gramsci, names shared ways of being and living that have come into existence as a result of the interaction of a myriad of historical forces, and that remain subject to history. Certain cultures may appear to persist unchanged for long periods of time, nonetheless they are always inherently in flux: coming into being, undergoing transformation, passing away. The nature of their persistence or transformation can only be discovered by careful empirical study. Similarly, the degree to which they constitute coherent wholes, the degree to which they hang together, cannot be assumed. This, too, is an empirical question.

A brief look at the difference between the attitude to culture we find in the notebooks and that characteristic of anthropology may help clarify what

Gramsci understands by "the cultural factor" and "cultural activity." And why he insists on the need for "a cultural front."

Culture in Anthropology and Culture in the Notebooks

The importance the concept of culture has for this Sardinian Marxist is one reason so many anthropologists have been attracted to his work. As Clifford Geertz observed in a famous essay, culture was the concept "around which the whole discipline of anthropology arose" (Geertz 1973, 4). The problem is that while the concept of culture has been defined by anthropologists in many different ways, their motivation for studying it and their attitude to its preservation have not been those of Gramsci. We do not, for instance, find anthropologists arguing for "the necessity for a cultural front." To understand anthropologists' attitude to culture, we need to go back to the discipline's origins, in Europe and North America.

In Europe, the discipline's origins were rooted in that continent's expansion into new and unfamiliar worlds. While there was a desire to dominate these new worlds, there was also recognition that success depended on understanding them. And this gave rise, even if often indirectly, to a desire to understand these unfamiliar "others" in their own terms. Anthropologists may often have failed to live up to this ideal, but whatever their faults, colonial anthropologists tended to be more concerned to understand and preserve the "cultures" they studied rather than transform them—one reason why colonial administrators often found the work of anthropologists of little practical use. In North America, an expanding settler state's confrontation with indigenous people gave a somewhat different slant to the anthropological project: a focus on preserving some record of ways of life that were seen as inevitably doomed once they encountered more "advanced" Euro-American culture. In the 1970s, this approach would be termed, rather disparagingly, "salvage anthropology."[4] In the course of their history, both the European and the North American anthropological tradition, however, would develop a strong commitment to cultural relativism and a belief in the value of cultural diversity. Cultures, it tends to be assumed, have a right to exist simply because they are distinct cultures. Gramsci, committed as he is to the project of revolutionary transformation, has no such automatic reverence for existing cultures. Part of what subalternity means for him is being trapped in a world that reinforces and

4. The phrase *salvage anthropology* was coined by Jacob Gruber in his "Ethnographic Salvage and the Shaping of Anthropology" (1970).

reproduces a culture of subordination. Overcoming subalternity necessarily involves cultural change.

All of us come to consciousness as members of particular cultural worlds, and one of the ways the realities of class inequality are lived is through culture. The contours of our cultural worlds, including their hierarchies of power and their associated tangles of commonsense notions, are likely to appear to us as beyond question, so obviously real that it would be absurd to ask for evidence or proof: this is just the way the world is. Disparities of wealth and power, for instance, may be thought of as manifestations of the laws of economics or of divine will; they may be celebrated or railed against, but to those who inhabit a world structured by these disparities it is hard to imagine that things could be other than as they are. For there to be fundamental social change, therefore, there needs to be cultural transformation, "that is to say a new common sense and with it a new culture" (*SPN*, 424), that enables subalterns to imagine another reality. Otherwise, challenging existing power structures is likely to seem as absurd as Don Quixote charging windmills.

As an activist-intellectual working toward social transformation, Gramsci was committed to bringing about cultural change. This is very different from the respect for existing cultures so deeply ingrained in the anthropological tradition. To some anthropologists, calls for cultural change can have an uncomfortable echo of the exhortations of the modernization theorists of the 1960s, who argued that underdevelopment was the result of "traditional" cultures, which held back progress. The kind of cultural change envisaged by this Marxist writing in the early twentieth century, however, is one that represents a subordinated class overcoming its subordination, not a capitalist North imposing its economic culture on a South perceived as backward. The concern with culture and common sense that we find in the notebooks is rooted in the conviction that a vital dimension of the overcoming of subalternity is the creation of a new culture and a new common sense. This creation is the cultural front that Gramsci sees as so necessary. He stresses, however, that the precise forms the new culture and the new common sense will take cannot be known in advance; they will be determined in the course of history. All we can say is that they will be the result of dialogue between a subaltern group and its intellectuals, and will build on the good sense that exists within common sense.

Cultural transformation rarely happens overnight, although change can appear to be sudden. In the summer of 2015, the Supreme Court of the United States, reflecting the extraordinarily rapid shift in American attitudes to same-sex marriage, ruled that the Constitution guarantees a right to same-sex marriage. In reality, this recognition was the culmination of decades of work by

LGBT activists. A key moment seems to have been the adoption of a narrative structured around a claim that LGBT people were being denied a basic civil right: All adults have the right to marry, why was this denied to gays and lesbians? The LBGT community had, we might say, tapped into one of the most powerful American commonsense beliefs about their society, enshrined in the Declaration of Independence: "We hold these truths to be self-evident, that all men are created equal." The appeal to common sense is indeed foundational to American political discourse. As Thomas Jefferson later explained, his aim in drafting the declaration was "to place before mankind the common sense of the subject, in terms so plain and firm as to command their assent" (quoted in Tindall and Shi 1999, 235).

The ongoing struggle to transform culture can be seen as part of what Gramsci termed the war of position, as opposed to the war of movement, the kind of frontal attack that is rarely possible for a subaltern class, precisely because it is subaltern.[5] The distinction between a direct seizure of power and the slow, incremental struggle characteristic of subaltern classes echoes Engels's argument in his introduction to Marx's *The Class Struggles in France 1848–1850*, written in 1895. The proletariat, Engels explains, is "a long way from winning victory with one mighty stroke, it has slowly to press forward from position to position in a hard, tenacious struggle" (Marx 1964, 16). A key part of that struggle is the struggle for cultural change.

Common Sense and History

In English, common sense, whether understood as a universal sense, or as the incontrovertible knowledge that such a sense gives us, is generally thought of as unchanging and true across space and time. It is seen, so to speak, as outside history. For Gramsci, however, the "fragmentary, incoherent and inconsistent" heterogeneity that is common sense is always the product of a tangle of different historical processes. Common sense, he writes, "is a collective noun, like religion: there is not just one common sense, for that too is a product of history and a part of the historical process" (*SPN*, 325–26). Just as material debris gradually accumulates in any area of human habitation in a somewhat random fashion, so too do beliefs and ideas; there are always new ideas continually drifting down to join the existing agglomerate of common sense. Some only remain there momentarily, others for somewhat longer, while some manage to embed themselves in seemingly more secure ways. At the same time, to

5. See *SPN*, 229–41.

continue with the metaphor, the bits and pieces that make up common sense are also subject to processes of erosion and other forms of destruction. Certain ideas lose their plausibility and are discarded. Not so long ago, for instance, it was common sense that marriage meant a union between a man and a woman. The aggregate that is common sense is never stable but continually changing in piecemeal ways.

For Gramsci, the task of the analyst confronted with the confusion of common sense, like that of the archaeologist confronted with the material debris of the past, is to sort through the mass of beliefs and opinions. They need to identify the different elements that make up this mass, and trace out the links between particular assumed truths and social realities. As with material strata, the forces acting to consolidate or destroy the various elements of common sense are multiple and the results of their interactions are always unpredictable. Nonetheless, there are reasons why some elements persist and some do not; understanding this process in any actual context requires empirical analysis. We need to look at how the different elements are disseminated. What is it that makes them so self-evident, and self-evident to whom? Whose common sense (men's, women's, poor people's, the better off, the more educated, the less educated, the old, the young, particular religious groups, and so on) are they? What are the mechanisms through which they are, or are not, internalized by individuals—what, indeed, does it mean to internalize them? To what extent do different elements hang together? Do individuals pick and choose between them? How do they choose between them? And on and on.

Just as physical landscapes are shaped by geological forces, biological processes, and human activity, the landscapes of common sense are shaped both by deep structural forces and more contingent history. For Gramsci, as a Marxist, the tectonic plates grinding against each other deep below the visible landscape of common sense are a society's fundamental class cleavages. It is in those underlying cleavages that the questions that seem most pressing to the philosophers of a given historical moment have their ultimate origins. And the initial way those questions express themselves, albeit in a naive form, is in popular common sense. The history of philosophy should not be seen as consisting of the succession of a series of great minds, we need to look at the connection between ideas and their historical context. If, Gramsci writes, "philosophy develops because the general history of the world (and thus the social relations in which men live) develops, and not at all because a great philosopher is succeeded by a greater one and so on, it is clear that the practical work of creating history also creates 'implicit' philosophy, which then becomes 'explicit.' This will be the case in so far as philosophers elaborate it coherently, in so far as problems of knowledge ensue which, over and above the 'practical' form of solution, sooner or later find theoretical form through the work of specialists, after having immediately found their naïve form in popular common sense, i.e. among the practical agents of historical transformations" (*FSPN*, 387).

Ultimately, as this passage makes clear, for Gramsci it is the everyday reality of subaltern experience that gives birth to the implicit philosophies to be found within common sense. Progressive intellectuals have the task of articulating these philosophies in a coherent form. Fundamental social change comes about when such philosophies are embodied in social movements. The "practical agents of historical transformations" are subalterns, but their effectiveness depends on their bringing into being, as they emerge from subalternity, their own organic intellectuals. Together, subaltern experience and the intellectuals that are born of it give rise to a new culture and a new common sense, a common sense with deep roots in subaltern experience that carries the emotional charge of traditional beliefs while reflecting a coherent, rational philosophy. For this to happen, however, there needs to be a dialogue in which the emergent intellectuals genuinely listen to popular common sense, not humbly (as Arendt insists), but attentively and critically, mining its good sense.

The value of Gramsci's concept of common sense is that it offers us a way of thinking about the texture of everyday life that encompasses its givenness—how it both constitutes our subjectivity and confronts us as an external and solid reality—but that also acknowledges its contradictions, fluidity, and flexibility. For all its apparent solidity, it is continually being modified by how actual people in actual places live it. We can think of his notion of common sense as naming the comfortable, predictable certainties that provide all of us with much of our basic mental furniture. The fact that it does not define the nature of that furniture is what makes the concept such a useful way of approaching the empirical analysis of the lived reality of subalternity. On the one hand, this approach allows us to hear the contradictory, multiple voices that speak through popular knowledge; on the other, without romanticizing common sense, it helps us discover the good sense contained within its confusion. The next chapter explores the content of popular knowledge, and the nature of the relationship between subalterns and their organic intellectuals in more detail.

4

What Subalterns Know

[C]an modern theory be in opposition to the "spontaneous" feelings of the masses? ("Spontaneous" in the sense that they are not the result of any systematic educational activity on the part of an already conscious leading group, but have been formed through everyday experience illuminated by "common sense," i.e. by the traditional popular conception of the world . . .) It cannot be in opposition to them. Between the two there is a "quantitative" difference of degree, not one of quality. A reciprocal "reduction" so to speak, a passage from one to the other and vice versa, must be possible. — SELECTIONS FROM THE PRISON NOTEBOOKS, 198–99

The previous three chapters have explored Gramsci's concepts of subalternity, intellectuals, and common sense. This chapter explores how, taken together, these three concepts provide us with a flexible yet structured approach to the problem of the relationship between the experience of inequality and the political narratives that emerge from it.

Can Subalterns Speak?

Left hanging at the end of my discussion of Gayatri Spivak and James Scott in chapter 1 was the question, where does the author of the prison notebooks stand on the issue of subalterns' ability to speak? We are now ready to return to it. As I hope has become clear, contra Spivak, Gramsci's concern throughout the notebooks is on collective rather than individual manifestations of subaltern speech. Ultimately, for him, the important question is how subaltern narratives are transformed into effective challenges to an existing hegemony. It is important to stress *effective* here; he is perfectly well aware that subalterns complain about their oppression and their exploitation, and often see it as unjust. The problem is that such rejection does not escape the prevailing hegemony: "Subaltern classes," as he puts it, "are subject to the initiatives of the dominant classes, even when they rebel; they are in a state of anxious defense" (*PNII*, 21). And here he is in agreement with Spivak: both dispute Scott's assertion that there are always spaces "outside the earshot of powerholders" where subalterns' "hidden transcripts" can be found. For Gramsci, as for Spivak, subalterns inhabit a world in which the major conceptual structures available to them are themselves inextricably bound up with the hegemonic narratives of the dominant classes. This is part of what defines the condition of subalternity.

Relevant here is the notebooks' rejection of what we might call the billiard-table model of society, which imagines societies as collections of distinct and autonomous individuals who interact with each other like billiard balls on a billiard table. Rather, Gramsci suggests, we should think of human beings as ensembles of social relations, ensembles that come into being in specific historical contexts. In a note entitled "Progress and Becoming," for instance, Gramsci reflects on the question of "what is man? what is human nature? If man is defined as an individual, psychologically and speculatively, these problems of progress and becoming are insoluble or remain purely verbal. But if man is conceived as the *ensemble* of social relations, it then appears that every comparison between men, over time, is impossible, because one is dealing with different, if not heterogeneous, objects" (*SPN*, 359).

Once we move from thinking of individuals as autonomous entities and begin to see them instead as the sum of their relationships with the human and natural world, the very notion of subjectivity shifts. Subjectivity now becomes the product of our life experiences as social individuals; in the course of our particular histories, both as individuals and as members of various groups, our sense of who we are emerges as we navigate through the relationships we have with others and with the world. Crucially, however, we never experience what happens to us in a raw, unmediated way. We all carry with us whole bundles of sometimes shifting beliefs and assumptions that we use to make sense of our experience. We acquire these beliefs and assumptions as a result of the myriad forms of socialization to which we are exposed: home, neighborhood, school, work, the mass media, social media, and on and on. Not that we simply accept the explanations we have internalized; rather, whether explicitly or implicitly, we engage with them.

The American artist Cindy Sherman's *Untitled Film Stills*, produced in the late 1970s, provides a compelling visual exploration of how we are both caught by, but also in dialogue with, the social narratives that surround us. In the photographs of *Untitled Film Stills*, Sherman presents herself in a series of invented personas and situations that in an almost uncanny way capture the mood and feeling of various film genres, such as film noir, melodrama, and so on. Even though we know that none of Sherman's images are actual stills from actual films, it is often hard to banish the sense that we are seeing a scene from a film we once saw and half remember. We can see these supposed film stills as dramatizing how the images of popular culture help produce our subjectivity. They confront us with women performing preassigned roles. In palpable form, they show how powerfully the repertoire of images presented to us in films and other forms of popular culture define the options women see as available to them. Reflecting on the series more than thirty years after they were first shown, the art critic Hal Foster noted that "the ingénues in the [*Untitled Film Stills*] are not simply the victims of imposed roles, as some of us wrote at the time. These are scenes less of ideological interpellation from the outside than aspirational identification from within: the young women struggle to approximate the scripted types, not to escape from them" (Foster 2012, 12).

We should note that while Sherman focuses on the scripted types presented to women, men, too, confront a repertoire of scripts. One significant difference, however, is that the scripts available to women are the product of a male-dominated world. The young women portrayed by Sherman are essentially women as seen through male eyes, something that becomes increasingly apparent as the filmic worlds Sherman drew on in *Untitled Film Stills* recede ever further into a seemingly distant and almost quaint past that predates second-wave feminism. And insofar as even the privileged women of the Global North have found themselves continually having to perform scripts written by men, they too, at least in this respect, inhabit a subaltern reality. Living in a world where the dominant scripts on offer have not been written by people like you is one of the defining characteristics of subalternity. Subalterns live in a commonsense world rooted in the narratives of those who dominate them.

This is not to say that subaltern groups have no collective, shared narratives but rather that such "hidden transcripts," generated as they are under the shadow of others' hegemonic narratives, tend to be fragmentary and hard to interpret. Unvalued and unrecorded by the society at large, they are not so much transcripts as traces. And since such traces often fail to conform, either in their language or their content, to the prevailing hegemonic norms, they tend to appear—particularly to a society's dominant groups—incoherent and unintelligible.

Gramsci's attitude to subalterns' own narratives of the worlds they inhabit is complex. On the one hand, he sees such narratives as confused and chaotic, laden with superstition and governed by emotion rather than reason; on the other, he sees them as the ultimate source of genuinely new narratives, narratives with the power to inspire revolutionary change. We might remember here his rhetorical question: "Is it possible that a 'formally' new conception can present itself in a guise other than the crude, unsophisticated version of the populace?" (*SPN*, 342). In other words, crude and unsophisticated as it may be, subaltern common sense is the ultimate source of new political narratives capable of effectively challenging those of the capitalist hegemony. It is this conviction that explains why Gramsci is so insistent that progressives seek out and listen to that common sense. In the notebooks, he gives many examples of where subaltern common sense, albeit often in fragmentary form, can be found. But while he takes common sense extremely seriously, he refuses to romanticize it. His complex, double attitude to subaltern "knowledge" is revealed in some of his reflections on Italian dialects and their relation to the national language. Before looking in more detail at where Gramsci suggests we search for expressions of subaltern common sense, it is instructive to tease out some of that doubleness.

Language and Subalternity

Language, for Gramsci, the former linguistics student, is never a neutral and transparent medium for transmission of content: "every language is an integral conception of the world and not just an outer garment that functions indifferently as a form for any content" (*PNII*, 366). The linguistic gulf between the educated and the "popular element" in the Italy of Gramsci's time was exacerbated by the fact that so many Italians did not speak Italian but one of the many regional dialects. One widely cited history of the spread of Italian after unification in 1861 estimates that at the time of unification no more than 2.5 percent of the population were Italian speakers. For the remaining 97.5 percent, Italian was a foreign language; their language was one of the many regional dialects (figures quoted in Tosi 2001, 5). By the early twentieth century, Italian was still only used habitually by some 20 percent, although an estimated 50 percent "could use Italian of some sort" (Richardson 2001, 69). The question of how Italian could be made a genuinely national language remained a hotly debated topic throughout Gramsci's lifetime.

Growing up in a small provincial town in Sardinia, mastery of the Italian language did not come easily to the future author of the notebooks. In an evocative essay, Pier Paolo Pasolini, the filmmaker and Gramsci admirer, reflects on those linguistic struggles, tracing out the slow progress toward "the security, the richness, the absolute quality of so much of his writing" (1982, 185). This is how he imagines the young Sardinian's early encounters with Italian:

> [Gramsci's] infancy and early adolescence were spent in a peasant milieu, in which Italian must have struck the ear as a language foreign to the Sardinians of Ghilarza, more in contact with America than Italy. Gramsci would have heard his first, resounding Italian out of the mouths of his "self-styled" professors of literature, teachers at the private grammar school of Santa Lussurgiu. (And, given that they must prove themselves accredited, even though not required to, their Italian would naturally be a constant, caricatural effort to approximate a purist, pompous humanism.) Gramsci, as the poor, set-apart little boy, experienced and profoundly interiorized every event of his childhood; and since, throughout his life, he suffered the shame, the impediment of his early self-sacrifice, that encounter with an official Italian which stood for culture and liberation must also have marked him deeply. (180–81)

The set-apart little boy would go on to study linguistics at Turin University, and these studies helped shape him as an intellectual. Indeed, Peter Ives, in his insightful study *Gramsci's Politics of Language*, argues persuasively that Gramsci's "studies in linguistics are central to his entire thought" (2004, 16). A particularly strong influence was Matteo Bartoli, one of his professors in Turin and a pioneer in the newly emerging field of neolinguistics. For Gramsci, as for Bartoli, language is rooted in culture and no language can be understood in isolation from its culture. The very term *language* encompasses far more than the purely linguistic. Language is one dimension of culture; it is "essentially a collective term which does not presuppose any single thing existing in time and space. Language also means culture and philosophy (if only at the level of common sense) and therefore the fact of 'language' is in reality a multiplicity of facts more or less organically coherent and co-ordinated. At the limit it could be said that every speaking being has a personal language of his own, that is his own particular way of thinking and feeling. Culture, at its various levels, unifies in a series of strata, to the extent that they come into contact with each other, a greater or lesser number of individuals who understand each other's mode of expression in differing degrees, etc." (*SPN*, 349).

According to this broad definition of language, how we experience the world and how we act in it are not only continually mediated by language; they are to an important degree the product of language. As another note puts it, "[L]anguage = thought. The way one speaks indicates not only the way one thinks and feels, but also the way one expresses oneself, the way one makes others understand and feel" (*SCW*, 129). In other words, language is one of the most important ways we engage with the world.

Gramsci's attitude to his country's regional dialects echoes his attitude to popular culture. He has no doubt that standard Italian provides its speakers with access to an intellectual richness that a dialect lacks. Reflecting his basic progressivism, he sees standard Italian as representing a more advanced world-view than that of dialect, writing in one note:

> If it is true that every language contains the elements of a conception of the world and of a culture, it could also be true that from anyone's language one can assess the greater or lesser complexity of his conception of the world. Someone who only speaks dialect, or understands the standard language incompletely, necessarily has an intuition of the world which is more or less limited and provincial, which is fossilised and anachronistic in relation to the major currents of thought which dominate world history. His interests will be limited, more or less corporate or economistic, not universal. While it is not always possible to learn a number of foreign languages in order to put oneself in contact with other cultural lives, it is at the least necessary to learn the national language properly. A great culture can be translated into the language of another great culture, that is to say a great national language with historic richness and complexity, and it can translate any other great culture and can be a world-wide means of expression. But a dialect cannot do this. (*SPN*, 325)

Here Gramsci's condemnation of dialect as confining its speakers within a "limited and provincial" understanding of the world is unambiguous. Elsewhere, however, he insists just as strongly on the emotional richness of dialect and the importance of allowing, indeed encouraging, children to speak it. In a letter he wrote to his sister Teresina, for instance, he literally begs her to let her young son Franco speak Sardinian:

> Franco looks very vivacious and intelligent: I'm sure that he already speaks fluently. In what language does he speak? I hope that you will let him speak Sardinian and will not make any trouble for him on that score. It was a mistake, in my opinion, not to allow Edmea [the daugh-

ter of Gramsci's elder brother Gennaro] to speak freely in Sardinian as a little girl. This harmed her intellectual development and put her imagination in a straightjacket. You mustn't make this mistake with your children. For one thing Sardinian is not a dialect but a language in itself, even though it does not have a great literature, and it is a good thing for children to learn several languages, if it is possible. Besides, the Italian you will teach them will be a poor, mutilated language made up of only the few sentences and words of your conversations with him, purely childish; he will not have any contact with a general environment and will end up learning two jargons and no language: an Italian jargon for official conversation with you and a Sardinian jargon learned piecemeal to speak with the other children and the people he meets in the street or piazza. I beg you, from my heart, not to make this mistake and to allow your children to absorb all the Sardinian spirit they wish and to develop spontaneously in the natural environment in which they were born: this will not be an impediment to their future, just the opposite. (*PLI*, 89)

These two passages, one from the notebooks, one from a letter, describe two very different ways of engaging with the world and through that engagement understanding it. The first passage, arguing for the superiority of standard Italian, comes from the same note (quoted in chapter 3) that castigates the narrow parochialism and backwardness of the kind of rural area in which Gramsci himself was raised, insisting that while we may have no choice about our place of birth, we can, and should, struggle to transcend its limitations. If we are to arrive at an understanding of the world based on reason, we need to begin by challenging the incoherent mass of commonsense certainties we have inherited, bringing reason and more advanced ideas to bear on them, raising our thought "to the level reached by the most advanced thought in the world" (*SPN*, 324). For an Italian, this requires a knowledge of the standard language; those who speak only dialect will have a "fossilised and anachronistic" understanding of the world. To understand the world in a considered, critical way, based on reason, we need the knowledge embodied in a language that has been shaped by a "great culture."

Gramsci's Italy, however, was a country where standard Italian was not the language the mass of the people grew up speaking. And not only did dialect-speakers not have the opportunity to acquire a mastery of the national language as they were growing up, that national language did not offer the secure home that the dialect spoken within the family and local community did. Someone without secure emotional and imaginative roots in their language will be in some sense crippled, as had happened, Gramsci believed, in the case of his niece Edmea. Forbidding Edmea from speaking Sardinian had prevented her from developing intellectually and "put her imagination in a straightjacket." Before we can raise our thinking "to the level reached by the most advanced thought in the world," we need to have a solid foundation in a language in which we feel at home. Throughout his life, Gramsci seems to have maintained a deep emotional connection to the language and culture of his birthplace. And, as the tone of the letter to his sister indicates, his appreciation of the Sardinian language was not the result of abstract reason, but had deep, visceral roots.

Gramsci's attitude to common sense echoes his attitude to dialect; he both criticizes its limitations and recognizes its emotional power. But common sense, for him, is also a site where the seeds of a new conception of the world are to be found, a narrative of reality with the power to challenge the existing hegemony. These seeds are the still incoherent expression of the world as viewed from the vantage point of a subaltern group beginning to overcome its subalternity. Those working to bring about social transformation need to seek out all traces of such subaltern conceptions of the world, however unsophisticated they may be. This is not an easy task, not only because of their fragmentary nature, but also because subaltern narratives are rarely recognized by those who maintain a society's authorized archives. If recorded at all, such narratives are found only in the margins of the official record, and even then only as the ears of those in power have heard them. Nonetheless, traces exist and, taking subaltern common sense as our guide, it is possible to map out some key contours of subaltern conceptions of reality. The notebooks suggest the places we need to look. These include folklore, serial novels, and other forms of popular culture, readers' letters to newspapers, diaries, and other autobiographical writings left by subaltern individuals. We can think of such sources as constituting something like an alternative archive within which traces of subaltern conceptions of the world have been deposited. We should not search in the notebooks, however, for detailed examples of these traces. What their author gives us is rather a guide as to where we should look. A tour through Gramsci's archive helps reveal what common sense is for Gramsci, and the linkages he sees between common sense, subalterns, and intellectuals.

Gramsci's Archive of Subaltern Conceptions

An important source of subaltern conceptions of the world is folklore. Gramsci's attitude to folklore is often extremely critical, as in his scorn for "the little old woman who has inherited the lore of the witches" (*SPN*, 323). But he is by no means simply dismissive: he takes folklore extremely seriously. For Gramsci, who grew up in a peasant environment that was, in the words of one of his biographers, "riddled with witchcraft, spell-casting and belief in the super- natural" (Davidson, 1977, 18), folklore could never be the quaint and pictur- esque remnants of a bygone age. The world of his childhood was one in which people had no doubt that living among them were women who transformed themselves at night into creatures that "sucked the blood from babies," and that "[g]hosts returned as Will-o'-the-wisps to squat on the breasts of sleeping people" (Davidson 1977, 18). Daily life for the Gramsci family's peasant neigh- bors involved constant vigilance against powerful, malignant forces, and it was these forces that people tended to blame for the various misfortunes that befell them: children or livestock dying or failing to thrive, crop failures, and any of the host of ills endemic to peasant communities. In Gramsci's eyes, such folklore acts to blind people to the real sources of their oppression and exploitation. The reason to study it is so as to challenge it more effectively. And here the schoolteacher is an important agent of change. Teachers need to com- bat the retrograde beliefs of folklore and replace them with a more "modern" outlook, but this requires those teachers to have a genuine understanding of the folklore-saturated world of their pupils:

> For the teacher, then, to know "folklore" means to know what other conceptions of the world and of life are actually active in the intellectual and moral formation of young people, in order to uproot them and replace them with conceptions which are deemed to be superior. . . . The teaching of folklore to teachers should reinforce this systematic process even further.
>
> It is clear that, in order to achieve the desired end, the spirit of folk- lore studies should be changed, as well as deepened and extended. Folk- lore must not be considered an eccentricity, an oddity or a picturesque element, *but as something which is very serious and is to be taken seri- ously*. Only in this way will the teaching of folklore be more efficient and really bring about the birth of a new culture among the broad popular masses, so that the separation between modern culture and popular culture of folklore will disappear. (*SCW*, 191; emphasis mine)

Just how seriously Gramsci took this cultural struggle is clear from the next sentence, with which he ends the note: "An activity of this kind, thoroughly carried out, would correspond on the intellectual plane to what the Reformation was in Protestant countries."

Though folklore, for Gramsci, contains much that needs to be "uprooted and replaced," he also sees it as a manifestation of common sense and, as such, as containing elements of good sense. It is significant, for instance, that he writes here about the birth of a new culture. It is not simply a matter of progressive teachers bringing an already fully formed modern culture to the backward masses, but rather the bringing into being of a new culture that draws from the good sense embedded in folklore and common sense as a whole.

Folklore is also an important source of evidence for how subalterns have seen the worlds in which they live, at different historical moments. Folklore, rather than being studied as some exotic and picturesque curiosity, "should . . . be studied as a 'conception of the world and life' implicit to a large extent in determinate (in time and space) strata of society and in opposition (also for the most part implicit, mechanical and objective) to 'official' conceptions of the world (or in a broader sense, the conceptions of the cultured parts of historically determinate societies) that have succeeded one another in the historical process" (SCW, 189). The conceptions of the world to be found in folklore, however, are necessarily incoherent. Gramsci continues:

> This conception of the world is not elaborated and systematic because, by definition, the people (the sum total of the instrumental and subaltern classes of every form of society that has so far existed) cannot possess conceptions which are elaborated, systematic and politically organized and centralized in their albeit contradictory development. It is, rather, many-sided—not only because it includes different and juxtaposed elements, but also because it is stratified, from the more crude to the less crude—if, indeed, one should not speak of a confused agglomerate of fragments of all the conceptions of the world and of life that have succeeded one another in history. In fact, it is only in folklore that one finds surviving evidence, adulterated and mutilated, of the majority of these conceptions. (SCW, 189)

And folklore is not confined to the traditional, as conventionally understood: "Philosophy and modern science are also constantly contributing new elements to 'modern folklore' in that certain opinions and scientific notions, removed from their context and more or less distorted, constantly fall within the popular domain and are 'inserted' into the mosaic of tradition. (*La scoperta de l'America* by C. Pascarella shows how notions about Christopher Columbus and about a whole set of scientific opinions, put about by school textbooks and the 'Popular Universities,' can be strangely assimilated)" (*SCW*, 189).[1]

Every time and place has its own contradictory bundle of common sense and good sense notions containing not only notions carried over from the past, but newly minted ones. The focus should be on the relationship between specific threads of common sense and specific life-worlds. Gramsci takes to task various Italian authors of his own day who "lump together pell-mell all the generic folklore motifs that in reality have very distinct temporal and spatial characteristics" (*SCW*, 306).

For Gramsci, the basic structuring opposition in any society is not that between the traditional and the modern but, as the concept of subalternity itself indicates, that between the dominated and the dominant.[2] His refusal to reify the traditional as the site of some kind of privileged authenticity helps explain his openness to popular culture in all its forms. The popular culture he had available to him in his prison cell was essentially limited to printed matter, the serial novels and other publications aimed at a mass readership to be found in the prison library, mass-circulation newspapers, and so on. Nonetheless, given the right attitude, as he explains in one of his letters to Tatiana, a prisoner can find riches in even the meager and unscholarly resources of a prison library. The letter is a response to a request from the wife of a political prisoner, passed on to him by Tatiana, for advice for her husband on how best to study in prison. Gramsci writes:

[M]any prisoners underestimate the prison library. Of course prison libraries in general are a jumble: the books have been gathered at random, from donations by charitable organizations that receive warehouse remainders from publishers, or from books left behind by released prisoners. Devotional books and third-rate novels abound. Nevertheless I believe that a political prisoner must squeeze blood even from a stone. It is all a matter of setting a purpose for one's readings and of knowing how to take notes (if one is permitted to write). I'll give two examples: in Milan I read a certain number of books of all kinds, especially popular novels . . . Well I found that even Sue, Montepin, Ponson du Terrial,

1. "La scoperta de l'America" (The discovery of America) is a burlesque poem by Cesare Pascarella, written in 1894, telling the story of Columbus's voyage in Roman dialect.

2. Crehan (2002) develops this point.

etc. were sufficient when read from this point of view: why is this sort of literature almost always the most read and the most published? what needs does it satisfy? what aspirations does it answer? what emotions and points of view are represented in these trashy books for them to be so popular? How is Eugene Sue different from Montepin? And does Victor Hugo too belong in this series of writers because of the subjects he deals with? And are *Scampolo* or *L'Aigrette* or *Volata* by Dario Nicodemi perhaps not the direct descendants of this late 1848 romanticism?[3] etc etc. The second example is this: a German historian, Gruithausen, has recently published a big book in which he studies the links between French Catholicism and the bourgeoisie during the two centuries before 1889. He has studied all the devotional literature of these two centuries: collections of sermons, catechisms from the various dioceses, etc. etc. and he has put together a magnificent book. (*PLI*, 262–63)

Nowadays the study of popular culture along the lines suggested here has become common in a number of disciplines, but in the 1920s and 30s it was a rare scholar who thought such stuff worthy of study. Decades after his death, Gramsci would be a key figure in the development of what came to be called cultural studies. *Antonio Gramsci: Selections from the Prison Notebooks*, edited by Hoare and Nowell Smith (1971), for instance, would be a major influence on the research group at the Centre for Cultural Studies at University of Birmingham, who under Stuart Hall's leadership established cultural studies as a distinct field in Britain.

His advice to the political prisoner makes it clear that Gramsci's motivation in searching the jumble of the prison library is to discover shared subaltern concepts of the world. His letter centers on the question of why popular literature is popular. What emotional needs does it satisfy? What conceptions of the world are represented in these "trashy books"? The supposed "transformation of the Gramscian idea insofar as the subaltern . . . would call out in a collective voice" (see chapter 1) that Spivak attributes to Guha is surely not a transformation but an accurate reflection of his focus on the collective.

It is worth noting that Gramsci's recognition of the value of popular literature makes no aesthetic claims for it: these are "trashy books." As regards his own tastes, he was a man of high culture. The authors he responded to on an aesthetic level tended to be literary giants such as Dante, Shakespeare, Tolstoy,

3. Dario Nicodemi (1874–1934) was a popular playwright and novelist. *Scampolo*, *L'Aigrette*, and *Volata* are three of his plays.

and Pirandello. But these, too, he saw not as existing outside political and economic realities, but as shaped by their particular historical moment. His insistence on this point is reflected in a note in which he discusses "utopias" and "so-called philosophical novels." For him, "one of their most interesting aspects to consider is [such novels] unwitting reflection of the most elementary and profound aspirations of even the lowest subaltern social groups, albeit through the minds of intellectuals preoccupied with other concerns" (*SCW*, 238).

The value of popular literature, and popular culture in general, lies in what it can tell us about the commonsense world of subalterns. Gramsci's distinction between aesthetic value and the beliefs and values embodied in works of art transforms the prison library's trashy books from bad literature into valuable documents in the archive of subaltern conceptions of the world. Popular literature can provide important clues to the worlds in which subalterns live; this is what makes that literature important and why, as a form of modern folklore, it should be taken seriously by those seeking traces of subaltern voices.

Particularly interesting to this intellectual in search of subaltern worldviews was the popularity of that quintessential nineteenth-century literary form, the serial novel. Indeed, as we saw, "the serial novel and popular taste in literature" is one of the four topics he lists in the letter to Tatiana in which he first lays out his plans for his prison studies. What explains, for instance, the appeal of Alexandre Dumas's *The Count of Monte Cristo*, first published in France in serial form from 1884 to 1885? From the moment the first installments started appearing, the book was a runaway success, and it would go on to become one of the nineteenth century's most popular novels, not only in France but throughout Europe and indeed beyond. Even today, it remains a staple of popular culture. The novel tells the story of a man falsely imprisoned for many years, who escapes, and through his discovery of a treasure hoard becomes enormously wealthy. He then proceeds to exact vengeance on those responsible for his imprisonment while rewarding those who helped him. For Gramsci, it is the archetypal serial novel. It can be seen as reflecting the frustrations and fantasies of the common man: "The serial novel is a substitute for (and, at the same time, it stimulates) the fantasies of the common man; it really is daydreaming. . . . In this case, one could say that the fantasies of the people stem from a (social) 'inferiority complex' that is the source of fantasies about revenge, punishing those responsible for their adversities, etc. *The Count of Monte Cristo* contains all the ingredients to induce these flights of fancy and hence to administer a narcotic that dulls the sense of pain, etc." (*PNIII*, 106).

The common man (or common woman) is not, however, one undifferentiated entity. The diversity of the subordinated is another leitmotif in the notebooks. We need to pay attention to the specific forms of subalternity that exist in specific contexts. There is no single subaltern, but always particular subaltern groups or classes. Different kinds of popular literature appeal to different audiences. Another note explains why chivalric romances, such as *Guerin Meschino*, were so popular with the peasants of southern Italy: "*Guerino*, together with a whole list of similar books (*Il Reali di Francia, Bertoldo*, tales of bandits, knights, etc.) typifies a particular type of popular literature: the most rudimentary and primitive type of literature that circulates among the most backward and 'isolated' strata of the population, especially those in the south, in the mountains, etc. Those who read *Guerino* do not read Dumas or *Les Misérables*, much less Sherlock Holmes. There is a specific kind of folklore, a particular type of 'common sense' that corresponds to these strata" (*PNIII*, 147).[4] Gramsci goes on to remark, "One could analyse *Guerino* as an 'encyclopedia' to gather information on the mental coarseness and the cultural indifference of the vast stratum of people who still feed on it" (*PNIII*, 148).

Central to his reflections on popular culture is Gramsci's challenge to the distinction between "authentic" and "inauthentic" popular culture, between works produced by "the people" and those created for them. He homes in on one Ermolao Rubieri, who had proposed a threefold classification for popular songs. According to Rubieri, as paraphrased by Gramsci, there are: "1) songs composed by the people and for the people; 2) songs composed for the people but not by the people; 3) songs written neither by the people nor for the people, but which the people have nevertheless adopted because they conform to their way of thinking and feeling." To which Gramsci responds: "It seems to me that all popular songs could and should be reduced to the third category, since what distinguishes popular song, within the framework of a nation and its culture, is not its artistic element or its historical origin, but its way of conceiving of the world and life, in contrast with official society" (*PNII*, 399–400). In other words, what is important is whether a song, a novel, or any other work of popular culture resonates with subalterns, the degree to which it appears to them to reflect the world as they know it. Just because a work has been produced by commercial interests does not mean that it does not reflect traces

4. Joseph Buttigieg provides the following glosses: "*Guerin meschino* (The humble guerino) and *I reali di Francia* (The monarchs of France) are the best-known and most popular chivalric romances by Andrea da Barberino (ca. 1370–ca. 1431)" (*PNII*, 406). "Bertoldo, a coarse, ungainly, but astute and crafty peasant, and his slow-witted son Bertoldino are the main characters in the popular tales by Guilio Cesare Croce (1550–1609), a Bolognese storyteller" (*PNIII*, 483).

of subaltern conceptions. So-called commercial literature also has its place in the archive of subaltern conceptions. In a note reflecting on what makes art interesting, Gramsci elaborates on the meaning of *commercial*:

> What makes it "commercial" is the fact that the "interesting" element is not "candid," "spontaneous," intimately fused with the artistic conception, rather it is sought after from the outside, mechanically, and it is doled out industrially, as a sure element of immediate "success." Still this means that even commercial literature must not be neglected in the history of culture. Indeed, it is extremely valuable, precisely from the point of view of the history of culture, for the success of a work of commercial literature is indicative (and often it is the only existing indicator) of the "philosophy of the age," that is, of the mass of sentiments {and conceptions of the world}[5] prevalent among the "silent" multitude. This literature is a "narcotic" of the people, an "opium."

The note continues with an elaboration of just how this "opium" works among those who no longer believe, as they once did, in divine retribution. *The Count of Monte Cristo* once again provides a concrete example: "A. Dumas's *Count of Monte Cristo*, which is perhaps the biggest opiate of the popular novels, could be analyzed from this perspective. What man in the street does not believe he has been treated unjustly by the powerful and does not fantasize about the 'punishment' to inflict upon them? Edmond Dantès [*The Count of Monte Cristo*'s protagonist] offers him the model, 'intoxicates' him with excitement, replaces the belief in a transcendental justice in which he no longer 'systematically' believes" (*PNII*, 313). Perhaps rather surprising to the reader in the twenty-first century, Gramsci includes opera among such narcotic popular art. In Italy, however, opera in the nineteenth and early twentieth century had a strong popular following. Opera is, indeed, a good example of how what is popular culture in one time and place can be transformed into high culture in another, a process helped if, as with Italian opera outside Italy, it involves a foreign language. For the author of the prison notebooks, who seems always to have responded more to the written word than music, opera is yet another form of escapist art:

> The baroque and the operatic seem, to many common people, an extraordinarily fascinating way of thinking and behaving that helps them

---

5. "And conceptions of the world" was subsequently inserted by Gramsci in the text of the notebook.

escape whatever they consider coarse, mean, despicable in their lives and education, so that they may enter a more exclusive sphere of high sentiments and noble passions. The serial novel and maidservant literature (all saccharine, mellifluous, mournful literature) provide heroes and heroines, but opera is the most contagious because words set to music are easier to memorize—they become like matrices in which the fluidity of thought is moulded into shape. Observe how many common people write: they recycle clichés.

On the other hand, sarcasm is too corrosive. One must bear in mind that this is not factitious snobbery but something that is deeply felt and experienced. (*PNIII*, 263–64)

I want to draw attention to the final paragraph here. Gramsci clearly had a horror of sentimentality; his distaste for anything with even the slightest hint of the saccharin runs through both the notebooks and the prison letters. But while he may have been a man of high culture with fastidious personal tastes, he also recognized the genuine emotion that lay behind common people's love of trashy art and saw its value. One of the letters to Tatiana contains a remembrance of Giacomo Bernolfo, a man who had once been his bodyguard, which is very revealing:

I am very sorry and much aggrieved by Giacomo's death; our friendship was much deeper and intense than you could possibly have realized, also because outwardly Giacomo was not very expansive and a man of few words. He was a rare person I assure you . . . When I met him right after the war, his strength was Herculean (he was a sergeant in the mountain artillery and used to carry cannon parts of great weight on his shoulders) and his courage was utterly fearless, though without boastfulness. And yet his emotional sensitivity was remarkably acute, even taking on melodramatic accents, which however were sincere, not affected. He knew a great number of verses by heart, but all of them belonging to that third-rate romantic literature loved so much by simple people [*popolo*] (along the lines of opera librettos, which are mostly written in a very peculiar baroque style with disgustingly pathetic mawkishness, which however seem to be astonishingly appealing), and he liked to recite them, though he would blush like a child caught in error whenever I joined the audience to listen to him. This memory is the most vivid aspect of his character that insistently comes back to my mind: this gigantic man who with sincere passion declaims verses, in bad taste but that express robust and impetuous elementary passions, and who stops short and blushes when his listener is an "intellectual" even though a friend. (*PLII*, 159)

Gramsci is always concerned with what actually appeals to common people. Intellectuals like himself might find much popular culture "disgustingly pathetic and mawkish," but it provides a series of glimpses of subaltern worlds with their "robust and impetuous," but "sincere" emotional landscapes. The need for progressive intellectuals to pay serious attention to that which resonates with the subalterns they wish to reach is another of the notebooks' leitmotifs.

Another potential source of objective data on this is research on public libraries: "The literature on the public libraries in Milan should be studied to obtain some 'real' ideas about popular culture: which kinds of books and authors are read most, etc.; publications of the public libraries, their character, tendencies, etc." (*PNI*, 331). More direct traces of subaltern voices are to be found in the letters to the editors of newspapers. Such letters constitute "one of the most typical documents of Italian popular common sense" (*PNI*, 108). As *typical* here indicates, it is always the commonalities that interest Gramsci.

The occasional diary or other autobiographical writing by a subaltern individual provides a rarer trace: "In *La Lectura* of 1928, Pietro Nurra published the previously unpublished diary of one of the combatants in the five days of Milan, Giovanni Romani from Mantua . . . The diary consists of a sort of notebook with 199 numbered pages, of which 186 are filled with writing in crude calligraphy and horrible wording."[6] It is interesting "because the common people are not given to writing such diaries, especially 80 years ago" (*PNI*, 341). It is not, however, Romani as an individual that interests Gramsci, but what his diary reveals about the thinking of the common people of his day. And once again we see him distinguishing between the information to be gleaned from such sources and their literary shortcomings.

Subaltern Common Sense and Subaltern Knowledge
Whereas Gramsci's archive of subaltern conceptions of the world provides a guide to where we can find, as he writes in the note quoted at the end of the previous chapter, the "implicit philosophy" of subalterns in its "naïve form in popular common sense," his concept of organic intellectuals theorizes the passage from implicit to explicit philosophy. And at the heart of the notion of

---

6. In May 1848, the Milanese rose against their Austrian rulers and drove them out of the city. This came to be called the Five Days insurrection.

organic intellectuals is a strong epistemological claim: the ultimate source of the foundational political narratives produced by those subaltern groups who escape their subalternity and achieve hegemony is the inchoate conceptions of the world born of the day-to-day experience of living in a given subaltern location. Organic intellectuals elaborate this implicit philosophy into a coherent explicit philosophy, but they do not originate it. As intellectuals, their organicity consists in their having "worked out and made coherent the principles and the problems" that have arisen out of the "practical activity" of the group that has produced these particular intellectuals (*SPN*, 330). In other words, the reason why intellectuals need to pay serious attention to common sense is not simply because effective political narratives need to resonate with existing common sense, although that, too, is important, but because only when the philosophy of the intellectuals has genuinely emerged from subaltern experience is it possible for subalterns and their intellectuals to come together as a cultural and social unity. Only then do they become a historical bloc with the power to bring about social transformation.

The passage from the implicit good sense embedded in the confusion of common sense to a coherent and explicit "philosophy" is long and complicated, however: "Creating a group of independent intellectuals is not an easy thing; it requires a long process, with actions and reactions, coming together and drifting apart" (*SPN*, 395–96). And, it should be stressed, its endpoint is never predetermined. Gramsci ridicules any simplistic progressive teleology (see, for example, *SPN*, 168). While subaltern experience gives rise to critiques of oppression, the condition of subalternity, by definition, works to mute and diffuse such critiques. Subalterns live under the rule of those who exploit and oppress them in a world organized through institutions and practices that sustain and reproduce that rule, a world suffused with hegemonic narratives that explain—from the vantage point of the dominant—why things cannot be other than they are. As a result, the knowledge that emerges from the experience of living the reality of subalternity on a daily basis necessarily takes the incoherent form of common sense. Subalterns know the reality of their subalternity but in a fragmented, distorted form; they see, as it were, through a glass darkly. It is only as they develop their own intellectuals, those knowledge producers "'specialised' in conceptual and philosophical elaboration of ideas" (*SPN*, 334), that they begin to see clearly and are able to express what they see in coherent form. And this knowledge is by definition collective. The intellectuals so laboriously produced by a rising subaltern class can be seen as midwives who help to bring forth a shared philosophy and culture gestated in the womb of subaltern experience. This is always a collective endeavor, and one that necessarily includes diffusion of that philosophy and culture: "Creating a new culture does not only mean one's own individual 'original' discoveries. It also, and most particularly, means the diffusion in a critical form of truths already discovered, their 'socialisation' as it were, and even making them the basis of vital action, an element of co-ordination and intellectual and moral order. For a mass of people to be led to think coherently and in the same coherent fashion about the real present world, is a 'philosophical' event far more important and 'original' than the discovery by some philosophical 'genius' of a truth which remains the property of small groups of intellectuals" (*SPN*, 325).

The incoherent knowledge inherent in subaltern experience needs to find coherent forms of expression, based on reason, that strike those subalterns as simple common sense. As Gramsci argues in a passage, quoted in chapter 3 but which bears repeating, there is a need "for new popular beliefs, that is to say a new common sense and with it a new culture and a new philosophy which will be rooted in the popular consciousness with the same solidity and imperative quality as traditional beliefs" (*SPN*, 424). Subalterns, we might say, can speak, but if they are to speak in politically effective ways, they need to develop their own organic intellectuals—intellectuals who transform their implicit knowledge into an explicit philosophy and culture that includes a new common sense. But what does this process look like in actual historical contexts? Part 2 of this study takes the concepts of subalternity, intellectuals and common sense to three case studies, each illustrative of an aspect of the passage from incoherent common sense, born of subaltern experience, to coherent political narratives.

PART II. *Case Studies*

5

Adam Smith

A BOURGEOIS, ORGANIC INTELLECTUAL?

Almost immediately after the appearance of Smith's work, *An Inquiry into the Nature and Causes of the Wealth of Nations*, all previous or contemporary economic writings were forgotten. This work, with its immense success and influence, was a guidebook for future generations of economists, and the starting point for most of their analyses. — MAURICE ALLAIS

The genius of *The Wealth of Nations* lies in Adam Smith's abilities as a great synthesizer, great observer, and great storyteller.
— ALAN KRUEGER, introduction to *The Wealth of Nations*

This chapter explores, through a concrete example, the process by which an emerging class "creates together with itself" its own organic intellectuals. The class is the bourgeoisie. My example is historical rather than contemporary because structural patterns are only revealed with hindsight. Politics at any one moment is, as Gramsci observes, "the reflection of the tendencies of development in the structure, but it is not necessarily the case that these tendencies must be realised. A structural phase can be concretely studied and analysed only after it has gone through its whole process of development, and not during the process itself, except hypothetically and with the explicit proviso that one is dealing with hypotheses" (*SPN*, 408).

Epigraph: From Allais's chapter in *Adam Smith's Legacy: His Place in the Development of Modern Economics*, edited by Michael Fry (Allais 1992).

The Embeddedness of Intellectuals

In chapter 2, I quoted a passage in which Gramsci ridicules Croce's belief that he is writing "a history from which every element of class has been exorcised," whereas in reality his account describes the process by which "a particular class manages to present and have the conditions for its existence and development as a class accepted as a universal principle, as a world view, as a religion" (*FSPN*, 353). The notebooks reject completely any Benda-like notion of the universal intellectual, whose production of knowledge exists within some empyrean beyond class. The knowledge produced by intellectuals, while not determined by the class realities of the world they inhabit, is always entangled with those realities. In the case of traditional intellectuals, the links may be complex and indirect but they exist nonetheless; with organic intellectuals, they are more direct. The very concept of organic intellectuals is intended to draw attention to the nature of the connection between specific knowledge producers and specific classes. At the heart of the concept is a narrative of class formation that sees history as opening up new economic spaces that create commonalities of interest. Such commonalities of interest, termed by Marx class-in-itself, create the potentiality, but only the potentiality, for the emergence of new self-conscious classes, what Marx referred to as class-for-itself.[1] A prime example of such a transition from class-in-itself to class-for-itself is the dissolution of feudalism and the emergence of a new bourgeois class. Together with itself, this emerging class created its own organic intellectuals: the knowledge producers who would give it "homogeneity and an awareness of its own function not only in the economic but also in the social and political fields" (*SPN*, 5).

The new, capitalist account of reality laid out "the necessary conditions of existence" for an economic system based on the production of commodities.[2] Crucially, it also explained, as must any potentially hegemonic narrative, why such a system would be in the interests of society as a whole. It should be stressed that this was not some carefully planned project carried out by intellectuals who had this as their conscious aim. Some may have, but many, like Croce, undoubtedly thought of themselves as disinterested seekers after truth, independent of any political project. The point is that in the context of a given historical moment, the individual and collective endeavors of a wide range of intellectuals, from the most distinguished to the popularizers and the hacks, whatever their self-defined aims, constitute the assemblage of knowl-

---

1. For the distinction between class-in-itself and class-for-itself, see *The Poverty of Philosophy* (Marx 1963, 173).

2. Karl Marx's *Capital* provides the classic account of such an economic system.

edge that underpins the dominance of a given ruling class. These intellectual endeavors mesh together with the material realities to form a historical bloc in which infrastructure and superstructures are entwined in a unified, if fractured, entity.

My empirical example of the creation of a new strata of organic intellectuals takes us back to the eighteenth century, and the historical moment when the bourgeoisie is beginning to emerge as a distinct class. I focus on Adam Smith, regarded by many as the thinker who first articulated the essence of capitalism, even if, as Emma Rothschild convincingly argues, this image of Smith as the patron saint of capitalism grossly distorts his argument (Rothschild 2011). The complex ways Smith was an intellectual of his time, and the journey his thought would take after his death to become a cornerstone of a hegemonic capitalist narrative, provide an illuminating context in which to explore the process by which a rising class creates its organic intellectuals.

It might be objected that in defining intellectuals Gramsci stresses that what is important is the "ensemble of the system of relations" within which knowledge production in all its forms takes place. In other words, he shifts the emphasis from intellectuals as individuals to the processes by which recognized, authoritative knowledge is produced. Does not focusing on a single intellectual, therefore, go against the spirit of the notebooks? My answer to this objection is that while intellectuals are shaped by their time and place, they are not mere automata generated by their historical context. The analyst's task is to trace out the particular nature of the relationship, in particular historical contexts, between "the general complex of social relations" in which producers of knowledge are embedded, and of which they can be regarded as personifications (*SPN*, 8), and the intellectual trajectories of specific lives. If we want to understand knowledge production in a given time and place, we need to map out the institutions and practices within which intellectuals operated, and the specific ways these shaped their work as intellectuals. Smith's geographical and historical location as a knowledge producer provides an especially interesting case.

The Scots Inquiry into the Science of Man
The historical moment that produced Smith was that of the Scottish Enlightenment, and to understand his intellectual trajectory during his lifetime, and the ways his thought was taken up after his death, we need to understand the world he inhabited. I should, however, begin with a disclaimer: I am an anthropologist, not a historian, and certainly not a specialist of eighteenth-

century Scotland. I approach the Scottish Enlightenment as a disciplinary outsider, and my account of Smith and his world is based on secondary sources.[3]

During the eighteenth century, Scotland saw an extraordinary flowering of innovative scholarship across a wide range of fields. Much later this would come to be termed the Scottish Enlightenment. The Scottish intellectuals who became major figures, not simply in their homeland but further afield, include philosophers, theologians, inventors, engineers, and those we would now call scientists, although the term scientist would only be coined much later. Adam Smith, David Hume, Thomas Reid, Henry Home (later Lord Kames), Dugald Stewart, Adam Ferguson, John Millar, William Robertson, Hugh Blair, Colin Maclaurin, James Watt, Joseph Black, and James Hutton are just some of the notable names. Based in the three university cities of Edinburgh, Glasgow, and Aberdeen, the Scottish Enlightenment was both part of the larger Europe-wide Enlightenment, but also specifically Scottish.[4] Experts in this field point to three major factors that contributed to Scotland's intellectual flowering: the economic and political realities of early eighteenth-century Scotland; its knowledge-producing institutions and the character of its intellectual life; and, particularly relevant in the context of this book, the sense of subalternity that many Scottish intellectuals felt when they looked south to their more powerful neighbor.

First, there was Scotland's poverty. The country had always been poor, with few natural geographical advantages. In the eighteenth century, less than 10 percent of its land was arable, while its mountainous terrain and lack of navigable rivers hampered transport and the development of industry. By the late seventeenth century, many Scots had already recognized that, as one historian writes, "if the country was to prosper, men would need to be trained, the economy improved and science brought to bear on problems" (Emerson 2003, 11). The project of national development, or in the language of the day "improve-

3. Some of the main sources I have drawn on are Roger Emerson's "The Contexts of the Scottish Enlightenment," in *The Cambridge Companion to the Scottish Enlightenment* (Broadie 2003); Emma Rothschild's *Economic Sentiments: Adam Smith, Condorcet, and the Enlightenment*; Nicholas Phillipson's essay "The Scottish Enlightenment," in *The Enlightenment in National Context* (Porter and Teich 1981) and his biography of Adam Smith; Ian Simpson Ross's biography of Adam Smith; and E. C. Mossner's biography of David Hume. Other works are referenced below.

4. Nicholas Phillipson's essay "The Scottish Enlightenment," in *The Enlightenment in National Context* (Porter and Teich 1981) explores the Scottishness of the Scottish Enlightenment.

ment," provides an important context for much of what Scottish intellectuals would achieve in the eighteenth century. These were thinkers who were very much concerned with practical questions, such as increasing the amount of cultivated land and improving agricultural productivity, developing industry and fostering trade.

The major political reality of early eighteenth-century Scotland was the 1707 Act of Union.[5] Although ruled by a single monarch for the previous century, up to this point England and Scotland had been independent kingdoms, each with its own parliament. Now there was a single state, dominated by England. The Act of Union allowed Scotland to retain its own independent legal system, but it abolished the Scottish parliament, replacing it with a limited number of Scottish representatives in the English parliament. The Scots were prepared to accept union with England, even in some quarters to welcome it, in part because of the country's increasingly dire economic situation. To many Scots it seemed that "the solution to Scottish economic woes was closer union with England and access to the English and imperial markets in which Scots were already successful interlopers" (Emerson, 12). The loss of its own independent political institutions was, nonetheless, traumatic for the Scottish political community. Scottish historian and Adam Smith biographer Nicholas Phillipson argues that

> one way of looking at the Scots inquiry into the Science of Man is to think of it as a critique of the classic language of civic morality undertaken by a group of men living in a sophisticated but provincial community which had been stripped of its political institutions at the time of the Act of Union in 1707 and still hankered after an understanding of the principles of virtue which would make sense of their present provincial condition. . . . the Scots' concern with the principles of virtue can be related to the traumatic effect of the Act of Union on the Scottish political community. In a long, sophisticated debate about the political and economic crisis in which the country was engulfed in the early years of the century, the Scots discovered that the language of contemporary politics was not well suited to making sense of their present predicament. In the three decades which followed the Union philosophers, politicians and men of letters set out to fashion an alter-

5. Technically, this was not an act of parliament but a treaty of union (Walker 1988, 85–86), but since it is generally referred to as the Act of Union, I too use this terminology.

native language of civic morality. By the 1760s the process was complete, and a new language of civic morality had been created which provided the Scots with a new understanding of civic virtue. (Phillipson 1981, 22)

The Scots inquiry into the Science of Man, we might say, emerges from a vantage point of subalternity.

For Phillipson, "the principal intellectual achievement of the Scottish Enlightenment" is "that its philosophers were able to show how this provincial language of civic morality could be used as an instrument for discussing the moral, political and economic organization of commercial civilization at large" (1981, 28). Note here that the civilization this language was so suited to describe was a commercial civilization. As we shall see, it is precisely this language of civic morality that Adam Smith would use in his extraordinarily influential work, *An Inquiry into the Nature and Causes of the Wealth of Nations.*

Another reason why this impoverished corner of Britain produced such a profusion of world-class thinkers in the eighteenth century was the quality of its knowledge-producing institutions and its vibrant intellectual life. The main centers of enlightenment scholarship were its three universities, Edinburgh, Glasgow, and Aberdeen, all three of which, but especially Edinburgh and Glasgow, were radically reorganized in the late-seventeenth and early-eighteenth centuries. Prior to this, these universities were "little more than seminaries, designed to prepare young men of relatively humble background for the kirk and to give the sons of the gentry a smattering of classics and philosophy" (Phillipson 1981, 28). They now became centers of the most advanced secular scholarship of the day. Their transformation had included the introduction of new, more effective teaching methods, and the establishment of chairs in new subjects such as humanity, history, mathematics, oriental languages, law, botany, medicine, and chemistry. The changes were the result of a demand for more relevant education. In the first thirty years of the eighteenth century, the universities of both Edinburgh and Glasgow "had become increasingly responsive to the educational needs of a civic-minded gentry and professional class" (Phillipson 1981, 28). Using a Gramscian perspective, we might say that they had implicitly recognized that the economic and political realities of the day demanded new forms of education capable of producing new kinds of intellectuals (*intellectual* here being understood in its wide Gramscian sense). One new kind of intellectual who would emerge over the next century or so would be the economist, a category of expert unknown to the eighteenth century. It is often forgotten just how late the coinage of this term was; the earliest citation in the OED for *economist*, used in the modern sense of a specialist in matters having to do with the understanding and management of a society's financial and other resources, is 1804.

The reorganized Scottish universities were undoubtedly superior to England's two universities, Oxford and Cambridge. Not that the bar here was particularly high. It was commonly acknowledged that far from being centers of learning, Oxford and Cambridge were the haunt of lazy, venal dons, less interested in teaching their students than in extracting money from them through complex systems of fees. Smith, who spent six years at Oxford as a student, was one such critic. Decades later, in his discussion of education in the *Wealth of Nations*, he would write: "In the University of Oxford, the greater part of the public professors have, for these many years, given up altogether even the pretence of teaching" (Smith 1976, 761). Even in the late eighteenth century, according to Eric Hobsbawm, Oxford and Cambridge continued to be, "intellectually null" (Hobsbawm 1962, 30). A significant point here is that, unlike the less wealthy Scottish universities, Oxford and Cambridge—financially independent thanks to their huge endowments—had been able to fend off any external demands for change.

The universities, however, were not the only places in Scotland where new Enlightenment knowledge was produced. There were also the many learned societies and clubs: "Throughout the eighteenth century Scottish intellectual life, and that of Edinburgh in particular, was to be meshed into a complex and constantly changing network of clubs and societies devoted to the improvement of manners, economic efficiency, learning and letters" (Phillipson 1981, 27), not that the creation of learned societies was an exclusively Scottish phenomenon. The eighteenth century saw the establishment of a profusion of such societies and clubs throughout Europe and the New World. They might take many different forms, but all shared a general aim of providing opportunities for the discussion and dissemination of new advances in knowledge—knowledge that encompassed many different fields. At this time, the boundaries between what are now considered different disciplinary fields were still very fluid. What seem to us the separate disciplines of philosophy, economics, law, historiography, social science, linguistics, mathematics, chemistry, engineering, and geology, for instance, were seen rather as different aspects of an ultimately unitary field of knowledge. And what are now thought of as clearly distinct areas of knowledge, such as economics or social science, had yet to be defined as discrete disciplines. It is worth remembering that Smith was first Professor of Logic and Metaphysics, and then of Moral Philosophy. In his own time, he was never referred to as an economist, a specialization that did not yet exist. Even the distinction between arts and sciences had yet to emerge. It is only during the eighteenth century that the term *science* acquires its modern meaning as "the theoretical and methodological study of nature" (Williams 1983, 278). The opposition between the "sciences" and "arts and humanities," which now seems so basic, also emerges in the eighteenth century. Interestingly, the term *scientist* was not coined until the mid-nineteenth century; the OED's earliest citation for *scientist* as meaning "a person with expert knowledge of a science; a person using scientific methods" is 1834. The citation (from an article in the *Quarterly Review*) reflects the hesitant gestation of this new concept. The *Quarterly Review* author begins by noting "the want of any name by which we can designate the students of the knowledge of the material world collectively." The anonymous author continues: "We are informed that this difficulty was felt very oppressively by the members of the British Association for the Advancement of Science, at their meetings . . . in the last three summers . . . *Philosophers* was felt to be too wide and too lofty a term, . . . ; *savans* was rather assuming . . . ; some ingenious gentleman proposed that, by analogy with *artist*, they might form *scientist* . . . but this was not generally palatable." We can see here a new form of knowledge and a new type of intellectual, struggling for recognition

Edinburgh, Aberdeen, and Glasgow all had important learned societies. All were lively cities that would expand significantly in the eighteenth century. Edinburgh's population grew from thirty-five thousand in 1707 to over fifty thousand by midcentury, and as Scotland's capital city, it had a particularly vibrant social mix. This included "military men, genteel judges, civil administrators and office holders. [As well as] noblemen and gentry who made the capital their resort and marriage market" (Emerson 2003, 21). Edinburgh's two most significant learned societies were the Philosophical Society (1737–83), which developed into the still existing Royal Society of Scotland, and the Select Society (1754–63), of which David Hume and Adam Smith were founder-members. These societies would "provide Edinburgh's enlightenment with its institutional and ideological definition" (Phillipson 2010, 119). In Aberdeen, considerably smaller than Edinburgh, intellectual life was dominated by individuals associated with its two small universities. The most prominent society was the Wise Club, or Philosophical Society (1758–73), but there was also the Gordon's Mill Farming Club (1758–after 1765), concerned, as its name suggests, with agricultural improvement. The fact that a number of the members of the Wise Club were also members of the Gordon's Mill Farming Club is evidence of the importance accorded to such practical concerns.

Glasgow, like Aberdeen, a port city, had its own specific character. During the eighteenth century its population exploded from around twelve thousand at the beginning of the century to eighty thousand by its end. A major source of its eighteenth-century prosperity was the slave trade. While Glasgow merchants had a relatively small presence in slave trading itself, they grew rich from the trade in lucrative slave-produced crops, first sugar and tobacco, and later cotton, which were shipped back to Europe from the New World in vessels that had unloaded their cargoes of African slaves. Closely connected to its agricultural hinterland, Glasgow was also a center for the livestock trade. Although for much of the century it was essentially a merchants' town, industry, too, was developing, spurred on in part by the needs of local agriculture. Also important were the processing opportunities offered by the imported goods of the Atlantic trade, and the demand for manufactured goods that could be sent back across the Atlantic and sold to buy yet more plantation crops. For Glasgow's entrepreneurial merchants and manufacturers, scientific and practical knowledge was highly valued: How might Scotland's economy, so "backward" in comparison to that of its southern neighbor, be "improved?" Town and gown, however, were more sharply divided in Glasgow than in Edinburgh, a division reflected in its learned societies, such as the Glasgow Literary Society (of which Adam Smith was a founder-member), which drew their membership primarily from university circles. There was, however, one significant exception, the Political Economy Club, founded in the 1740s by Lord Provost Andrew Cochrane, a prosperous tobacco merchant with intellectual interests. In this club, merchants dominated. Adam Smith, a regular attendee, was one of only two professorial members. Cochrane's aim was to provide a forum for merchants to exchange experience and ideas. Its members were specifically encouraged to inquire "into the Nature and the Principles of Trade in all its Branches, and to Communicate their Knowledge and Views on that Subject to each other" (Phillipson 2010, 129).

The Enlightenment's learned societies and clubs, in Scotland and elsewhere, were established to provide spaces where their members could exchange knowledge, but they were also committed to spreading knowledge to the wider society. We only have to think of that great monument of Enlightenment scholarship, the *Encyclopédie*, to recognize the stress laid on the dissemination of knowledge by Enlightenment thinkers. A related concern, particularly strong perhaps in the case of the Scottish societies, was that knowledge should be useful. We need to bear in mind, however, that "in the Enlightenment, the concept of 'usefulness' encompassed both practical, economic benefit and a sense of utility related to the moral or intellectual improvement of the individual" (Wood 2003, 103). The interest in improvement was widely shared. Edinburgh's Philosophical Society, for example, had begun as a medical research group before widening its remit to include "scientific knowledge generally and Scottish antiquities, also improvement in agriculture, manufactures and technology" (Ross 2010, 80). To the society's founders, all these topics fell within the general heading of "philosophy." The Select Society, in turn, gave birth in 1755 to the Edinburgh Society for Encouraging Arts, Sciences, Manufactures, and Agriculture in Scotland. Even earlier, there was the Society of Improvers in the Knowledge of Agriculture in Scotland. Founded in 1723, again in Edinburgh, this society had a membership of approximately three hundred, consisting of a mix of landowners and intellectuals with a shared interest in agriculture and its dependent industries. It saw itself as providing, in Emerson's words, "a forum for the discussion of economic changes in a society still overwhelmingly agrarian." And, as Emerson notes, these ideas did not remain at the level of pure speculation: "What may have mattered as much as its discussions and occasional publications were the demonstrated benefits of what it argued for. These could be seen in the increased productivity of those estates which had begun to increase arable land through the introduction of more animals, better crop regimes, and the adoption of practices such as longer restrictive leases" (2003, 19–20).

In general, these clubs and societies were organizations of knowledge production that were equally interested in what we tend today to see as the distinct fields of pure and applied knowledge—a distinction that was far less marked in the eighteenth century. The intellectuals of the Scottish Enlightenment, very conscious of the "backwardness" of their homeland, were far from being isolated, ivory-tower thinkers. The problems they sought to address were those their country's would-be improvers were confronting. We might think here of Gramsci's criticism of what he termed "the so-called 'Popular Universities,'" which in his view would only have been successful "if the intellectuals had been organically the intellectuals of those masses, and if they had worked out and made coherent, the principles and the problems raised by the masses in their practical activity, thus constituting a cultural and social bloc" (*SPN*, 330). Transposing this formulation to an earlier historical period, when the emerging class was that of the bourgeoisie, we might see Phillipson's "complex and constantly changing network of clubs and societies devoted to the improvement of manners, economic efficiency, learning and letters" (Phillipson 1981, 27), precisely as working out and making coherent the principles and the problems raised in the practical activity not of "the masses," but of an emerging capitalist class.

For Gramsci, an emerging class in the process of its formation always produces new kinds of intellectuals. The scientist, a specialization only named in the nineteenth century, is a good example of a new type of intellectual linked to the rise of the bourgeoisie. What is new here is the stress on knowledge derived from experimental methods of inquiry. As Steven Shapin, a historian of science, explains, "Advocates of the new experimental science in seventeenth-century England were simultaneously arguing for a new type of knowledge, a new type of knower, and a new mode of relationship between the knower and what was to be known" (Shapin 2010, 158–59). The development of this new form of knowledge, science, would give birth not only to a new category of intellectual, the scientist, but also to that other key figure in modern knowledge production, the disinterested "expert." In time the scientist as expert would come to displace the earlier dominant model of the knowledge producer as Christian philosopher and gentleman-scholar. As Shapin puts it, "By the 1830s, a new utilitarian culture articulated political demands for the professionalization of the scientific role and the state subvention of science . . . because it was materially useful to society. What was now asked for and achieved was state support, not for underwriting the role of the Christian philosopher and gentleman-scholar, but for that of the scientific *expert*" (179).

Traditional intellectuals—to adopt the terminology of the notebooks—who had taken the form of the Christian philosopher and gentleman-scholar, were being supplanted by a new type of intellectual, one organically linked to a developing industrial society. The learned societies of the later seventeenth and eighteenth centuries were one of the seedbeds from which the new, emerging form of knowledge, science, and the new knowledge producer, the scientist, developed.

A crucial form of knowledge in the rise to dominance of capitalist-based economic systems is what came to be termed "economics," which emerges as a distinct discipline practiced by a distinct kind of intellectual, the economist. As I have noted, neither economics nor the economist existed as recognized categories during Smith's lifetime. In line with this, while there is an entry for the term *political economy* in the index to the *Wealth of Nations*, there is none for *economy*, and the entry for *economists* (spelled "Oeconomists" and capitalized) refers to the school of French thinkers led by François Quesnay, nowadays known as the physiocrats. We can see economics and the economist as a branch of knowledge and a particular expert that, as Gramsci puts it, "the capitalist entrepreneur creates alongside himself" (*SPN*, 5). This process of creation takes time; it is over the course of the nineteenth century that *economics* and *economist* gradually acquire their modern meanings, but the swirling maelstrom of intellectual production that is the Scottish Enlightenment played a major role in generating these new categories so central to the emerging capitalist system.

We Are Slaves to the Language We Write

Looking back from a twenty-first-century vantage point, the intellectual achievements of such eighteenth-century giants as David Hume, Adam Smith, and the other Scottish virtuosi unquestionably represent one of the high points of modern European thought. But this was not always so clear to those men themselves; the patterns of history only become clear in hindsight. Scottish intellectuals living in the eighteenth century could not think of themselves as part of a distinct Scottish Enlightenment; the term *Scottish Enlightenment* was only coined in 1900 (Broadie 2003, 3), not that men like Hume or Adam Smith lacked confidence in themselves as intellectuals. The Scottish literati were highly cosmopolitan and well aware that they could more than hold their own in Europe's Republic of Letters. And it was not necessarily to England that these thinkers looked: "Philosophical, medical and scientific ideas came from France and Holland as readily as from England; toleration and liberal theology were Dutch and Swiss as well as English; polite standards of taste owed as much to the French as to Addison [editor of the enormously influential *Spectator*]" (Emerson 2003, 18). At the same time, however, they never forgot that they were citizens of an impoverished and economically backward nation that had surrendered its political independence to England. Union with England may have been recognized by many as economically advantageous to Scotland, but it was also, to use Phillipson's term, traumatic. Looming over Scottish intellectual life was the giant shadow of their powerful neighbor to the south, a neighbor whose disdain for the Scots and Scotland was often palpable, as evidenced, for instance, by the many disparaging remarks about the country and its inhabitants made by Samuel Johnson and recorded by the Scot James Boswell in his celebrated life of the great man. Many of these aphorisms would become famous, such as the comment that the "noblest prospect which a Scotchman ever sees, is the high road that leads him to England!" (Boswell 1846, 137). For the Scottish literati, the shadow of subalternity was an inescapable reality.

A telling indication of the Scots' internalized sense of inferiority during this period is the embarrassment felt by so many Scottish intellectuals because of what they saw as the deficiencies of their language. The language of educated Scots men and women was English. Except in the Highlands, few Scots had any knowledge of Gaelic, or much interest in the Gaelic tradition: the model for English was the language spoken in polite English society. But this was not the language of most Scots. Not only was there the distinct Scottish accent, often unintelligible to those south of the border, the English written and spoken by the Scots also differed in its grammar, syntax, vocabulary, and idioms from that of the educated English man or woman. Smith was fortunate that, thanks to six years of study at Oxford, he had acquired the spoken and written English of England. Hume's English by contrast was always that of a Scotsman, and he never lost his strong Scottish accent. He might be acknowledged across Europe as one of the intellectual titans of the age, but until the end of his life, he remained anxious about "Scotticisms" in his writings, relying on English friends to check his manuscripts before publication so any such blemishes could be removed. His spoken language he regarded as beyond hope of Anglicanization. In the 1750s, when he was already well established as a European scholar, he would write in one letter: "I am still jealous of my Pen. As to my Tongue, you have seen that I regard it as totally desperate and Irreclaimable" (quoted in Mossner 1980, 370). On the one hand, Hume has no doubts about Scottish literary achievement; on the other, he seems to take for granted the inferiority of Scots English, as in this passage from another letter in which he marvels, "At a time when we have lost our princes, our Parliaments, our independent Government, even the Presence of our chief Nobility, *are unhappy in our Accent & Pronunciation, speak a very corrupt Dialect of the Tongue which we make use of;* is it not strange I say, that, in these Circumstances, we should really be the People most distinguish'd for Literature in Europe?" (quoted in Mossner 1980, 370; emphasis mine). Note also Hume's acknowledgment here of England's political hegemony over Scotland. We can see the unquestioned acceptance of linguistic inferiority by eighteenth-century Scottish intellectuals as one of the effects of this very real hegemony.

As Ernest Campbell Mossner, author of the standard biography of Hume, explains, the Union made Scots English newly problematic for those anxious to participate in public life beyond the confines of their native land. Scotland now had parliamentary representatives in the English parliament rather than its own parliament, and those Scottish representatives were often incomprehensible to the English members. As one prominent Scot despairingly reported of a Scottish peer who had addressed the House of Lords, "Deil *ae* word, from beginning to end, did the English understand of his speech." Another Scots peer, whose witty anecdote fell flat at a dinner with English lawyers, appealed to a fellow Scot at the table: "My story is not understood, Adam; for God's sake translate for me, as I can utter no sound like an Englishman but sneezing" (both examples quoted in Mossner 1980, 371). This failure of communication was seen by both Scots and English as the Scots' problem; if they wanted to participate in English political and cultural life, then they would have to learn to speak the English spoken in those circles.

The educated English of England set the standard for written English. And writing well in English was crucial once English and other European vernacular languages had replaced Latin as the language of scholarship. But for the Scots, as Mossner observes, this was not an English in which they felt at home. Noting that the first chair in English in Britain was established by Edinburgh University in the mid-eighteenth century, Mossner comments, "Perhaps for the very reason that English was still, in Scottish ears, almost a foreign language" (371). In the later eighteenth century, the Scottish philosopher James Beattie wrote a very revealing letter to an Englishman describing the problems faced by those who may know a language well, yet do not feel they own it. Subaltern anxiety oozes from the letter.

> We who live in Scotland are obliged to study English from books, like a dead language. Accordingly, when we write, we write it like a dead language, which we understand but cannot speak; avoiding perhaps all ungrammatical expressions and even the barbarisms of our country, but at the same time without communicating that neatness, ease, and softness of phrase, which appears so conspicuously in Addison, Lord Lyttleton, and other elegant English authors. Our style is stately and unwieldy, and clogs the tongue in pronunciation, and smells of the lamp. We are slaves to the language we write, and are continually afraid of committing *gross* blunders; and, when an easy familiar, idiomatic phrase occurs, dare not adopt it, if we recollect no authority, for fear of Scotticisms. In a word, *we* handle English as a person who cannot fence handles a sword; continually afraid of hurting ourselves with it, or letting it fall, or making some awkward motion that shall betray our ignorance. An English author of learning is the master, not the slave of his language, and wields it gracefully, because he wields it with ease, and with full assurance that he has the command of it. (Quoted in Mossner, 374; Beattie's emphasis)

The anxiety manifested here runs like a thread through the Scottish Enlightenment as a whole. An awareness of Scottish subalternity, shared by the Scots themselves and their powerful southern neighbor, was a persistent sore that never healed. It was also, however, an irritant that helped produce the proverbial pearl. As Phillipson argues, one way of approaching "the Scots inquiry into the Science of Man" is precisely as a response to the trauma of 1707, which brought home to the Scots the undeniable reality of their subalternity. What interests me here is how that inquiry would also provide some key building blocks for what would become the hegemonic narrative of capitalism. I explore this through a consideration of one of the most prominent intellectuals of the Scottish Enlightenment, Adam Smith, the author of the *Wealth of Nations*.

Nowadays, Smith's masterwork is often seen, as by Maurice Allais, Nobel laureate in economics (see epigraph to this chapter), as the original guidebook for economists, a work that articulates universal truths that transcend any geographical or temporal specificities. It is also, however, the work of a Scottish intellectual who lived at a time when modern industrial capitalism was just beginning to emerge. How does Smith appear if we approach him as an intellectual organically linked to a rising bourgeois class, whose thought helped to give that class "homogeneity and an awareness of its own function not only in the economic but also in the social and political fields" (*SPN*, 5), and whose shifting posthumous reputation seems to track that class's rise to power? To answer this question I want to go back to the moment of the genesis of the *Wealth of Nations*, and the historical context that shaped its author as an intellectual, beginning with an overview of Smith's biography, not so much his personal biography—it is not this that defines the "organicity" of an intellectual—but his formation as an intellectual, and the context of that formation.

My account here draws on the work of a number of Smith scholars, including Phillipson (1981, 2010), Ross (2010), Donald Winch (1978), and Fonna Forman-Barzilai (2010). I am especially indebted to Emma Rothschild's *Economic Sentiments: Adam Smith, Condorcet, and the Enlightenment*. Rothschild is not a Marxist and her theoretical starting-point is somewhat different from mine, but she too is interested in the origins of one of the dominant narratives that would come to underpin the capitalist regime, laissez-faire. Tellingly, as she notes, nowhere in the writings of Smith himself, nowadays so revered as its great champion, does the term *laissez-faire* appear; nor, we might add, does the word *capitalism*. Indeed, *capitalism* "as a word describing a particular economic system" only emerges in the early nineteenth century (Williams 1983, 50).

A Scottish Enlightenment Intellectual

Reviewing the Phillipson biography, Colin Kidd notes how Smith nowadays is "popularly identified as the founder of economics, an apostle of capitalism and honoured prophet of the new right" (Kidd 2010, 21). A number of recent scholars, however, including Kidd, reject this characterization as not merely a gross simplification, but a fundamental misreading. If we want to understand the argument in the *Wealth of Nations*, and Smith's intellectual project as a whole, we need, they insist, to situate him in his historical context.

Smith was very much a Scot and it was the Scottish Enlightenment that formed him as a thinker. Born in 1723 in the small town of Kirkcaldy, ten miles from Edinburgh, a few months after his father's death, he was raised by his devoted mother with input from James Oswald, appointed in his father's will as the boy's tutor and guardian. His mother never remarried and Smith himself remained single. Throughout his life his bond with his mother seems to have been his closest emotional tie. The families of both his parents belonged to the minor gentry and "had connections with the law, the army and the world of office-holding on which the routines of Scottish public life and politics depended" (Phillipson 2010, 9). At the age of fourteen, a fairly normal age to go to university in this period, he left Kirkcaldy for Glasgow University, relatively recently reorganized, and now an intellectually exciting and progressive place. Francis Hutcheson, Professor of Moral Philosophy, would have a particularly significant and lasting influence on Smith's thought.

After three years at Glasgow, Smith was awarded a Snell Exhibition for up to eleven years of study at Balliol College, Oxford. In the event, he would only stay for six years. Supposedly, Snell exhibitors were Glasgow University students who were preparing to take holy orders, but this had ceased to be enforced. Smith was distinctly unimpressed with Oxford's intellectual life, as his later comments in the *Wealth of Nations* indicate. Nonetheless, his years there gave him an opportunity to engage in rigorous, self-directed study. It also, as I have already noted, enabled him to acquire the written and spoken English of polite English circles. Unlike his close friend Hume, this Scotsman never had to worry about Scotticisms marring his prose.

On his return to Scotland, he first settled in Edinburgh, where his family connections and existing friendships ensured a welcome for him in the city's intellectual circles. Throughout eighteenth-century Europe, patronage played a dominant role in intellectual life. The Scottish patronage network was particularly tight-knit, since the country "was governed by a very small class of landowners and merchants—perhaps 1,300 in 1700 and no more than double that number in 1800" (Emerson 2003, 15). Smith initially established his intellectual reputation through two series of public lectures, one on rhetoric, and one on jurisprudence. Public lectures on topics such as the law, medicine, the natural sciences, and classical languages, advertised in advance and open to anyone prepared to pay the stipulated fee, were a significant feature of eighteenth-century Edinburgh's cultural and intellectual life (Phillipson 2010, 89).

The impetus for the lecture series and the choice of topics came from one of Scotland's most powerful intellectual patrons, Henry Home (ennobled in 1752 as Lord Kames), one of the founder-members of Edinburgh's Select Society.

Home had a particular interest in young scholars whom he would mentor and befriend, using his patronage to advance their careers. The importance of Kames is indicated by Smith's response when asked many years later by James Boswell what he thought accounted for Scotland's intellectual creativity. Even though Smith did not have a high opinion of Kames's writings, his answer was unambiguous: "We must everyone of us acknowledge Kames for our master" (quoted in Phillipson 2010, 87). He had been introduced to Home by his close friend James Oswald, the son of his former guardian and now an up-and-coming member of parliament. Home, impressed by Smith's intellect and innovative thinking, immediately adopted him as one of his protégés. Two major influences on both patron and protégé were Hutcheson, Smith's former professor at Glasgow, and Hume, who, although controversial and considered scandalous by some for his religious skepticism, was acknowledged throughout Europe as one of the age's leading thinkers. As part of the attempt "to fashion an alternative language of civic morality" (Phillipson 1981, 22), which Phillipson sees as at the heart of the Scots inquiry into the Science of Man, both Home and Smith were concerned to develop "a science of man based on the study of the sentiments and affection" (Phillipson 2010, 88). They saw rhetoric and jurisprudence as central to this new science and neither, in Home's view, were adequately taught at Edinburgh University. Since his new protégé had studied both topics intensively during his time at Oxford, he seemed an ideal choice for lectures reflecting a more progressive scholarship that drew on Hutcheson and Hume.

The lectures were first given in 1749. Smith then repeated them for the following two years. They proved to be very successful, attracting a number of Edinburgh's prominent literati and immediately "establishing him as a leading member of the younger literati of ministers and lawyers around whom the life of the capital would increasingly revolve" (Phillipson 2010, 119). It was during this period that Smith and Hume became friends (Ross 2010, xxiii); the two men would remain extremely close until Hume's death, in 1776. After three years in Edinburgh, however, the young lecturer's growing reputation led to his appointment at Glasgow University, first as Professor of Logic and Metaphysics, and then from 1752 to 1764 as Professor of Moral Philosophy. He would prove to be a hard-working and dedicated teacher, as well as an able administrator. He would also become an engaged member of a number of learned societies in both Glasgow and Edinburgh, and a full participant in Glasgow's social and cultural life. Despite all the demands on him, he still managed to find the time to write the book that would be his first major success, *The Theory of Moral Sentiments*, published in 1759. Described by Phillipson as "Smith's extraordinary attempt to develop a coherent and plausible account of the processes by which we learn the principles of morality from the experience of common life without descending into wanton religious skepticism, Mandevillian cynicism [as elaborated in Bernard Mandeville's *Fable of the Bees*], or Rousseaunian despair" (Phillipson 2010, 148).

The *Theory of Moral Sentiments* was an immediate literary sensation. The first edition rapidly sold out, and the book became a talking point in literary circles across Europe. In terms of Smith's future, one important effect of the book was that it brought him to the attention of Charles Townsend, a prominent English politician looking for a tutor to travel abroad with his stepson and ward, the Duke of Buccleuch, whom Townsend was bent on preparing for a political career in England. Finding tutors among university professors was a common practice among eighteenth-century aristocrats. The financial inducements were considerable, not only a far higher salary but often a lifetime pension once they had completed their few years of tutoring duties. Townsend's offer was certainly generous. As a professor, Smith's annual income was between £150 and £300; Townsend was offering him an annual salary of £500 while he was tutoring the young duke, to be followed by an annual pension of £300. Nonetheless, Hume, among others, seems to have been surprised how readily he accepted the offer. It seems, however, that by the early 1760s Smith was finding the demands of his university duties increasingly onerous. In addition, travelling with Buccleuch offered an opportunity to engage with fellow thinkers beyond the confines of his own small country. However glittering eighteenth-century Scottish intellectual life may appear in hindsight, to its participants it could apparently seem parochial. Around this time, we find Smith complaining in one letter that the country was "barren of all sorts of transactions that can interest anybody that lives at a distance from it" (quoted in Ross 2010, 209).

Townsend's plan was that Smith would accompany the young duke, then a youth of eighteen, on a version of the customary Grand Tour taken by aristocratic young men to round out their education. Despite his acknowledged social awkwardness, this shy professor seemed to Townsend to have the intellectual qualities necessary to prepare his ward for a life in politics. In the event, Townsend's premature death shortly after tutor and his pupil returned from their travels put paid to these plans. With Townsend gone, Buccleuch, who seems always to have been ambivalent about the future sketched out for him, returned happily to his Scottish estates.

Smith and the young duke would travel together for three years, and their relationship soon became a genuine friendship that continued until the former's death. In later years, Buccleuch would frequently turn to Smith for advice on managing and improving his estates. Their time abroad was spent mainly in Toulouse and Paris but they also stayed for two months in Geneva, where they visited Voltaire, one of Smith's heroes. One remembrance of Smith recounts his admiration for Voltaire's unsparing critiques of "fanatics and heretics of all sects." This same remembrance records his commenting that Voltaire had "done much more for the benefit of mankind than those grave philosophers whose books are read by a few only. The writings of Voltaire are made for all and read by all" (quoted in Phillipson 2010, 190). This reported comment brings to mind Gramsci's question (quoted above, in chapter 1): "Is a philosophical movement properly so called when it is devoted to creating a specialised culture among restricted intellectual groups?" (SPN, 330). Smith may have had the character of an unworldly academic but this committed and inspiring teacher of undergraduates, many no more than fourteen, fifteen, or sixteen years old, seems always to have valued accessible scholarship capable of reaching a wide audience.

The years Smith spent traveling with Buccleuch—the only time he left Britain—gave him a valuable opportunity to study economic and political events in France firsthand, and to exchange ideas with leading French intellectuals. The timing was particularly happy since Scottish philosophy and letters had become highly fashionable in the France of the 1760s. In addition, prior to his arrival, his great friend Hume, lionized by the Parisians, had been assiduous in providing introductions for tutor and pupil. This, coupled with Smith's own reputation as the author of The Theory of Moral Sentiments, ensured that he found a warm and appreciative welcome among the French literati. Of particular interest to him were François Quesnay and his circle of physiocrats. During his time in Paris, Smith met regularly with this group and clearly found their discussions stimulating. He was, however, skeptical of a number of physiocratic assumptions, in particular their insistence that agriculture was "the sole source of the revenue and wealth of every country" (Smith 1976, 664), while commerce and industry were essentially unproductive. It is not surprising, perhaps, that someone who had spent so much time in a commercial hub like Glasgow, and discussed improvement with merchants in learned societies, should reject the wholesale dismissal of all forms of production other than agriculture.

After his return from France in 1766, Smith spent a few months in London before moving back to his mother's house in Kirkcaldy. Financially secure, thanks to the Buccleuch pension, he was now free to devote himself to the composition of the book that would be his enduring legacy, the Wealth of Na-

tions. Writing the book would take him more than nine years. When it finally appeared, in the spring of 1776, it was immediately recognized as a major intellectual achievement. By the end of his life it had become a bestseller; five more editions, the earlier ones with significant revisions and additions, would appear in his lifetime. In the quarter century after his death, in 1790, however, what the book was taken to mean would undergo some interesting shifts.

Smith himself saw the *Wealth of Nations* as merely one element of a far broader intellectual project of the development of a new Science of Man, a project that had begun with his Edinburgh lectures on rhetoric and jurisprudence. In Phillipson's words, Smith "believed that it was now [that is, in the light of recent philosophical advances] possible to develop a genuine Science of Man based on the observation of human nature and human history; a science which would not only explain the principles of social and political organization to be found in different types of human society, but would explain the principles of government and legislation that ought to be followed by enlightened rulers who wanted to extend the liberty and happiness of their subjects and the wealth and power of their dominions" (Phillipson 2010, 2). *The Theory of Moral Sentiments* represented the first published element of this project and the *Wealth of Nations* the second. He had planned to write two further volumes: "A sort of Philosophical History of all the different branches of Literature, of Philosophy, Poetry and Eloquence" and "a sort of theory of History of Law and Government" (quoted in Phillipson 2010, 3). But although he would live for another fourteen years, these volumes would never appear. Ever the perfectionist, shortly before his death Smith ensured that all his preparatory work toward them was destroyed. One reason the volumes were never completed was his appointment, thanks to Buccleuch, as a commissioner on Scotland's Board of Customs. While his duties were not particularly onerous, he took them very seriously and they made heavy demands on his time.

The *Wealth of Nations* is undoubtedly Smith's most famous book; nonetheless, it is reported that Smith himself "always considered [*The Theory of Moral Sentiments*] as a much superior work" (Ross 2010, 188). He continued to revise and produce new editions of *The Theory of Moral Sentiments* throughout his life. The current consensus among Smith scholars is that the two books should be seen as two aspects of a single, unified project. The judgment of posterity, however, has overwhelmingly favored the *Wealth of Nations*. But just what is the argument of this much cited but not always well understood text?

Adam Smith's Freedom

In the two centuries since Smith's death, the *Wealth of Nations* has come to be seen as one of the ur-texts of capitalism, but, as often happen to such sanctified texts, it is treated more as a revered monument to be admired from afar rather than actually read. In the popular imagination, its five books and close to a thousand pages of thoughtful, nuanced argument have shrunk to a single sound bite: all that is required for a society's economic well-being is that market forces are allowed to operate freely; the market itself will do the rest with its all-powerful "invisible hand." This, however, is a gross caricature of this multilayered and complex text. To get beyond the caricature, it is necessary not only to read the *Wealth of Nations* seriously, but to locate both the book and its author in its historical context. A historian who has done this with particular care is Emma Rothschild in her study of Smith and his French contemporary the Marquis de Condorcet, *Economic Sentiments: Adam Smith, Condorcet, and the Enlightenment*, a book that, as she tells us in her opening sentence, takes as its subject "laissez faire when it was new" (Rothschild 2001, 1). My account of the *Wealth of Nations* draws heavily on Rothschild, although I make no claims to do more than pull out a few of the threads she identifies. Also, my theoretical starting-point and the questions with which I am concerned are a little different.

In chapter 2, I quoted Gramsci's reading of Croce's account of Italian history as providing a particular class with a narrative that "manages to present and have the conditions for its existence and development as a class accepted as a universal principle, as a world view, as a religion" (*FSPN*, 353). We might see the *Wealth of Nations* as similarly providing a particular class narrative, even if this was not its author's intention.

The book has two faces: one that looks to the past, one to the future. The one turned to the past is focused on the fetters of feudal restrictions and encumbrances. A key benefit of Scotland's union with England, in Smith's view, had been the resulting eclipse of the Scottish aristocracy: "By the union with England, the middling and inferior ranks of people in Scotland gained a compleat deliverance from the power of an aristocracy which had always before oppressed them" (Smith 1976, 944). The face turned to the future is concerned with demonstrating how once freed from obsolete feudal fetters, the new, freer economic system struggling to be born—a system based on an ever increasing division of labor—will lead to "general opulence" (Smith 1976, 25). What the condemnation of feudal residues and the vision of a better, more prosperous future share is an idea of freedom. "The idea of freedom is central to everything that Smith wrote" (Rothschild, 70). And his notion of freedom is not limited to economic freedom: "Freedom consisted, for Smith, in not being interfered with by others: in any of the sides of one's life, and by any outside forces (churches, parish overseers, corporations, customs inspectors, national governments, masters, proprietors). Interference, or oppression, is itself an extraordinarily extensive notion; Smith at times talks of inequality as a form of oppression, and of low wages as a form of inequity" (Rothschild, 71).

Smith continually contrasts the ideal of freedom with the dependency inherent in feudal societies, a dependency he saw as profoundly corrupting. As he was reported to have said in his lectures on jurisprudence at Glasgow University, "Nothing tends so much to corrupt and enervate and debase the mind as dependency and nothing gives such noble and generous notions of probity as freedom and independency" (quoted in Phillipson 1981, 35–36). His own view of the centrality of his critique of the encumbering residues of the past to the *Wealth of Nations* is revealed in a celebrated letter commenting on the response to his account of Hume's death. To the outrage of many, Smith's account made it clear that Hume retained his religious skepticism to the end. This "single" and to Smith, "very harmless Sheet of paper," he complained, "brought upon me ten times more abuse than the very violent attack I had made upon the whole commercial system of Great Britain" (quoted in Phillipson 2010, 247). "Commercial system" here refers to the whole panoply of outmoded institutions and practices he saw as holding back the "natural" progress of economic life to what he termed ever greater opulence.

Smith's argument in the *Wealth of Nations*, as in his other writings, is underpinned by an assumption of human progress. Like so many eighteenth-century thinkers, Smith's historical narrative is evolutionary. He assumes that in the course of their history, human societies advance, achieving in the process ever greater levels of opulence. He identifies four basic stages of human development, each defined by its mode of subsistence. First comes hunting. Out of this develops pastoralism, then agriculture, until, finally, a society reaches the highest stage, commerce. The most explicit discussion of the four stages in the *Wealth of Nations* is in the first two sections of book 5 (Smith 1976, 689–723), but a general assumption of progress pervades the whole text. Once it is assumed that progress is, as it were, natural, the question then becomes what holds back this progress. This question runs through the *Wealth of Nations*. As R. H. Campbell and A. S. Skinner put it in their introduction to their authoritative edition of the *Wealth of Nations* (1976), "The belief in the natural progress of opulence, almost its inevitability, is so strong throughout the WN that, when dealing with a contemporary problem, Smith's main objective is to isolate those barriers which lay in the path of natural progress as he saw it, and to advocate their speedy removal" (Campbell and Skinner 1976, 59).

For Smith, the story of his own time was one of economic advance, with the emergence of new forms of social organization, liberated from the fetters of the feudal and prefeudal past, and based on freedom. Smith's critique in the *Wealth of Nations* of the regulations governing the corn trade are well known. There is another critique in the book, however, to which Smith devotes considerable space, but which is often overlooked, even though, in Rothschild's view, it is "at the heart of [Smith's] view of economic reform" (Rothschild 2001, 87). This is Smith's attack on the apprenticeship system.

Real Encroachments upon Natural Liberty
The European apprenticeship system originated with the medieval guilds; it ensured that guild members maintained control over who was allowed to enter a given trade, how they were trained, and who would be allowed to become guild members with the right to practice as an independent master craftsman. In the mid-sixteenth century, the Statute of Artificers was enacted, which shifted some control from the guilds to the state. This statute regulating apprenticeship remained technically in force until 1814. By the time the *Wealth of Nations* was written, however, the whole system was in decline, with the development of new trades and industries that did not have guilds, and the growing importance of new urban centers that were not incorporated and therefore not subject to guild control. Nonetheless, the apprenticeship system still controlled the lives and working conditions of large numbers of young workers. And in Smith's eyes it was both inefficient and oppressive.

It was inefficient because, as a form of monopoly, it tended to keep both profits and wages artificially high. Interesting and perhaps surprising to the modern reader, given this thinker's status as "honoured prophet of the new right" (Kidd 2010, 21), it was the high profits that Smith saw as the major problem. "He was," Rothschild writes, "much more disturbed by high profits than by high wages" (Rothschild 2001, 93). And he saw workers as having far less power to combine to raise wages than employers had to raise prices, writing in the *Wealth of Nations*, "We have no acts of parliament against combining to lower the price of work; but many against combining to raise it," and noting that "masters are always and everywhere in a sort of tacit, but constant and uniform combination, not to raise the wages of labour above their actual rate" (Smith 1976, 84). Employers he sees as, in general, one-sided and self-interested: "Our merchants and master-manufacturers complain much about the bad effects of high wages in raising the price, and thereby lessening the sale of their goods both at home and abroad. They say nothing concerning the bad effects of high profits. They are silent with regard to the pernicious effects of their own gain. They complain only of those of other people" (Smith 1976, 115).

Another inefficiency inherent in the apprenticeship system is that it "obstructs the free circulation of labour from one employment to another" (Smith 1976, 151). Since only those who had served an apprenticeship in a given trade were allowed to practice it, it was difficult for workers to move between trades, even when one was declining and one rising. Smith uses the example of wool and silk weaving, declining in his day, and the rising trade of linen weaving. In all three weaving trades, "the operations are so much alike, that the workmen could easily change trades with one another, if those absurd laws did not hinder them" (Smith 1976, 151).

Apprenticeship was also inefficient as a form of education. An apprentice is "a servant bound to work at a particular trade for the benefit of a master, during a term of years, upon condition that the master shall teach him that trade." In reality, however, "Long apprenticeships are altogether unnecessary" (Smith 1976, 139). No one actually needed the years of an apprenticeship to acquire the skills of an established trade. The primary beneficiaries of an apprenticeship system were the masters who profited from the years of unpaid apprenticeship labor (Smith 1976, 140).

Apprenticeship was not merely inefficient; it was unjust. Today, Smith may be chiefly remembered as a passionate advocate of free trade, but his denunciations of injustice and inequity in the *Wealth of Nations* are just as passionate. "Servants, labourers and workmen of different kinds," he notes, "make up the far greater part of every great political society," and he goes on to make this impassioned plea for their right to a decent life: "No society can surely be flourishing and happy, of which the far greater part of the members are poor and miserable. *It is but equity*, besides, that they who feed, cloath and lodge the whole body of the people, should have such a share of the produce of their own labour as to be themselves tolerably well fed, cloathed and lodged" (Smith 1976, 96; emphasis mine). The argument here is far from simply economic efficiency, although Smith certainly believes that an equitable system would be more efficient. What is involved is a basic and undeniable right: "it is but equity." Both the statute of apprenticeship and the "exclusive privileges of corporations [guilds]" by contrast, represent "real encroachments upon natural liberty" (Smith, 1976, 470). "Freedom, for Smith, is," as Rothschild argues, "an end in itself, of a self-evident sort" (Rothschild 2001, 70).

"Natural liberty," in the *Wealth of Nations*, is bound up with property, and the most fundamental form of property is labor. A famous passage summarizes the argument: "The property which every man has in his own labour, as it is the original foundation of all other property, so it is the most sacred and inviolable. The patrimony of a poor man lies in the strength and dexterity of his hands; and to hinder him from employing this strength and dexterity in what manner he thinks proper without injury to his neighbour, is a plain violation of this most sacred property. It is a manifest encroachment upon the just liberty both of the workman, and of those who might be disposed to employ him" (Smith 1976, 138). Apprenticeship is basically unjust in that it is a form of unfree, bonded labor: "During the continuance of the apprenticeship, the whole labour of the apprentice belongs to his master" (Smith 1976, 119). An apprentice is not only a servant but one bound "to work at a particular trade for the benefit of a master" (Smith 1976, 139). The very inequality of the relationship poisons it. Smith believed passionately in the basic equality of human beings and explicitly rejected any notion of "natural," inborn inequality. In the first book of the *Wealth of Nations*, he espouses a particularly strong version of inherent equality:

> The difference of natural talents in different men is, in reality, much less than we are aware of . . . The difference between the most dissimilar characters, between a philosopher and a common street porter, for example, seems to arise not so much from nature, as from habit, custom, and education. When they came into the world, and for the first six or eight years of their existence, they were, perhaps, very much alike, and neither their parents, nor play-fellows could perceive any remarkable difference. About that age, or soon after, they come to be employed in very different occupations. The difference of talents comes then to be taken notice of, and widens by degree, till at last the vanity of the philosopher is willing to acknowledge scarce any resemblance. (Smith 1976, 28–29)

In other words, we are all born equal; it is only the division of labor that creates the illusion of "natural," or god-given inequality. In the nineteenth century, such radical equalitarianism, and the associated denunciation of established privilege, would tend to be airbrushed out of accounts of the argument to be found in the *Wealth of Nations*.

Smith also saw the apprenticeship system through its linkage with settlement law as central to the essential arbitrariness of the law at the level of the parish. Settlement law fixed in which parish an individual had a "settlement." This was the place to which they were seen as belonging and therefore entitled to poor relief and other benefits, all of which were parish-based. Apprenticeship was one of the most common ways of acquiring a settlement (Snell 1996, 308). The laws governing both settlement and apprenticeship, however, were far from straightforward; whether or not a particular individual did or did not have a settlement, and where that settlement was located was often disputed. Parishes were inherently anxious to avoid their obligations to pay poor relief, and keen to restrict competition for local employment, housing, common land, and so on, access to which was also based on settlement law. The complex and confusing patchwork of laws encouraged contestation. To Smith, the tangle of regulation was, as Rothschild puts it, "an oppressive combination of public laws and corporate bylaws—a 'corporation spirit'—in which laws are enacted for the benefit of the powerful, and enforced at the caprice of magistrates, masters, overseers, and churchwardens" (Rothschild 2001, 88–89). The denunciations of this corporation spirit that so blantantly manipulated the laws in the interests of the powerful would also be airbrushed out of later accounts of the *Wealth of Nations*. In essence, Smith saw apprenticeship as part of a premodern, feudal world in which individuals, whether rich or poor, were not free, autonomous agents, but bound into complex networks of obligation and entitlement, some formal and enshrined in law, many informal and customary, although not necessarily for that reason less binding. This was a world in which everyone was woven into a web of institutions and practices: "Work, training, socialization, finance and exchange, local political eligibility and involvement, family life and such concerns were all mutually integrated" (Snell 1996, 305). For Smith, this feudal world was inefficient in economic terms, hampering the natural increase in opulence, but equally it was profoundly unjust. And dominated as it was by the rich and powerful, it prevented the poor and powerless from challenging the arbitrary and unjust regime under which they lived.

The Freedom to Truck, Barter, and Exchange

Smith's critique of apprenticeship represents the face of the *Wealth of Nations*, turned to the oppressive and inefficient residues of the past. His much better known celebration of free trade reflects the face that looks to a future in which an economy freed from the restrictive encumbrances of the past will lead to increased prosperity across society. The magic mechanism here is the division of labor, which stems in a famous formulation from the uniquely human "propensity to truck, barter, and exchange one thing for another" (Smith 1976, 25). The assumption is that, given its rootedness in this most basic of human characteristics, and the inherent tendency of societies to progress, the new economic system will develop naturally. And, it will develop without the need for any divine intervention. The story told by the *Wealth of Nations* is a resolutely secular one.

Smith himself was always very circumspect as regards his religious convictions, and his own religious beliefs remain unclear. His caution is understandable at a time when even the suspicion of religious skepticism could be dangerous. As recently as 1697, the teenage Thomas Aikenhead had been hanged after he had done no more than "orally ridiculed some passages in the Old Testament" (Mossner 1980, 354). While his two modern biographers, Ross and Phillipson, agree that Smith shared his friend Hume's distaste for the rigidities and intolerance of much organized religion, they differ on the question of whether or not he was a believer. Ross reads the scanty evidence left by Smith as indicating that he "was not prepared to contemplate the notion of a world lacking a creator" (Ross 2010, 117), while Phillipson sees him as sharing Hume's skepticism (Phillipson 2010, 244). What is clear is that, as Campbell and Skinner observe, "The break with the tradition of Christian authority [in the *Wealth of Nations*] is obvious; even historical parts of the Bible and its apparent relevance to the discussion of a nomadic life are virtually ignored, with only the most incidental of references to the Old Testament" (Campbell and Skinner 1976, 51). And, whether or not he was a believer, the economic system laid out in the *Wealth of Nations* has no place for a divine presence. Similarly, the exploration of the emergence of morality out of the experiences of everyday life in *The Theory of Moral Sentiments* is precisely the elaboration of a moral system that has dispensed with divine revelation. Smith's intellectual project assumes that we do not need God to arrive at an economically efficient and morally just world; what impedes progress is simply the lingering remnants of feudal and prefeudal restrictions. It is because he sees apprenticeship as a prime example of an outmoded restriction of individual freedom that his critique of it is central to the argument of the *Wealth of Nations*. By contrast to the inefficiency and injustice of apprenticeship, and of the whole legal panoply in which it is embedded, the new economic system struggling to be born, a system based on free exchange, represents not only freedom but efficiency and justice.

Such an economic system is efficient because it increases the productivity of human labor. Through the magic of the division of labor and the associated "invention of a great number of machines which facilitate and abridge labour, and enable one man to do the work of many" (Smith 1976, 17), an ever increasing stream of goods can be produced, and this abundance allows everyone, including the poorest, to live better. The first chapter of the first book of the *Wealth of Nations* gives a rhapsodic account of the benefits of the division of labor. The celebratory tone, combined with down-to-earth concreteness, is characteristic of Smith's accessible narrative style. Presupposing no specialist knowledge on the part of his reader, he tells his story in a way that carries the reader along with him. We might say of him, as he was reported to have said of Voltaire, that his writings were "made for all" (see the passage above, quoted from Phillipson). "Observe the accommodation of the most common artificer or day-labourer in a civilized and thriving country," Smith begins, "and you will perceive that the number of people of whose industry a part, though but a small part, has been employed in procuring him this accommodation, exceeds all computation. The woollen coat, for example, which covers the day-labourer, as coarse and rough as it may appear, is the produce of the joint labour of a great multitude of workmen. The shepherd, the sorter of the wool, the wool-comber or carder, the dyer, the scribbler, the spinner, the weaver, the fuller, the dresser, with many others, must all join their different arts in order to complete even this homely production" (22). Smith then lists the many different kinds of labor necessary to create the ships that transport all the different goods required for even the simplest coat, exclaiming at one point: "What a variety of labour too is necessary in order to produce the tools of the meanest of these workmen!," before continuing to pile on more and more specific examples of the diverse forms of labor that go into providing the "very meanest person" in a "civilized country" with the necessities of life (23). In this way, he builds up to his triumphant conclusion, celebrating the benefits of the division of labor: "Compared, indeed, with the more extravagant luxury of the great, his [the very meanest person's] accommodation must no doubt appear extremely simple and easy; and yet it may be true, perhaps, that the accommodation of an European prince does not always so much exceed that of an industrious and frugal peasant, as the accommodation of the latter exceeds that of many an African king, the absolute master of the lives and liberties of ten thousand naked savages" (23–24).

To unleash the full power inherent in the principle of the division of labor, however, there needs to be freedom of commerce. The abolition of restrictions on labor, such as the apprenticeship regulations, is one key element here, another is the removal of the regulations governing the corn trade. Taken together, the critique of apprenticeship regulations and the better known one of the corn trade regulations can be seen as constituting, in Rothschild's words, "an inclusive system of commercial freedom: for industry and for agriculture, and for the commerce in labor as well as for the commerce in commodities"

(87–88). An economic regime based on freedom, one from which outmoded restrictions have been stripped away, would not only be more productive and lead to greater prosperity, it would be more just. And justice is, for Smith, an absolute value: "it is but equity" (96) that the mass of the population who furnish society with its basic needs should themselves have access to a decent life. This is only possible, however, in a society with an advanced economy capable of production on the necessary scale.

Smith's celebration of the division of labor is not unalloyed, however; he also points out its less desirable effects. Take, for instance, his famous example of pin making, which by his time had been broken down into something like eighteen different operations, performed by different workers with each worker's contribution reduced to the same simple task, or set of tasks, endlessly repeated (Smith 1976, 14–15). Those condemned to such monotonous work lives are likely to suffer both mental and physical stunting.

> [T]he understandings of the greater part of men are necessarily formed by their ordinary employments. The man whose whole life is spent in performing a few simple operations, of which the effects too are, perhaps, always the same, or very nearly the same, has no occasion to exert his understanding, or to exercise his invention in finding out expedients for removing difficulties which never occur. He naturally loses, therefore, the habit of such exertion, and generally becomes as stupid and ignorant as it is possible for a human creature to become. . . . The uniformity of his stationary life . . . corrupts even the activity of his body, and renders him incapable of exerting his strength with vigour and perseverance, in any other employment than that to which he has been bred. His dexterity at his own particular trade seems, in this manner, to be acquired at the expence of his intellectual, social and martial virtues. But in every improved and civilized society this is the state into which the labouring poor, that is, the great body of the people, must necessarily fall, unless government takes some pains to prevent it. (Smith 1976, 781–82)

It would seem that a degree of stunting of the mass of the population, however regrettable, is an inevitable cost of civilization unless the government steps in. Given his popular image as the great champion of laissez-faire, we should note his implicit argument here that it is the government's responsibility to "take some pains to prevent" this stunting. And, indeed, he goes on to advocate that "the most essential parts of education . . . to read, write and account" should be made available even to poor children who must necessarily begin working at an early age. As he sees it, "For a very small expence the publick can facilitate, can encourage, and can even impose upon almost the whole body of the people, the necessity of acquiring those most essential parts of education" (785).

Significantly, the rationale is not that of efficiency. The "labouring poor" do not need such education to perform their allotted tasks. Given that their employment in "civilized" societies involves no more than the endless repetition of the same few simple tasks, education is not required to generate productive workers. Rather, the argument for educating "the whole body of the people" stems from the conviction that without education a human being is a sad, stunted being. Someone "without the proper use of the intellectual faculties of a man . . . seems to be mutilated and deformed," lacking an "essential part of the character of human nature" (Smith 1976, 788). And I think we can assume that just as Smith believes that the mass of the population has a right to be "tolerably well fed, cloathed and lodged," so, too, he sees them as having the right to a certain level of education. As a man of his time, he saw any form of formal public education as essentially concerned with the education of boys. Women, he felt, could obtain the education they needed within the context of the family (Smith 1976, 781). This may seem somewhat dismissive to modern ears, but given the importance he attached to the moral education we all receive from our family and circle of friends—a key theme in his *Theory of Moral Sentiments*—it is less patronizing than it sounds.

He also stresses the value of education for the creation of properly informed and rational citizens. Education is necessary to combat "the gross ignorance and stupidity which, in a civilized society, seems so frequently to benumb the understandings of all the inferior ranks of people" (788). An educated population will not be subject to the "delusions of enthusiasm and superstition" and will recognize the reasonableness of government. Like other eighteenth-century intellectuals, Smith believed in the power of reason: "An instructed and intelligent people . . . are always more decent and orderly than an ignorant and stupid one. . . . They are more disposed to examine, and more capable of seeing through, the interested complaints of faction and sedition, and they are, upon that account, less apt to be misled into any wanton or unnecessary opposition to the measures of government" (Smith 1976, 788).

The confidence here that the poor, provided they are "instructed" and their intelligence developed, will not only understand the "measures of government" but will happily accept them, reflects both a firm belief in their basic intellectual capacity and the assumption that the measures of the kind of progressive government and economic system he advocates will necessarily be in the interests of the mass of the population. All that is required is that the poor are given the education necessary for them to understand government's rational explanations. Writing before the French Revolution and the development of large-scale industrial, factory-based production, Smith has none of the fear of the poor and dispossessed that haunts the writing of so many later commentators.

Part of the brilliance of the *Wealth of Nations* is that Smith gives us both a coherent but somewhat abstract theoretical system, and an accessible and concrete account of its implications in the real world. Smith tells a story that, at least in its broad outline, is easy for the nonspecialist reader to grasp. This story combined a "plea for liberty [that] accorded with the intellectual presuppositions of the eighteenth century" (Campbell and Skinner 1976, 47) with the laying down of a path as to how we might get there. Later historians have challenged the accuracy of Smith's narrative. "The eighteenth century, *pace* Adam Smith," according to Snell, a historian of the eighteenth century, "was not a time of parochially closed internal labour markets" (Snell 1996, 310). For the purposes of my argument, however, it is not important whether or not Smith's narrative is historically accurate. The key point is that Smith articulates a narrative that would be adopted by a rising bourgeois class.

Prior to the publication of the *Wealth of Nations*, a number of Smith's friends feared that its intellectual sophistication would prevent it finding a wide readership. Their fears, however, proved unfounded, and the book was an immediate and continuing success. What his friends seemed to have missed was that it did far more than provide an account of a theoretical system. "There was," as its modern editors explain, "another side to the WN, a more pragmatic, down to earth side, which gave the work a practical relevance in the eyes of many to whom the intellectual system was perhaps a mystery or merely irrelevant." Smith "commanded respect because the practical conclusions which followed from the chief elements of his system were evidently related to the economic problems of the middle of the eighteenth century" (Campbell and Skinner 1976, 42–43). Here was a thinker, it seemed, deeply knowledgeable, but with a practical understanding of the concerns of his time and place. Campbell and Skinner give as an example the book's discussion of the Navigation Acts: "The protection afforded by the Navigation Acts provided a firm and unfettered basis for Glasgow's success as an entrepot in the tobacco trade. Hence to read the practical discussion in Book IV of the WN, whether to accept or to reject its conclusions, was to read an account highly relevant to the contemporary economic scene. The Book discusses the stuff of which contemporary economic policy was made" (Campbell and Skinner 1976, 46).

Smith was never an intellectual who was cut off from the day-to-day concerns of his world. We saw how he was an active participant in various learned societies, which included among their members not only academics, but merchants, and other "practical" men. There was, for instance, the merchant-dominated Glasgow's Political Economy Club, founded to generate and disseminate knowledge of "the Nature and the Principles of Trade in all its Branches" (Phillipson 2010, 129). One of only two professorial members, Smith was a regular attendee, presumably valuing the merchant-eye view it provided. Smith clearly intended the *Wealth of Nations* to be a book that, like those of his hero Voltaire, was made for all, one to be read by merchants, manufacturers, and legislators as well as scholars. It was, as Phillipson puts it, "a call to his contemporaries to take moral, political and intellectual control of their lives and the lives of those for whom they were responsible" (Phillipson 2010, 238).

Over time, Smith would come to be seen as embodying the quintessentially bourgeois project of laissez-faire, but, as Rothschild demonstrates, this is a gross oversimplification. How did this distortion happen? To answer that question, we need to look at the transformations in meaning his text underwent in the decades after his death as certain threads of Smith's complex and nuanced argument were pulled out, while others were ignored or even denied.

Adam Smith and the Rise of Economics

Smith died in 1790, almost exactly a year after the storming of the Bastille. As the turbulent events unfolded in France, many in Britain looked apprehensively across the channel, fearing the spread of revolution. But there were also many who celebrated what they saw as the coming of a new age of reason: "Bliss was it in that dawn to be alive . . . When Reason seemed the most to assert her rights," as Wordsworth would enthuse. Opinions were particularly divided in Scotland, and Smith himself became a polarizing figure: to the "liberal young of Edinburgh" he was a hero, while to those who did not share their liberalism, the doctrine of Free Trade could smack of revolution (Rothschild 2001, 56). Alarmed by what seemed the spread of a dangerous radicalism, the British state began a series of prosecutions of those alleged to be spreading seditious views. In Scotland, the sedition trials resulted in particularly severe sentences, including transportation for life. In their defense a number of the accused appealed to Smith's arguments on Free Trade, a more equitable tax system, and freedom of the press. Such arguments cut little ice with the prosecutors, however, serving rather to confirm their view that such doctrines were indeed seditious.

This was the context in which a memoir of Smith appeared that was destined to become "by far the most important biographical work about Smith, as well as an early source of Smith's conservative renown" (Rothschild 2001, 57). Published in 1793, the author was Smith's friend Dugald Stewart, characterized by Phillipson as "the philosopher of a new influential and singularly unsubtle idea of citizenship. He was the apostle to the expert, confident and instructed, willing to assist in the ordinary process of government, concerned above all with increasing its managerial efficiency in the interests of preserving public order in an increasingly turbulent age" (Phillipson 1981, 39–40). In line with his celebration of the apolitical expert, Stewart's memoir endorses Smith's advocacy of economic freedom in the *Wealth of Nations*, but is far more circumspect as regards his views on political liberty. According to Stewart, Smith argues that, as long as a country's laws are just, that country's people "would have little reason to complain, that they were not immediately instrumental in their enactment" (Stewart 1980, 310). "Stewart's defence of Smith," as Rothschild explains, "was part of a far more extensive discussion, in the mid-1790s, about the distinction between politics and political economy, and about the definition of freedom. His object, in the memoir, seems to have been to show that political economy was an innocuous, technical sort of subject. Smith was a retiring, innocuous sort of person, quite unconcerned to influence public opinion, and interested only in offering hints on policy to 'actual legislators'" (Rothschild 2001, 58).

A couple of years later, in the context of a sudden rise in food prices, the reform-minded MP Samuel Whitbread unsuccessfully introduced a bill in parliament that would have instituted a minimum wage. Both supporters and opponents of the bill appealed to arguments to be found in the *Wealth of Nations*. At this point, Smith was still seen by many, as he had been during his lifetime, as sympathetic to the poor. Indeed, in 1798 Malthus would write disapprovingly of Smith's unrealistic concern with "the happiness and comfort of the lower orders of society" (quoted in Rothschild 2001, 82). In the next few years, however, it would be the conservative reading of the *Wealth of Nations* that would win out. By 1800, the liberal and potentially seditious Smith had been eclipsed; he had become "the modern hero of commerce" (Rothschild 2001, 64).

Key to Smith's transmutation was the separating out of political economy as a distinct discipline, a process that was complete by the middle of the nineteenth century. As Gramsci noted, "The capitalist entrepreneur creates alongside himself . . . the specialist in political economy" (*SPN*, 5). And once it has been established, a new discipline seems to do no more than acknowledge a naturally existing topic of study. For John Stuart Mill, writing in 1836, the recognition of political economy as "a science with its own territory, its own definition, and its own methods of investigation" was simply an indication of the historical advance of knowledge (Rothschild 2001, 218). From this perspective, Smith becomes a forerunner, a genius, certainly, but one groping his way toward the clear light of a discipline yet to be revealed, a genius still encumbered with all kinds of extraneous and irrelevant baggage. But to see Smith in this way is to distort his argument. It both misrepresents the *Wealth of Nations* and ignores the broader project to which that text belongs. Smith's investigations into the "Nature and Causes of the Wealth of Nations" are the product of a time before economics was walled off in its own disciplinary territory. They are part of "an earlier and less bounded scene," as Rothschild puts it, "in which the territory of economic life extends in all directions" (Rothschild 2001, 218). With the triumph of political economy, and then later economics, Smith and the *Wealth of Nations* become reconfigured. We might compare the retrospective recasting of the argument of the *Wealth of Nations* with the reconfiguring of the history of European painting in the nineteenth century after the triumph of modernism. After that triumph, the history of the visual arts comes to be seen as a teleology that culminates in modernism. Allais's assessment of Smith (used as an epigraph to this chapter) illustrates the recasting of Smith, who wrote before economics as a discipline existed, as the original economist, the font from which the discipline flows. Before this could happen, however, a separate and distinct economic realm had to be defined as the subject matter of a new discipline, the discipline of economics.

The Organicity of Adam Smith

Does the centrality of the *Wealth of Nations* to the fundamental capitalist narrative make Smith an organic bourgeois intellectual? As I hope this chapter has made clear, Smith would certainly not have seen his intellectual project as that of providing a rationale for unfettered capitalism. He would probably be horrified to see merchants and manufacturers, not to mention the finance capitalists who have succeeded them, claiming the *Wealth of Nations* as a foundational text. Nonetheless, the book's critique of feudal economic fetters, coupled with its vision of potential opulence for all once those fetters are struck off, would in time, once certain arguments had been removed and others highlighted, provide an emerging bourgeois class with its vision of a future founded on economic "freedom." Smith, we might say, shows the rising bourgeoisie their future as a class. On the one hand, he gives them a charge:

clear away all the lingering feudal restrictions holding back the full flowering of free commerce! On the other, he lays out the prospect of a shimmering and enticing future of increasing wealth for all—provided, that is, the charge is fulfilled in a responsible way under the mindful eye of progressive legislators. This is the class, the book implies, that can bring about a future of universal opulence.

To answer the question of Smith's organicity, it is important to remember Gramsci's insistence that in studying intellectuals, our focus should be on the process of knowledge production rather than on the particular qualities of individual intellectuals. We need to look at the "ensemble of social relations" out of which forms of collective knowledge emerge, teasing out the links—often highly mediated—between basic economic relations and conceptualizations of reality. Intellectuals are always shaped by their environment. Like other Scottish Enlightenment thinkers, Smith was in many ways a cosmopolitan intellectual, part of an international republic of letters, but he was also a Scot. As Alexander Broadie, editor of the *Cambridge Companion to the Scottish Enlightenment*, puts it: "A Scot writing on politics, economics, social structures, education, law or religion will think in terms of the politics, economics, society, education, law or religious dimension of his country, and it is impossible for his thought not to be affected by these distinctive features of his national context. The point is not that the Scottish models contribute irresistibly to the agenda from which Scottish thinkers work, though those models surely will be on their agenda. It is rather that the thinkers write as Scots, who have therefore lived in, worked with, and in large measure been formed by those institutions" (Broadie 2003, 2).

One inescapable reality for any Scot growing up in the early eighteenth century was that they lived under the shadow of English hegemony. Theirs was, we might say, a subaltern location. And, partly in response to the new economic and social realities, Scotland's knowledge-producing infrastructure underwent a transformation during this period: universities were reformed with the introduction of new, more effective teaching methods, and the recognition of a range of new disciplines. There were also the many learned societies and clubs that sprang up in all the major cities. The close-knit fraternity of Scottish virtuosi was far from exclusively academic. It included progressive-minded merchants, landowners, and other practical men, all of whom shared a concern with finding solutions to the many problems facing their country; in their gatherings, improvement, what it entailed and how it might be achieved, was a frequent theme of discussion. And the vantage point from which they viewed Scotland's predicament tended to be that of Scotland's progressive landowners, merchants, and other men of business. Such men (and this was an almost exclusively male world) may have represented a Scottish elite, but they were still subaltern in relation to the English power elite.

The author of the *Wealth of Nations* was a product of this intellectual environment, and the book reflects its genesis within a subaltern location. It is written in explicit opposition to an existing regime of power. Smith, we should remember, saw it as a "very violent attack . . . upon the whole commercial system of Great Britain" (quoted in Phillipson 2010, 247). The *Wealth of Nations* transforms the experience of Scotland's practical men of business into a coherent political narrative. This extraordinarily rich text "was a product of many things," but a key element was "Smith's close contact with the merchant class of Glasgow" (Broadie 2003, 5). While many of those merchants were well-educated men, whose common sense may have been more coherent than that of Gramsci's *semplici*, they did not, as a class in formation, as yet have their own coherent narrative that explained how the specific interests of merchants and manufacturers could be seen as reflecting a vision beneficial to the whole of society. The power of the *Wealth of Nations*, as James Buchan, author of *The Authentic Adam Smith*, writes, "is that, like Fra Pacioli's treatise on double-entry bookkeeping in 1494, it reproduces commercial knowledge and practice in the vernacular, and like that great work provides them with respectability" (Buchan 1995, 13).

It took time, however, for the book's confident vision of ever-expanding opulence, based on commercial freedom, to reveal itself as the source of the kind of organizing vision Gramsci sees as essential for any emerging class. In Smith's lifetime, and for some decades after his death, the message of his masterwork was far less clear and much disputed. Particularly distasteful to many merchants and manufacturers was Smith's insistence that enlightened governments have an obligation to rein in the self-interest of those very merchants and manufacturers. It was not inevitable that this text, considered by its author a work of moral philosophy, would be a foundational text for the new capitalist world order. It took work by other thinkers and popularizers to mould Smith's argument into an organizing vision for an emerging bourgeois class. It was only long after his death that Smith ceased to be seen as a moral philosopher and was redefined as an economist, and not merely an economist but a point of origin for the whole discipline of economics—a discipline that comes into being together with capitalism. Only with the benefit of hindsight does the organicity of the author of the *Wealth of Nations* become clear.

Chapters 6 and 7 of this book move forward in time from the eighteenth to the twenty-first century, and from a focus on the concept of the organic intellectual to that of common sense. The chapters explore two very different attempts, from opposite ends of the political spectrum, to mould common sense into a particular shape: the Tea Party and the Occupy Wall Street movement. The two projects are very different. The Tea Partiers' common sense has its roots in the past. It can be seen as an outgrowth of the capitalist narrative to which Smith gave such articulate form—even if he might be dismayed by the oversimple market triumphalism now associated with his name. The Occupy movement, by contrast, was perhaps groping its way, however unsteadily, toward a new common sense that genuinely challenges the prevailing hegemony that there is no way but the capitalist way.

6

The Common Sense of the Tea Party

The really dangerous bull [in the rodeo] isn't [Glenn] Beck, it's a whole slew of once "fringe" ways of looking at the world that have become what he calls "common sense." The idea that civil rights are special rights and regulations are theft, that taxes are bad for the economy and the poor are best helped by helping the rich. — LAURA FLANDERS

This chapter looks at an example of political mobilization from the extreme right of the political spectrum: the Tea Party. It focuses on a particular aspect of the Tea Party phenomenon: its attempt to frame the current woes of the American economy, and what should be done to remedy them, in terms of a specific, easily graspable narrative. In other words, I explore the Tea Party as a project to make a given narrative common sense.

As we have seen, *senso comune*, in the notebooks, is that comforting set of certainties in which we feel at home, and that we absorb, often unconsciously, from the world we inhabit. These are the basic realities we use to explain that world. Initially such certainties are those of the environment in which we grow up and are socialized; later, particularly if we are exposed to wider worlds, our stock of common sense will be modified and augmented. And the common sense of those different worlds is itself subject to change; over time its tangle of often contradictory assumptions shift as new realities establish themselves, and old ones are discarded. We tend, however, to be blind to this mutability, experiencing our everyday world as undergirded by a web of fixed, commonsense realities that only a Don Quixote could deny. For those seeking to bring into being a historical bloc with the potential to overturn the existing hegemony, common sense is necessarily a key site of struggle. We can think of it as one front in the long, slow war of position fought by subaltern classes as they begin to overcome their subalternity and cast off their "mind-forged manacles." If they are to reach the mass of the population, progressive activists need to use language and narratives with which that mass is already familiar; the realities of lived experience need to be explained in ways that resonate with the good sense to be found in subaltern common sense.

Common sense, however, is not only a site of struggle for those trying to transform society. Dominant classes (who in their rise to power constituted their own historical bloc) may have the resources necessary to ensure that their worldview remains dominant—this is part of what defines hegemony—but their dominance is never completely won, never totally secure. It must be continually maintained and reproduced. This does not mean, however, the creation of new narratives by new organic intellectuals, but rather the effective dissemination of already existing narratives, recrafted to resonate with the concerns of a given historical moment. The simple, accessible common sense, on which such dissemination relies, remains rooted in the foundational narratives forged by the organic intellectuals the dominant class created in its rise to power. We can see the Tea Party phenomenon as an example of the effective dissemination of a common sense, grounded in some old capitalist verities, which at a particular historical moment resonated particularly strongly with certain sections of the American public.

Shifting America to the Right

The political influence wielded by the Tea Party since its emergence in 2009 is undeniable. Ronald Formisano's summing up in 2012 of its political influence in his "brief history" of the Tea Party remains true as of 2016: "It is too early to claim that the Tea Party has—or Tea Parties have—changed history, but the movement has had an enormous impact on the Republican Party, moving its center of gravity far to the right. It has severely constricted the maneuverability of the Obama administration and has shaped, perhaps more than any other current political force, the content of the nation's political agenda since 2009" (Formisano 2012, 2).

The scholars and journalists who have attempted to make sense of the Tea Party phenomenon have all commented on the suddenness with which it appeared, and its extraordinarily rapid rise to prominence. As Theda Skocpol and Vanessa Williamson write in a study published in 2012, *The Tea Party and the Remaking of Republican Conservatism*, Tea Party groups "burst onto the national scene, starting in early 2009, just weeks into the Obama presidency" (Skocpol and Williamson 2012, 5). Like giant mushrooms appearing after rain, it seemed that one day there was nothing, and then the next, there they were, fully formed: organized groups across the country with a shared commitment to "limited government, fiscal responsibility and free markets," to quote the motto of the Tea Party Patriots, an umbrella organization for local Tea Party groups. In 2010, the Tea Party Patriots "claimed to have 2,800 local cells in their network," and while independent investigators came up with far lower numbers (Formisano, 33), it was clear that something rather remarkable was going on.

But what did this sudden eruption of political discontent actually signify? Can it be seen as springing directly from the frustrations and fears of ordinary people? Those on the left and center-left have tended to be skeptical, dismissing the Tea Party as false populism. Far from representing the grass roots, this was Astroturf. As Nancy Pelosi, then speaker of the House of Representatives, put it: "It's not really a grassroots movement. It's astroturf by some of the wealthiest people in America to keep the focus on tax cuts for the rich instead of for the great middle class" (quoted in Formisano, 7). Her dismissiveness is shared by the academics Paul Street and Anthony DiMaggio, authors of *Crashing the Tea Party*. Their book is, they explain, an exposure of "an ugly, authoritarian, and fake-populist pseudomovement directed from above and *early on* by and for elite Republican and business interests" (Street and DiMaggio 2011, 9). The Tea Party, they insist, italicizing the phrase in case the reader has any doubts, "is *not a social movement*" (10).

Is the Tea Party authentic? For many, this seems to be the key question: "The main debate about the Tea Party," Formisano writes, "has to do with authenticity. To what extent has it emerged from the grassroots, from ordinary people, especially from those not previously involved in politics, or to what extent has it been created by corporations, billionaires, and right-wing media seeking to further their own agendas?" (Formisano, 6). But is authenticity in fact the central issue? Formisano answers his own question: "The simple answer is that the Tea Parties have been created by both kinds of populism, in part by the few—the corporate lobbyists from above—but also from the passionate many expressing real grassroots populism" (8). Skocpol and Williamson also stress the genuine emotional appeal of the Tea Party message. For their study, rather than relying simply on "surveys, news accounts, and public information," they visited different Tea Party groups, interviewing their members and engaging in participant observation: "We knew we needed to get out there and hear from Tea Party participants face to face" (Skocpol and Williamson, 14). Their research revealed the importance of feelings: "Issues and policies matter to Tea Party members, of course, as do their conceptions about American government . . . But we would be remiss not to underline, from the start, the *feelings* that came across so vividly when people spoke to us" (46–47). This would seem to be an example of the "feeling-passion" identified by Gramsci as a crucial element of any effective political movement (*SPN*, 418); whether of the left or the right, political movements need to harness such feeling. We can see the Tea Party as a highly successful bringing together of certain narratives, long propagated by right-wing intellectuals, with deeply felt anxieties of those Formisano terms the "passionate many." This chapter traces out this dialogue between organized and extremely well-funded elements on the right, and the more inchoate, but often passionate feeling of "ordinary people," manifested in the form of commonsense truths. I begin with Street and Dimaggio's elite Republican and business interests.

Shaping the Narrative from Above

Within the heterogeneous power bloc that constitutes the American capitalist class, there have been, virtually ever since Franklin D. Roosevelt's New Deal was enacted, those committed to roll back the gains won by working and middle-class Americans. Their task has, no doubt, been made easier by the decline of the American left after the Second World War. The reasons for this decline are complex and much debated. For the purposes of this chapter, the relevant point is the undeniable absence of a strong, popular left-wing movement in recent decades.

Intellectuals have played a crucial role in the project to reverse the gains of the New Deal. It is they who have provided the narratives necessary to make the case that any attempt to manage capitalist economies (along the lines suggested by John Maynard Keynes and his followers, for instance) are futile, and that free, unfettered markets are the only way to achieve prosperity across society. "A vast network of policy-oriented right-wing intellectuals, generously funded, has been," as Skocpol and Williamson note, "strategizing and writing for many years, awaiting the moment when political and electoral winds might shift just enough to allow their ideas to find a larger place on the mainstream agenda" (84).

These policy-oriented right-wing intellectuals cover a wide spectrum. At one end there are renowned academic economists such as Milton Friedman and Friedrich Hayek, who spent their working lives championing the unfettered market at elite universities in Britain, the United States, and Germany. Such intellectuals can be seen in Gramscian terms as traditional intellectuals, heirs to disciplines and knowledge-producing institutions that seem "to represent an historical continuity uninterrupted even by the most complicated and radical changes in political and social forms" (*SPN*, 7). At the other end of the spectrum there are popularizers like Glenn Beck, and the right-wing commentators on Fox News and other conservative media. The power wielded by such divulgators is evidenced by the rapid ascent to the number one spot on the Amazon bestseller list of Hayek's *The Road to Serfdom* after Beck championed it on his hugely popular radio program. We may wonder how many of his listeners made their way to the end of this dense tome from 1944, but that is another matter. Popularizers such as Beck are crucial if the narratives produced by sophisticated, specialized intellectuals are to be transmuted into easily graspable common sense. We should remember here Gramsci's inclusive definition of intellectuals: intellectuals include not only the producers of knowledge, but its distributors, even "the most humble 'administrators' and divulgators of pre-existing, traditional, accumulated intellectual wealth" (*SPN*, 13).

To understand the apparently sudden emergence of the Tea Party, it is helpful to look at the history of this long-incubating project. We need to go back quite far, to the years before the so-called Reagan revolution. In hindsight, this was a time of exceptional prosperity, when the federal minimum wage was at its highest and the unemployment rate was below 4 percent.[1] Nonetheless, there were those who saw danger looming. One such was the corporate lawyer Lewis Powell, who in 1971, two years after the federal minimum wage reached its peak, wrote a private memo to his close friend Eugene Sydnor Jr., Chair of the Education Committee of the U.S. Chamber of Commerce. The memo was written just a couple of months before President Nixon's nomination of Powell to the U.S. Supreme Court, although it only became public the following year, well after Powell had been confirmed.

In the memo, entitled "Attack on American Free Enterprise System," the future Supreme Court Justice gives voice to an anxiety shared by many members of the business elite that their control over the country's hegemonic narrative was slipping. During his tenure as a Supreme Court Justice (1972–87), Powell would gain a reputation as a moderate; his memo, however, even though writ-

---

1. In 1969 the federal minimum wage was $1.60 an hour ($10.10 in 2013 dollars). At the beginning of 2013 it was $7.25 (Piketty 2014, 309).

ten in calm and measured language, exudes fear. The topic was what he saw as a general undermining in the contemporary United States of what is "variously called: the 'free enterprise system,' 'capitalism,' and the 'profit system'" (these and all subsequent quotes from the memo are taken from the typescript copy of the memo in the Powell Archive, posted online). The reality and danger of the attack are, for him, undeniable. "No thoughtful person," he writes in his opening sentence, "can question that the American economic system is under broad attack." He goes on to enumerate the "varied and diffused" sources from which this attack stems: there are, of course, "the Communists, New Leftists and other revolutionaries who would destroy the entire system, both political and economic." But these "remain a small minority, and are not yet the principal cause for concern." What really worries this defender of the American economic system is the attack coming from a very different quarter: "The most disquieting voices joining the chorus of criticism come from perfectly respectable elements of society: from the college campus, the pulpit, the media, the intellectual and literary journals, the arts and sciences, and from politicians. In most of these groups the movement against the system is participated in only by minorities. Yet, these often are the most articulate, the most vocal, the most prolific in their writing and speaking." In the face of such attack, American business has been far too complacent; it needs to fight back. "[T]he time has come—indeed, it is long overdue—for the wisdom, ingenuity and resources of American business to be marshaled against those who would destroy it."

The memo was written for the Education Committee of the Chamber of Commerce; Powell stresses that the combating of "the chorus of criticism" needs to involve educational institutions from college campuses to high schools. But the business community should also be "reaching the public generally": there are dangerous ideas out there and they need to be challenged. One example of "the type of article which should not go unanswered," cited by Powell, is "'A Populist Manifesto' by ultra-liberal Jack Newfield." In his article, Newfield, the champion of the business community notes with alarm, "argued that 'the root need in our country is to redistribute wealth.'" Scholarly academic publishing may be important, but so too is more popular fare: "The newsstands—at airports, drugstores, and elsewhere—are filled with paperbacks and pamphlets advocating everything from revolution to erotic free love. One finds almost no attractive, well-written paperbacks or pamphlets on 'our side.' It will be difficult to compete with an Eldridge Cleaver or even a Charles Reich for reader attention, but unless the effort is made—on a large enough scale and with appropriate imagination to assure some success—this opportunity for educating the public will be irretrievably lost."[2] The business community is being urged, we might say, to mold common sense. Powell clearly shares Gramsci's belief in the importance of intellectuals to the articulation and dissemination of class narratives in accessible, commonsense form.

The memo also bemoans the lack of influence the business community has over Congress, invoking Roosevelt's "forgotten man," that great image of the depression and the New Deal: "Marxist doctrine," which Powell claims "has a wide public following among Americans," may argue that "the 'capitalist' countries are controlled by big business," nonetheless

> as every business executive knows, few elements of American society today have as little influence in government as the American businessman, the corporation, or even the millions of corporate stockholders. If one doubts this, let him undertake the role of "lobbyist" for the business point of view before Congressional committees. The same situation obtains in the legislative halls of most states and major cities. One does not exaggerate to say that, in terms of political influence with respect to the course of legislation and government action, the American business executive is truly the "forgotten man."
>
> Current examples of the impotency of business, and of the near-contempt with which businessmen's views are held, are the stampedes by politicians to support almost any legislation related to "consumerism" or to the "environment."

Whether or not the business community in 1970 was quite as powerless as Powell suggests is debatable, but leaving that question aside, read today, this lament from the years before the so-called Reagan revolution, seems to speak of a very distant political environment. This, however, is the political world in which the beginnings of the Reagan revolution are to be found, and a number of the memo's themes are still very much with us. There is, for instance, the memo's suspicion of "legislation related to 'consumerism' or to the 'environment.'" Such suspicion is an enduring thread that runs through right-wing attacks on unnecessary and harmful government regulation.

The six-thousand-word memo concludes in an interesting, contradictory

---

2. Cleaver was a writer and political activist, one of the early leaders of the Black Panther Party. Reich is a legal scholar and law professor. In 1970, while a law professor at Yale Law School (both Bill Clinton and Hillary Rodham Clinton were students of his at Yale), he published *The Greening of America*, a celebration of 1960s counterculture that became a best seller.

fashion. After insisting that "[I]t hardly need be said that the views expressed above are tentative and suggestive," and recommending that "a thorough study be done," the moderate and careful lawyerly tone is transformed into that of a prophet foreseeing doom. Any such study "would be an exercise in futility unless the Board of Directors of the Chamber accepts the fundamental premise of this paper, namely, that business and the enterprise system are in deep trouble, and the hour is late."

The private memo was publicized by the liberal columnist Jack Anderson, after it had been leaked by a member of the Chamber of Commerce. It immediately caused considerable controversy. But while it may have outraged liberals, others heard it as a rallying cry and much needed wake-up call aimed at a complacent business world, blind to the reality of the liberal onslaught. Forty years later, it remains the single most requested document in the Powell Archives (Powell Archive, accessed December 22, 2012).

The memo's origins are explained in a letter written, once the document had been leaked, by Powell's friend Sydnor to a fellow Chamber of Commerce member. Sydnor writes:

> Mr Powell and I have been friends for years, and we have both worked in public education in Virginia. When I became chairman of the Education Committee of the Chamber [of Commerce], I discussed with him various ways of providing for the public a more balanced view of the Free Enterprise System, which has been under considerable criticism for a number of years.
>
> At my request Mr Powell incorporated these possible approaches in a memorandum for the use of my committee. His suggestions covered a broad range of possible educational activities for study and consideration by the Education Committee, and if desired, by the Chamber's Board. (Sydnor letter, September 26, 1972, Powell Archive)

Initially dismayed by the leaking of the memo, Sydnor, as he wrote in a letter to Powell in October, soon began to see "a silver lining to the cloud in that [the memo had] received wide publicity and distribution." He continued, "The Chamber has already had a number of requests for the memorandum from individual business men as well as local and state chambers of commerce, and as we discussed on the telephone last week, there are plans for reprinting it and distributing it on a very wide scale throughout the country" (Sydnor letter, October 3, 1972, Powell Archive).

Sydnor had already developed this theme in a letter to a local newspaper, a copy of which, dated October 2, 1972, is in the Powell Archive (it is not clear if the letter was actually published). Anderson's attempt, by publicizing the leaked memo, "to pillory a great American may well prove a blessing in disguise. Hopefully the widespread publicity about the memorandum may wake up businessmen all over this country to the pressing need for prompt and effective implementation of these sound suggestions" (Sydnor letter, October 2, 1972, Powell Archive).

The memo did apparently have this effect, resonating with the fears of many in the business community, who perceived looming and threatening change; there was no shortage of volunteers eager to respond to Powell's call for "the wisdom, ingenuity and resources of American business to be marshaled against those who would destroy it." And a number of these volunteers had the kind of deep pockets necessary to finance such an effort. As a result, the next few years would see the establishment of a whole host of new public policy research institutes (popularly termed think tanks), many based in Washington, created explicitly to promote conservative agendas and influence government policy.

In themselves, think tanks were nothing new in Washington. One of the most venerable is the Brookings Institution, founded in 1927. Avowedly nonpartisan, Brookings declares on its website: "Research at the Brookings Institution is conducted to inform the public debate, not advance a political agenda" (http://www.brookings.edu/about/research, accessed December 23, 2012). For some on the right, however, Brookings seemed to lean left. In part to provide a counterbalance, in 1943, as the economist Murray Weidenbaum recounts in his history of Washington think tanks, the American Enterprise Institute for Public Policy Research (AEI) was founded. Weidenbaum would himself be closely associated with the AEI.

By the early seventies, however, around the time Powell wrote his memo, some on the right were voicing concerns that the AEI had been co-opted, that the institute, in their view, had become "so concerned about appearing respectable that it was no longer willing to take a stand for conservative principles," as one historian puts it (Phillips-Fein 2009, 171). Two men who shared these concerns were Joseph Coors, one of the brothers who owned the Coors Brewing Company, and Paul Weyrich, a conservative congressional aide who later many would credit with coining the term *moral majority*. Coors was a conservative of long standing who would go on to be a member of Ronald Reagan's "kitchen cabinet." Coors, as he told an interviewer many years later, had been, "stirred" by Powell's memo (Phillips-Fein 2009, 169). Both he and Weyrich agreed on the need for a new, more effective organization that would attack liberal thinking and promote a socially conservative and probusiness agenda. The result was what is nowadays perhaps the best-known and most influential right-wing think tank, the Heritage Foundation, established in 1973. Coors provided the initial financial backing ($250,000) and Weyrich the organizational expertise. Its explicitly political and conservative aims are laid out on its website. The mission of the foundation, "to formulate and promote conservative public policies based on the principles of free enterprise, limited government, individual freedom, traditional American values, and a strong national defense," foreshadows much of the Tea Party message.[3] The establishment of the Heritage Foundation and the transformation it brought about in the culture of Washington think tanks marks an important moment in the long-term cultural project of reversing the provisions of the New Deal and shifting America rightward. As Karlyn Bowman, a staff member at AEI and colleague of Weidenbaum, describes it, "The Heritage Foundation's emergence onto the think tank scene in 1974 changed the way all think tanks in Washington do business. . . . Think tanks were pretty sleepy places until this scrappy, energetic new organization arrived" (quoted in Weidenbaum, 31). David Vogel credits Heritage with turning isolated conservative intellectuals into a network "by providing a way for them to have a direct influence on the shaping of policy in Congress" (Vogel 1989, 224).

Coors was not the only businessman eager to provide major financial support to those seen as willing to engage in the struggle against what Powell termed the "Attack on American Free Enterprise System." Two particularly interesting and powerful figures are the Koch brothers, David and Charles, the billionaire owners of the oil-based company Koch Industries. In 2010 their combined fortune amounted to thirty-five billion dollars, exceeded only by Bill Gates and Warren Buffett. The brothers are famously secretive, but in 2010 Jane Mayer wrote an extended *New Yorker* profile of them, detailing their long libertarian crusade and their role as "the primary underwriters of hardline libertarian politics in America" (Mayer 2010, 48). Only after the publication of the *New Yorker* piece did the Kochs begin to attract any significant public scrutiny. My account here draws heavily on her article.

The Koch Brothers' Crusade

On the death of their father in 1967, David and Charles Koch and their siblings inherited the oil company he had founded. David and Charles soon bought out the other siblings' interests and, with Charles as CEO, Koch Industries

3. Heritage Foundation, http://www.heritage.org/about, accessed December 23, 2012.

would grow exponentially. The brothers had been raised by their father, Fred Koch (an original member of the extreme, right-wing John Birch Society) as both libertarian and conservative. In one interview, David Koch explained how libertarianism was "something [he] grew up with—a fundamental point of view that big government was bad, and imposition of government controls on our lives and economic fortunes was not good" (quoted in Mayer, 47). In 1977 the brothers' commitment to propagating libertarianism led to their providing the funds to launch the Cato Institute, termed by Mayer "the nation's first libertarian think tank." On its website, the institute defines itself as a think tank "dedicated to the principles of individual liberty, limited government, free markets and peace."[4] The institute sees its target audience as "'intermediaries' between formal decision makers and policy analysts—primarily staffs on Capitol Hill and in the administration as well as journalists" (Weidenbaum, 33). Between 1986 and 1993, this one think tank would receive $11 million from the Koch brothers (Mayer 2010, 50).

While the Koch brothers are committed to libertarianism in general, they also have particular concerns as the owners of an enterprise built around the extraction of oil. It is notable that the institute's scholars have consistently challenged the reality of climate change and argued that environmental regulation is both inefficient and unnecessary. A major oil company has a lot at stake; in 2012 Koch Industries was listed as one of the top five air polluters among U.S. corporations by the Political Economy Research Institute, University of Massachusetts, Amherst (PERI, 2012). A shift away from fossil fuels represents a serious threat to a company based on the extraction of oil. As Naomi Oreskes, a historian of science, writes, "If the answer is to phase out fossil fuels, a different group of people are going to be making money, so we shouldn't be surprised that [the Kochs] are fighting tooth and nail" (quoted in Mayer, 51). Support for climate change skeptics is one of the Koch brothers' strategies. And this support has been very generous: $61.3 million between 1997 and 2010. Greenpeace, which has dubbed Koch Industries "a financial kingpin of climate science denial and clean energy opposition," describes their modus operandi in the following terms: "The company's tight knit network of lobbyists, former executives and organizations has created a forceful stream of misinformation that Koch-funded entities produces and disseminates. This campaign propaganda is then replicated, repackaged and echoed many times throughout the Koch-funded web of political front groups and think tanks" (Greenpeace 2010, 6).

4. Cato Institute, http://www.cato.org/about, accessed December 23, 2012.

There may be consensus within the scientific community that climate change is real, human activity is a major factor, and that global warning threatens the future of our planet, but this has not yet become common sense outside that community. Simplistic, climate-science-denying narratives that tap into a widely shared suspicion of all-knowing "experts," can sound very persuasive to those who rely on the popular media for their science—particularly if the disseminators are backed by the almost unlimited funds of the Koch-funded lobby.

The denial of climate science, while one of the Koch brothers' major concerns, is part of a much wider libertarian project, just as the Cato Institute is only one of many recipients of their largesse. The range of organizations they fund demonstrates the scope of their libertarianism. The Heritage Foundation, between 2005 and 2008, received $1.6 million (Greenpeace, 22). Other organizations they have funded include "the Institute for Justice, which files lawsuits opposing state and federal regulations; the Institute for Humane Studies, which underwrites libertarian academics; and the Bill of Rights Institute, which promotes a conservative slant on the Constitution" (Mayer, 50). George Mason University has been the recipient of particularly generous donations. In the mid-eighties, the Kochs gave this public university the funds to set up a new conservative think tank, the Mercatus Center, which defines itself as "a university-based research center dedicated to bridging the gap between academic research and public policy problems."[5] The name *mercatus*, the Latin for market, was carefully chosen; the center's research, its website explains, "is focused on how markets solve problems." By 2010 the Kochs had given more than $30 million to George Mason, primarily to support the Mercatus Center, making it one of the best funded of the U.S. think tanks.

The influence of the right-wing narratives generated by think tanks like Heritage, Cato, and Mercatus is unquestionable, but the Kochs wanted more: "They needed a mechanism to deliver those ideas to the street, and to attract the public's support" (Mayer, 52). And in 1984 David Koch and Richard Fink, together with Matt Kibbe (later to become president of FreedomWorks, a Tea Party advocacy group), set up Citizens for a Sound Economy, a suitably grassroots-sounding name. Between 1986 and 1993, Citizens for a Sound Economy would be funded by the Kochs to the tune of $7.9 million. By 2004, however, internal rifts split the group apart. David Koch and Fink then es-

5. Mercatus Center, George Mason University, "About," accessed January 6, 2013, http://mercatus.org/content/about.

tablished a new group, Americans for Prosperity, while Citizens for a Sound Economy merged with another conservative organization, Empower America, to form FreedomWorks, which would become a key player in the Tea Party story.

In total, David and Charles Koch have, over the years, "quietly given more than a hundred million dollars to right-wing causes" (Mayer 2010, 44). And they keep a firm grip on those they fund, as David Koch explained to the libertarian and author Brian Doherty: "If we are going to give a lot of money, we'll make darn sure [the organizations funded] spend it in a way that goes along with our intent. And if they make a wrong turn and start doing things we don't agree with, we withdraw funding. We do exert that kind of control" (quoted in Doherty 2007, 409).

Funding is not the only connection between the Kochs and their think tanks. Both those who run the organizations and the researchers they employ frequently have close ties to the Kochs. Just how close those ties can be is illustrated by the Independent Women's Forum (IWF), one of the smaller organizations they support. The IWF was established in 1992, and between 2005 and 2008 it received $335,000 from the Kochs. The IWF, as it explains on its website, "is on a mission to expand the conservative coalition, both by increasing the number of women who understand and value the benefits of limited government, personal liberty, and free markets, and by countering those who seek to ever-expand government in the name of protecting women."[6] Exactly what, or who, the IWF is independent of, is not explained. The many attacks on "feminists" to be found in the articles on its website, however, suggest that it is feminism from which the IWF is anxious to distance itself.

Nancy Pfotenhauer, president of the IWF from 2001 to 2008 and current board member of the Cato Institute, is a good example of the kind of intellectual for whom the Koch network is a perfect home. Pfotenhauer graduated from George Mason University (home of the Mercatus Center) in 1987 with a master's in economics. The Mason Economics Program provides a profile of her as an exemplary alumna. Immediately after graduating, she became a senior economist at the Republican National Committee, and at age twenty-four served in the George H. W. Bush transition team as the economist for the Independent Regulatory Agencies task force, overseeing the policy, budget, and personnel recommendations for both the Federal Trade Commission and

6. Independent Women's Forum, "About," accessed January 6, 2013, http://iwf.org /about.

the Interstate Commerce Commission.[7] During the Clinton years, she worked for Koch Industries, and from 1996 to 2001 was their top Washington lobbyist. The 1990s also saw her cohosting a news show on the short-lived National Empowerment Television cable channel, founded by Paul Weyrich (cofounder of the Heritage Foundation).

As an organization, the IWF is very much about getting a certain message out. Using Gramscian terminology, we might see Pfotenhauer and the IWF researchers and bloggers as part of that stratum of minor intellectuals described in the notebooks as exercising "an organisational function in the wide sense," who "correspond to the NCOs and junior officers in the army" (*SPN*, 97). Closely allied with certain corporate interests, they work to influence policy in line with their market-centered view of the world. Pfotenhauer stressed the organization's goal of influencing policy when she gave testimony to the U.S. House of Representatives Committee on Education and Workforce in 2004. Anxious to clear up any misunderstandings about the group, she explained that the "IWF is a non-profit, non-partisan public policy organization that focuses on issues of importance to women." She then explained "what IWF is not." "It is not a grassroots organization focused on mobilizing large numbers of our fellow citizens. Rather we are a group whose members are legal scholars, economists, academicians, historians and foreign policy experts who hope to apply our professional experience to impact the formulation of public policy."[8]

Pfotenhauer's claim that the IWF is nonpartisan might seem at odds with its mission statement and the strongly promarket and antigovernment stance of the postings on its website, but not if this stance is defined as no more than obvious common sense. The IWF's Energy and Environmental Policy, for instance, argues for "common sense environmental policies that protect our natural resources." Rhetorically, *common sense* here is intended to shift discussion of the proposed policies beyond the domain of argument: these are not positions that need to be argued for or against, they are simple, undeniable facts that any "ordinary" person, not blinded by the sophistries of so-called experts or partisan blinders, can immediately recognize. As we might expect of a

7. George Mason University, "Meet an Alum," accessed January 6, 2013, http://economics.gmu.edu/programs/la-ma-econ/meet-an-alum/293.

8. Committee on Education and the Workforce, "Testimony of Nancy M. Pfotenhauer, President, Independent Women's Forum before the Committee on Education and Workforce Hearing On 'Examining Cash Balance Pension Plans: Separating Myth from Fact,' accessed January 6, 2013, http://archives.republicans.edlabor.house.gov/archive/hearings/108th/fc/pensions070704/pfotenhauer.htm.

beneficiary of Koch funding, the organization dismisses any form of government environmental regulation as misguided and futile. For the IWF, sound environmental policies will not come from the state: "IWF believes that the market will better identify promising, environmentally-sound energy sources than will politicians."[9] In 1971, Lewis Powell had called for "the wisdom, ingenuity and resources of American business to be marshaled against those who would destroy it." By the time the Tea Party burst onto the scene in 2009, Powell's call had been well and truly answered by corporate donors, who had poured millions into a network of conservative and libertarian think tanks. These included major players such as Heritage, Cato, and Mercatus, but also numerous smaller organizations like the IWF. There was a problem, however. As Bruce Bartlett, a conservative economist and historian and former employee of a Koch-funded Dallas think tank, put it, "The problem with the whole libertarian movement is that it's been all chiefs and no Indians. There haven't been any actual people, like voters, who give a crap about it. So the problem for the Kochs has been trying to create a movement." With the emergence of the Tea Party, "everyone suddenly sees that for the first time there are Indians out there—people who can provide real ideological power" (quoted in Mayer, 47). There was a concern, however, that the dominant narrative of this uprising reflect conservative, libertarian common sense. The Kochs, as Bartlett explained to Mayer, "are trying to shape and control and channel the populist uprising into their own policies" (Mayer 2010, 47). It is worth noting that while the Tea Party phenomenon may have fulfilled a libertarian fantasy, the conservative libertarian elite, as Bartlett's account indicates, was not able to bring such a movement into being on its own.

The Koch brothers and the other "roving billionaire advocates," as Skocpol and Williamson stress, were only one of the forces that came together at a particular historical moment in a way that gave the Tea Party "the ongoing clout to buffet and redirect the Republican Party and influence broader debates in American democracy" (Skocpol and Williamson, 13). Another force was grassroots activists. They were the Indians the libertarian chiefs had suddenly discovered.

9. Independent Women's Forum, "Energy," accessed January 7, 2013, http://www .iwf.org/issues/energy.

I Want My Country Back!

All movements have their origin stories. There seems to be a need for simple narratives that identify one clear source, Rosa Parks's refusal to move to the back of the bus as the spark that ignited the Civil Rights movement, for instance.[10] The birth of the Tea Party is commonly traced back to a passionate rant by the CNBC financial reporter Rick Santelli on February 19, 2009. Standing on the floor of the Chicago Mercantile Exchange, addressing the traders as well as the CNBC viewers, Santelli was incandescent with rage. His target was the recently elected Obama administration's plan to provide help to those whose mortgages were being foreclosed. The assumptions underpinning Santelli's rant about who is deserving of help and who is not, what is fair and what is not, are central to the Tea Party narrative. His tirade began like this: "The government is promoting bad behavior! How is this, president and new administration, why didn't you put up a website to have people vote on the Internet as a referendum to see if we really want to subsidize the losers' mortgages; or, would we like to at least buy cars and buy houses in foreclosure and give 'em to people that might have a chance to actually prosper down the road and reward people that could carry the water instead of drink the water. This is America! How many of you people want to pay for your neighbor's mortgage that has an extra bathroom and can't pay their bills?"[11]

As Formisano observes, "Santelli directed his anger, interestingly, at the low-income house buyers who had been scammed into taking on mortgages they could not afford rather than at the banks and investment firms that, by creating derivatives, had made huge bets on the failure of those mortgages—and then profited when they did fail" (Formisano, 26).

Right-wing bloggers across the internet—the internet was a crucial factor in the rise of the Tea Party—immediately picked up on Santelli's passionate outburst, as did Rupert Murdoch's Fox Network, where it was shown repeatedly. Organizations such as FreedomWorks (born out of the merger of the Koch-funded organizations Citizens for a Sound Economy and Empower America) were equally quick to recognize the opportunity they were being offered. "Within hours," Formisano notes, "FreedomWorks and similar Washington-

10. In reality the civil rights movement has a far longer history and more complex origins, and far from being a simple seamstress who was just tired that day, Parks, as documented in Jeanne Theoharis's biography of Parks, published in 2013, was the secretary of the Montgomery chapter of the National Association for the Advancement of Colored People.

11. Conservapedia, "Rick Santelli," accessed September 21, 2013, http://www.conservapedia.com/Rick_Santelli.

based groups realized their moment had come, that the economic meltdown and the change from a Republican to a Democratic administration had created the climate to launch into Tea Party organizing. In early 2009 economic, political and cultural shocks came together to activate ordinary persons across the country—mostly conservative Republicans, but also independents and others—to organize and mobilize" (Formisano, 27).

The Tea Party's origins, however, go back further than Santelli's rant on the floor of the Chicago Mercantile Exchange. The original Boston Tea Party of 1773, "about which so much is said and so little known" (Formisano, 118), has long served Americans as a powerful national myth of justified revolt by tax-paying citizens against tyrannical government. For a number of years, "corporate lobbyists had been suggesting antitax and antiregulatory Tea Parties" (Formisano, 26). However, it was the apparently unstoppable slide of the US economy and the government stimulus proposed by the newly elected Barack Obama, both deeply troubling to conservatives, that provided the necessary climate of fear and anger in which "ordinary people" were motivated to begin organizing. Santelli may have lit the match, but there was plenty of combustible timber ready to take fire: people like Keli Carender, for instance, a thirty-year-old, conservative blogger living in Seattle. Disillusioned with the Republican Party and profoundly critical of Obama, Carender, as she explained to the journalist Kate Zernike, "started thinking, what are we getting ourselves into?" Carender's response was simple and straightforward: "It didn't make sense to me to be spending all this money when we don't have it. It seems more logical that we create an atmosphere where private industry can start to grow again and create jobs" (quoted in Zernike 2010, 16). Particularly angered by the stimulus bill, the conservative blogger organized a small demonstration against it on February 16, the day before Obama was due to sign the bill and three days before Santelli's rant. A year later, Carender would begin working full time for the Tea Party Patriots.

Another person sometimes identified as the initiator of the Tea Party is Mary Rakovich. Laid off from her job as an electrical engineer in the auto industry and, like Carender, angry about the stimulus bill, Rakovich decided to attend a local training session on how to protest government spending, organized by FreedomWorks. Somewhat ironically, such FreedomWorks training "draws heavily on imitating liberal pressure groups such as MoveOn.org and urges Tea Party activists to read the writings of Saul Alinsky" (Formisano 2012, 70).[12]

---

12. Saul Alinsky was an American community organizer and radical, whose *Rules for Radicals* (published in 1971, a year before Alinsky's death) has become something of a bible for community organizers.

Spurred on by the training session, Rakovich decided, some nine days before Santelli's rant, to organize a protest at an upcoming Florida town hall meeting where President Obama was due to speak. The protest was tiny, consisting of no more than Rakovich, her husband, and a few family and friends, but it caught the attention of a number of reporters, including those from Fox Television. As she told these reporters, it was clear to her that Obama was promoting socialism "although he doesn't call it that" (quoted in Formisano, 25).

The accusation that Obama's policies represent socialism is one of the central tenets of the Tea Party. And while this may sound bizarre to many on the left, the idea that even the smallest challenge to the sovereignty of the free market is tantamount to either socialism or fascism is an enduring staple of the American right. It can be found, for example, in the Powell memo, where Powell bemoans the fact that "[t]here seems to be little awareness that the only alternatives to free enterprise are varying degrees of bureaucratic regulation of individual freedom—ranging from that under moderate socialism to the iron heel of the leftist or rightist dictatorship." A more recent example of seeing any deviation from free market principles as either socialism or fascism is the response of the libertarian CEO of Whole Foods, John Mackey, to that particular bête noire of libertarians and the Tea Party, Obama's Affordable Health Care Act. In 2009, in a *Wall Street Journal* op-ed, Mackey had equated Obama's health care proposals with socialism. By January 2013, however, the Affordable Health Care Act, he explained in an interview on National Public Radio, now seemed to him more like fascism (Wilstein 2013).

Wherever we want to locate the origins of the Tea Party, its growth was explosive. Just two months after Santelli's outburst, on April 15, the day when Americans' annual tax returns are due, Tea Party demonstrators mobilized thousands of protestors for a reported 750 separate Tax Day Tea Parties (Formisano, 27). And while the numbers were certainly swelled by the ceaseless promotion of these protests by Fox News and other right-wing media in the weeks leading up to April 15, the anger and frustration the media were tapping into was real. But with whom exactly did the Tea Party message of limited government, fiscal responsibility, and free markets resonate? The *New York Times* and CBS News, also in April 2010, carried out a large-scale poll that attempted to gauge the level of Tea Party support in the country as a whole, and to discover who the Tea Party supporters were and what they believed. According to this poll, "the 18 percent of Americans who identify themselves as Tea Party supporters tend to be Republican, white, male, married and older than 45" (CBS/New York Times poll, April 5–12, 2010). But while Tea Party supporters may be more likely to be male, at the grassroots level, Skocpol and

Williamson found that "women [were] dominating the organizing efforts" (43). In this, the Tea Party is following in a long tradition of American civic activism, which has always relied heavily on the voluntary labor of women.

Formisano cautions us against focusing too much on the differences between Tea Party supporters and other Americans: "Most analysts of the Tea Party, friends and foes alike, have tended to concentrate on how its adherents stand out from other citizens (being whiter, wealthier, older, and more educated than other Americans). But it can be equally instructive to examine how rank-and-file Tea Partiers resemble other Americans of whatever demographic group or political persuasion. Millions of Americans share the sense that they are losing control of their lives and that vast impersonal forces, some global in character, exert too much influence on their ability to live as they wish" (106–7). This echoes Skocpol and Williamson's argument that "the 'Tea Party' symbolism was a perfect rallying point since it brings to mind the original American colonial rebels opposing tyranny by tossing chests of tea into Boston Harbor. It signifies authentic patriotism, and has visceral meaning to people who feel that the United States as they have known it is slipping away. "I want my country back!" one Massachusetts man declared to Skocpol and Williamson (7), a sentiment that reflects the emotional sense of loss with which the Tea Party's symbolism connects (Skocpol and Williamson 2012, 7).

We are surely in the domain of feeling rather than thinking here, what Gramsci termed "the elementary passions of the people" (SPN, 418). The simple prescription of "limited government, fiscal responsibility and free markets" as the sole road to American prosperity, which certain business interests and libertarians have been pushing for decades, provides an accessible explanation of what is wrong with contemporary America, and how things might be fixed. It also resonates with a deeply felt moral sense of what is right and proper. And in the context of what Skocpol and Williamson term "the startling social changes and roiling politics that mark the United States in the early twenty-first century" (82), to many it is precisely that moral map that seems to be under attack.

According to this worldview there are those the government has a duty to help and those it does not. We can see here a distinction with deep historical roots, between those who have legitimate state entitlements, entitlements for which they have worked, and the undeserving recipients of government "welfare." These latter are those Mitt Romney would describe to potential funders of his 2012 presidential campaign as "dependent upon government, who believe that they are victims, who believe that government has a responsibility to care for them, who believe that they are entitled to health care, to food, to housing, you name it."[13] These leaked comments, which quickly became infamous, may have shocked many mainstream voters, but to Tea Party supporters this distinction is likely to seem obvious and beyond question, no more than common sense. As one activist explained to Skocpol and Williamson, "I've been working since I was 16 years old, and do feel like I should someday reap the benefit. I'm not looking for a handout. I'm looking for a pay out of what I paid into" (61).

The Tea Partiers' commonsense distinction between legitimate entitlements and unearned welfare "handouts" lies behind the much ridiculed sign seen at some Tea Party events, "Keep your government's hands off my Medicare." As Skocpol and Williamson explain, "Tea Party people know that Social Security, Medicare, and veterans' programs are government-managed, expensive, and funded with taxes. It is just that they distinguish these programs, which they feel recipients have 'earned,' from other social benefits, which they feel unnecessarily run up expenses, or might run up public costs in the future—placing a burden on hardworking taxpayers to make payments to freeloaders who have not earned public support" (60).

The Tea Partiers Skocpol and Williamson met may have been unambiguously in favor of "limited government" in the abstract, but at the same time they, like other Americans, "love the parts of government they recognize as offering legitimate benefits to citizens who have earned them" (Skocpol and Williamson, 63). Tea Partiers, who represent a generally older demographic, are often the recipients of Social Security or rely on Medicare. Or if they themselves are not beneficiaries, someone in their household probably is. Given this, it is perhaps not surprising that 62 percent of them, according to the CBS/*New York Times* poll, thought that "the benefits from government programs such as Social Security and Medicare [were] worth the costs . . . for taxpayers." And among all their many Tea Party interviewees, Skocpol and Williamson only encountered one who favored taking the Tea Party advocacy of free-market solutions to the logical extreme of privatizing Social Security and Medicare. This is despite the fact that FreedomWorks, Americans for Prosperity, and one of the Tea Party's favorite Republicans, Paul Ryan, have all urged such privatization. Grassroots Tea Partiers do not, it seems, accept blindly everything the movement's leaders propose; the top-down message is, as it were, in dialogue with some deep-seated, commonsense assumptions about what, to use Piketty's formulation, is just and what is not.

13. "Mitt Romney's '47 Percent' Comments," YouTube video, September 18, 2012, accessed January 24, 2013, https://www.youtube.com/watch?v=M2gvY2wqI7M.

Makers and Takers

The distinction between legitimate entitlements that recipients have "earned," and the unearned "handouts" given to welfare recipients and other "moochers," is entangled with another fundamental opposition, which Skocpol and Williamson see as basic to the Tea Party worldview: that between workers and nonworkers. "A well-marked distinction between workers and non-workers—between productive citizens and freeloaders—is central to the Tea Party worldview and conception of America. As Tea Partiers see it, only through hard work can one earn access both to a good income and to honorable public benefits" (65). An opposition between workers and non-workers, or producers and non-producers, stretches back a long way. "For much of American history," as Formisano describes, "reformers separated society into the 'toiling masses' or the producing many in opposition to the nonproductive but powerful and wealthy few. They defined their enemies not in terms of Marxist class warfare but rather as the parasites of economic society, the idle rich, the absentee owners but not the resident owner of an enterprise, dishonest lawyers, saloon keepers, financiers who gambled with other people's money—in short, the nonproducers.... Thus Tea Partiers do not so much see a conflict between big government and the freedom-loving individual but between 'workers' and 'people who don't work'" (20).

Underpinning the current anger on the part of those who see themselves as hardworking producers is the structural reality of the shrinking of the manufacturing sector. By 2012, employment in manufacturing had fallen from 18 million in 1988 to less than 12 million (Stiglitz 2012, 321). And in many cases the wages paid by manufacturing jobs today are not enough to sustain the same kind of middle-class lifestyle as in earlier decades. The auto industry is a good example of a sector where wages have recently declined, often precipitously: "As recently as 2007, the base wage of an autoworker was around $28 an hour. Now, under a two-tier wage system agreed upon with the United Automobile Workers union, new hires can expect to earn only about $15 an hour" (Stiglitz 2012, 57). It is not surprising that many formerly middle-class people see the world they grew up in slipping away from them.

The idea that Americans can be divided into makers and takers has been a recurrent theme in speeches by Paul Ryan, Mitt Romney's running mate in his 2012 presidential campaign, and who in 2015 would be elected House Speaker. In an interview published in 2011, he declared: "Right now, according to the Tax Foundation, between 60 and 70 percent of Americans get more benefits from the government than they pay back in taxes. So, we're getting toward a society where we have a net majority of takers versus makers" (quoted in Baumann 2013). As Nick Baumann points out, Ryan is only able to get to his figure of more than 60 percent of Americans as takers by including Medicare, Social Security, and national defense as taker programs. Most of Ryan's supporters, however, are probably not going to subject his claim to this kind of scrutiny; its effectiveness comes from that fact that it resonates emotionally with common-sense assumptions about who the recipients of government benefits are: those who don't work, the moochers, and the generally morally unworthy. And just who the moochers are tends to be entangled with a deep-seated, albeit implicit rather than explicit, racism. The historian Bruce Schulman put it like this to Zernike, "If you look at the tax revolt groups, a lot of it is, we're sick and tired of our tax money being used for 'them.' . . . 'Them' isn't always identified as blacks—these were middle class people who don't see themselves as racists, and they aren't—but it's clear that 'them' is racialized" (quoted in Zernike, 57).

Once the distinction becomes one between those who work and those who do not, in which "the resident owner of a business" is included among all the other deserving workers, it is easier to understand why "public opinion surveys indicate that Tea Party supporters, much more than other Americans, are unconcerned about corporate malfeasance or government favors to companies (otherwise known as corporate welfare), mainly in the form of low taxes and federal subsidies" (Formisano, 63). Indeed, some Tea Partiers go so far as to argue that "corporations need not pay taxes since corporations create jobs" (Formisano, 66). This sentiment is echoed by Mark Meckler (cofounder of the Tea Party Patriots) in response to a question about corporations that do not pay taxes: "We've been suggesting a corporate tax holiday to allow these companies to come in and create jobs" (quoted in Formisano, 65). The argument that corporations are the ultimate makers, that it is they who create jobs, and that taxing them is counterproductive for economic prosperity, is one that wealthy business interests in America have long propagated.

The Antitax Crusade

In the *New Yorker* article "Tax Time," published in 2012, Jill Lepore provides an instructive history of the long, antitax crusade waged by some of America's wealthiest. A key player in the boom years that led up to the stock market crash of 1929 and the Great Depression was the banker, industrialist and philanthropist Andrew W. Mellon. From 1921 to 1932, Mellon, one of America's richest men, served as Secretary of the Treasury under Republican presidents Harding, Coolidge, and Hoover. He played an important role in ensuring that capital gains were exempted from taxable income, that estate taxes were reduced, and that the top tax rate was capped at 25 percent. In 1924, when "the only Americans who paid more in taxes than Mellon were John D. Rockefeller, Jr., Henry Ford, and Edsel Ford" (Lepore, 26), Mellon laid out the case for limiting taxes on the wealthy in *Taxation: The People's Business*. The essence of Mellon's argument, one that would echo down the years to its present Tea Party incarnation, is that when the wealthy are taxed at high rates they cease to invest in productive enterprises. The high tax rates of the years following the First World War, he insists, "must be reduced to a point where capital is freed from the killing effect of these rates upon new investments" (Mellon 1924, 136). Achieving what he terms "a sound system of taxation," in other words, lowering taxes, would, he argues "increase the number of jobs and at the same time advance general prosperity" (137).

Even if the degree to which New Deal legislation succeeded in reigning in American capitalism is sometimes overstated, the economic fallout of the Great Depression and the rise of Roosevelt and his New Deal did change the political climate. For a time, the argument that left to themselves, free from the burden of excessive taxation, wealthy entrepreneurs would "advance general prosperity" rang somewhat hollow. Nonetheless, the policies of the New Deal did not go unchallenged. One such challenge was to the tax system funding government programs. It took the form of a twenty-year-long campaign to repeal the Sixteenth Amendment to the Constitution. The amendment, passed in 1913, granted Congress the right to levy an income tax. The campaign was launched in 1938 by two organizations, both funded by wealthy businessmen: the American Taxpayers Association and the Committee for Constitutional Government. Their strategy involved a campaign to persuade the necessary two-thirds of the states to call for a constitutional convention at which the amendment would be put to the vote. In reality, according to Isaac Martin, a historian of this movement, those behind the campaign "were gambling that the growing pressure would force Congress to take action on the Amendment before the campaign ever crossed the two-third majority" (Martin 2010, 12). This never happened, but the antitax activists were nonetheless remarkably successful, coming within just two states of achieving the two-thirds majority that would have compelled Congress to call a constitutional convention. Even more important, they succeeded in shaping a powerful antitax narrative that would to many seem no more than common sense. Martin argues that it was this campaign that "pioneered much of the antitax rhetoric that would come to dominate American politics at the dawn of the 21st century" (Martin 2010, 12). It is precisely this antitax narrative that resonates so powerfully with Tea Partiers. In addition, as Lepore notes, "it was during this campaign that the business lobby succeeded in redefining American citizens as 'taxpayers,' a practice that politicians have followed ever since, as if the defining act of citizenship were not casting a ballot but filing a return" (Lepore 2012, 27).

For those trying to implement New Deal legislation, the deep suspicion of taxation, particularly in the case of direct taxes, was a reality they could not afford to ignore. As the tax historian Molly Michelmore writes, "New Dealers recognized the need to manage popular opposition to new federal income taxes and to insulate the administration from the kind of taxpayer hostility that had produced a vibrant and powerful grassroots antitax movement in the 1930s" (Michelmore 2012, 5–6). It was this political calculation that led to the decision to fund the new unemployment and old age insurance programs through an indirect payroll tax rather than any increase in income tax, and to frame them not as government-provided welfare but as analogous to an insurance scheme into which individuals first paid their individual contributions, later receiving the benefits they had earned, this despite the fact that it was clear from the outset that those programs would also require contributions from the federal government. This reluctance to defend taxation to fund the new programs would help to lay the foundation for what would become the commonsense distinction between legitimately earned entitlements and unearned welfare handed out to the irresponsible and feckless—the distinction that has such visceral power for the Tea Partiers.

In general, Washington policymakers have remained queasy about taxation. Only during World War II did the government engage in a propaganda campaign actively promoting the benefits of taxation. The message was often delivered by Hollywood stars and other celebrities, and the central theme was one of shared sacrifice (Formisano, 104). But this was very much a wartime exception. In the 1960s, for instance, "The architects of [President Johnson's] War on Poverty, like the New Dealers before them, never defended a broad-based progressive income tax as a public good, in everyone's interest. Nor did they refer to Social Security, health care, and unemployment insurance as 'welfare'" (Lepore 2012, 28). And, beginning with Reagan, as Formisano argues, "the Republican Party and more recently the new right-wing media have implanted an antitax dogmatism at the very core of their reason for being" (104).

The obvious, commonsense distinction between makers and takers, between those who work and earn a legitimate recompense and those who simply rely on handouts from the government, is fundamental to the Tea Party narrative. The sentiment is succinctly summed up by the Tea Party bumper sticker that reads: "You are NOT ENTITLED to what I have EARNED" (Skocpol and Williamson, 66). "This moral social geography, rather than any abstract commitment to free-market principles," as Skocpol and Williamson stress, is what "underlies Tea Party fervor to slash or eliminate categories of public benefits seen as going to unworthy people who are 'free-loading' on the public sector" (Skocpol and Williamson, 66). The racialized figure of the "welfare queen," imagined as a woman of color, living a life of luxury on fraudulently claimed welfare benefits, conjured into being by Reagan during his 1980 presidential campaign, remains an enduring stereotype of everything that is wrong with welfare. To many, this moral social geography represents an incontrovertible truth about what the government should, and should not, be doing. And whatever we may think of the Tea Party narrative, in this instance the decades-long work of the right-wing heirs of Andrew Mellon, Lewis Powell, and other twentieth-century champions of low taxation, free markets, and limited government, has undoubtedly played a crucial role in braiding together a number of strands—strands deeply woven into the diffuse heterogeneity of American common sense—into an emotionally convincing narrative. This narrative, which rings so true to Tea Partiers, provides them with an explanation of why America, as it seems to them, is slipping away from hard-working Americans, and especially white Americans.

Hegemony and Dissemination

By definition, hegemony includes the power to disseminate a ruling class's worldview in ways that make it hard to challenge. This dissemination is achieved not only through formal educational institutions, schools and universities, but the whole panoply of media. The rise of the Tea Party has been greatly facilitated by the right-wing media. From the outset, the echo chamber of Fox News and other right-wing media has championed the Tea Party—a support amplified by new forms of internet-based, knowledge distribution, in particular social media and the blogosphere. For Skocpol and Williamson, "right-wing media purveyors" constitute a third force in addition to those of "policy-oriented right-wing intellectuals" and "grassroots activists," which together explain the Tea Party phenomenon (13).

The Fox News empire has been one of the most influential media outlets in recent years. Owned by the right-wing billionaire Rupert Murdoch and run by Roger Ailes, a longtime media consultant to the Republican Party, Fox News represents a new kind of news broadcasting, one that has abandoned any pretence of objective neutrality. The strident and partisan tone of its news presenters follows a model developed originally by the talk radio that has become such an influential platform for the dissemination of right-wing common sense. Talk radio not only reflects, but has helped to create this common sense. Its history helps explain the media landscape bestrode by the Fox colossus, which has played such a key role in fostering the Tea Party.

As the journalist Steve Rendall documents, right-wing talk radio has a longer history than is often assumed. According to the received narrative, it was the repeal by the Federal Communications Commission (FCC) of the Fairness Doctrine in 1987, part of the Reagan administration's push for deregulation, that unleashed stridently partisan radio. Paul Vitello, for instance, reiterates this claim in his *New York Times* obituary of Bob Grant, one of the pioneering hosts of this form of radio. In reality, however, the Fairness Doctrine, as administered by the FCC, never had much in the way of teeth. Rendall notes that "not one Fairness Doctrine decision issued by the FCC ever concerned itself with talkshows. Indeed, the talkshow format was born and flourished while the doctrine was in operation. Before the doctrine was repealed, right-wing hosts frequently dominated talkshow schedules, even in liberal cities, and none was ever muzzled" (Rendall 2007).

The origins of political talk radio lie, rather, in the tumult of the 1960s, when so many seemingly bedrock beliefs of cold-war America were being challenged. As with Lewis Powell's memo, it can be seen as a reaction to a fear that the old order was being overrun by out-of-control radicals while those who knew better were simply sitting on the sidelines letting it happen. The truth is that "political talk radio was largely born in a backlash, with conservative white male hosts railing against the progressive movements for civil rights, women's liberation and peace" (Rendall 2007). One difference between those hosts and Powell was that rather than adopting Powell's patrician tones, they spoke a populist language accessible to all. It was in this milieu that Bob Grant became a star host, and it was Grant and the other right-wing hosts who crafted what would become an enduring persona, a persona that gave voice to "the working stiff—the guy who pays $4 a day in bridge tolls just to go to and from work" (WABC program director Mark Mason, quoted in Rendall 2007). This angry persona, who so effectively and seemingly authentically channeled the frustrations of the "working stiff," was confined to the presenter's broadcasts; "Off the air Mr Grant was courtly and polite" (Rendall 2007). Grant's talk-radio model would help shape a myriad of right-wing talk radio programs. Both Rush Limbaugh and Sean Hannity "considered [Grant] a founding father of their radio format" (Vitello 2014). With the arrival of Fox News, the aggressive, take-no-prisoners persona would be translated into a visual format.

Watched by millions of Americans, Fox towers over its cable news rivals such as CNN and MSNBC, virtually drowning out MSNBC's liberal-slanted shows. For Skocpol and Williamson, "mostly what America has right now is a thousand-pound-gorilla media juggernaut on the right, operating nineteenth-century style, coexisting with other news outlets trying to keep up while making fitful attempts, twentieth-century style, to check facts and cover 'both sides of the story'" (126).

Surveys, such as those by the University of Maryland's Program on International Policy Attitudes, document how regular viewers of Fox News are more likely to be misinformed, believing, for instance, that most economists were predicting that the new Affordable Care Act, popularly known as Obamacare, will worsen the deficit, and that most scientists do not agree that climate change is occurring. Particularly telling is that these viewers also believed (usually mistakenly) that their own taxes had gone up, a nice example of the power of the media juggernaut even when it is providing information about things of which those watching have their own direct experience (all examples cited in Maloy 2010).

During their fieldwork, Skocpol and Williamson observed a particularly startling instance of the right-wing media's power to disseminate bizarre and paranoid information: "At a Tea Party meeting in Massachusetts, people discussed the possibility that the 'Smart Grid' (an infrastructure improvement to the electricity grid, a plan approximately as controversial as road repair) was in fact a plan that would give the government control over the thermostats in people's homes. We wondered how such an outlandish conspiracy theory could have been accepted by the intelligent and well-educated people at this meeting—until we checked the Fox News transcripts. Glenn Beck had indeed raised this weird possibility on his show" (202).

Among their generally conservative audience, Fox News and its right-wing hosts have established themselves as the source of authoritative and reliable information, providing "a constant drumbeat of news that shapes the American conservative worldview and keeps people on edge." In one of the states on which they focused, Virginia, "every single Tea Party member [Skocpol and Williamson] spoke to mentioned Fox News as a prime news source." Fox News, moreover, is seen as providing truths that other media conceal. As one interviewee explained, "If you watch the networks, you aren't informed about how bad off we are" (this and the preceding two quotations, Skocpol and Williamson 2012, 135). This fearful worldview is persuasive precisely because it resonates so powerfully with a gut feeling, shared by many, that the safe, familiar world in which they grew up, and in which they feel at home, is under attack.

Tea Party common sense and its populist paranoia may not align with the interests of every element of the business class, but its unwavering faith in free enterprise, its objection to taxation, and its commitment to untrammeled rights for all business owners, from the individual entrepreneur up to the largest corporation, represents a capitalist worldview, albeit a simplistic one. It is important to stress that there is not a single, homogeneous, capitalist narrative; the basic economic relations on which the whole capitalist edifice rests can accommodate many different variants, and many different justifications of those variants. The Tea Party narrative, a distant and distorted descendant of Adam Smith's vision of freedom, is one strand within a historical bloc in which material relations in the course of history, through struggle between different groups, have come to be expressed in particular accounts of "how the world is"—narratives that explain and justify why the world is as it is.

This capitalist historical bloc, which represents a particular "unity between nature and spirit (structure and superstructure)" (*SPN*, 137), while not necessarily invincible, has enormous power. Those who would challenge its dominant narratives are faced with a far harder task than those following the grain of entrenched capitalist assumptions. Those asumptions are now so deeply embedded at every level of knowledge-producing institutions that their original class origins have been buried. They have become simply knowledge, beliefs that underpin both the knowledge of intellectuals and the common sense of "ordinary people." Common sense, however, is not monolithic. It is, in Gramsci's words, "a chaotic aggregate of disparate conceptions," where it is possible to find "anything that one likes" (*SPN*, 422). There are always strands of good sense that refuse the hegemonic narratives to be found interwoven into this "chaotic aggregate." Progressives seeking radical change need to search out those strands and rebraid them into a new and compelling narrative. There is, as Gramsci writes, "a necessity for new popular beliefs, that is to say a new common sense and with it a new culture and a new philosophy which will be rooted in the popular consciousness with the same solidity and imperative quality as traditional beliefs" (*SPN*, 424). The next chapter approaches the Occupy Wall Street movement as perhaps the embryonic beginnings of one such attempt.

7

Common Sense, Good Sense, and Occupy

I'm so scared of this anti-Wall Street effort. I'm frightened to death. [The Occupy movement is] having an impact on what American people think of capitalism.
—REPUBLICAN POLLSTER FRANK LUNTZ

[Occupy Wall Street's] success to me is in changing the national narrative, naming the huge elephant in the room: economic inequality and a political system that's rigged to serve the few at the cost of the many. In a very short time this became the new common sense. —OCCUPY WALL STREET ACTIVIST, quoted in Milkman (2013)

The Occupy Wall Street movement (ows)[1] might seem a very different movement from the Tea Party, but it, too, can be seen as having at its heart a reconfiguration of certain strands of American common sense, although its narrative, unlike that of the Tea Partiers, reads the dominant capitalist narrative against the grain. It is this aspect of ows on which this chapter focuses. It asks the question: Can we see this movement as incubating the first stirrings of the kind of new common sense for which Gramsci called (*SPN*, 424)?

Adopting a Gramscian perspective, we could see the strands of common

1. My account of ows draws on a number of published accounts of the movement. These include Byrne (2012); Castells (2012); Gitlin (2012); Gould-Wartofsky (2015); Graeber (2013); Milkman, Luce, and Lewis (2013); Schneider (2013); and van Gelder et al. (2011).

sense that OWS rebraided as examples of the good sense that exists within the confused agglomerate of common sense. These particular strands have long been a part of American populism, even if they have tended to be marginalized in the decades since the Reagan revolution. An accessible, popular defense of American business of the kind called for by the Powell Memo was a crucial dimension of this revolution. And this defense, which appeals to feeling rather than reason, has been extraordinarily successful, overwhelming the older populist narratives of FDR's New Deal. A good example is the "It's morning in America" rhetoric of Reagan's first presidential campaign. Drawing on an imagined, idyllic past, this emotionally persuasive rhetoric conjured up a vision of an unfettered capitalism and a new coming of that lost golden land in which all prospered.

Two passages from the notebooks, both reflecting on the relation between thought and action, seem particularly relevant for an understanding of the achievement and limitations of OWS. In the first passage, Gramsci writes of the "contrast between thought and action, i.e. the co-existence of two conceptions of the world, one affirmed in words and the other displayed in effective action." When this coexistence goes beyond the self-deception of individuals and is found "in the life of great masses," such a contrast "cannot but be the expression of profounder contrasts of a social historical order. It signifies that the social group in question may indeed have its own conception of the world, even if only embryonic; a conception which manifests itself in action, but occasionally and in flashes" (*SPN*, 326–27). The problem for subaltern social groups, even if they consist of "great masses," is that in normal circumstances, even within those subalterns' own heads, the hegemonic narratives that explain so much of the reality they confront tend to drown out alternative conceptions of the world. Narratives that radically challenge the existing hegemony can only express themselves in action "occasionally and in flashes." We might see in OWS a normally submerged "conception of the world" that suddenly began to express itself in action, even if only as a momentary flash. Viewed in this light, can OWS be considered the first embryonic stirrings of an effective challenge to the hegemonic capitalist narrative?

The second passage from the notebooks that seems a good starting-point for this chapter is one in which Gramsci reflects on the relationship between the "philosophy" of intellectuals and "the popular 'mentality.'" The "philosophical activity" of intellectuals "is not to be conceived solely as the 'individual' elaboration of systematically coherent concepts, but also and above all as a cultural battle to transform the popular 'mentality' and to diffuse the philosophical innovations which will demonstrate themselves to be 'historically true' to the extent that they become concretely—i.e. historically and socially universal" (*SPN*, 348). What does OWS look like if approached as one aspect of "a cultural battle to transform the popular 'mentality'?"

Naming the Elephant

It is easy to condemn OWS for its lack of clear demands and to point to its relatively short-lived prominence as evidence of failure. Nonetheless, it did succeed—and there seems wide agreement on this—in forcing "inequality" to the forefront of political debate in the United States. "Within a few weeks," as Todd Gitlin, a veteran Vietnam War activist and academic, writes in his account of OWS, "The movement's friends and its enemies could agree that there was a new center of gravity in what we are pleased to call 'the national debate.' Inequality of wealth was now widely recognized—and seen as a problem, not a natural condition. 'The 1 percent' and 'the 99 percent' were commonplaces" (Gitlin 2012, 232).

A key point here is that, by definition, "commonplaces" or commonsense notions, do not need substantiation by argument or evidence: their truth is immediately apparent and beyond question. To many, the OWS slogan "We are the 99 percent!" seemed to do no more than express an obvious truth: there is something profoundly wrong with the ever-growing gulf between rich (the 1 percent) and the rest of Americans (the 99 percent), and this gulf is evidence that something has gone terribly wrong with the American system itself. The slogan seemed to encompass the many different ways a profound inequality manifests itself in the contemporary United States. The elephant in the room had been named.

For those who experience life from a position of subalternity, there is an inherent tension between what their day-to-day reality feels like and the hegemonic narratives of how the world is that saturate the world they inhabit. Those striving to bring into being narratives that challenge the accepted verities must continually struggle against the weight of the received wisdom. The Tea Partiers may be seen as political outliers but the assumptions that underlie their conception of the world are in line with a gospel central to American political discourse: government intervention in the economy is the problem rather than the solution; allocating resources and distributing the social product is best left to the free market. To deny that gospel tends to be seen not only as a denial of reality, but as tantamount to advocating the Stalinist gulag or the Nazi concentration camp. It is hard to bring into being a new common sense that, as the "We are the 99 percent!" slogan implicitly did, calls this gospel into question. It is much easier to refurbish an old capitalist narrative so it speaks to the fears and resentments of twenty-first-century Americans. The task of progressives is made all the harder when those who would question the existing hegemony lack the "roving billionaire advocates, and right-wing media purveyors" that propelled the rise of the Tea Party (Skocpol and Williams 2012, 13). Given this, the sudden and rapid emergence of ows is especially remarkable. Like the Tea Party, it seemed to come from nowhere and then be everywhere.

While ows may not have had backers with deep pockets, a supportive media, or a message in tune with capitalist nostrums, it did have Skocpol and Williamson's third force: grassroots activists. And these activists had available to them a substantial critique of capitalism with a long history, even if that critique is seldom to be found in the mainstream media. There was also the economic reality so many Americans were living in the wake of the Great Recession, which began at the end of 2007. Crucial to the rise of ows was an apparently ever-increasing inequality, accompanied by ever-dwindling prospects for upward mobility, overseen by a government that seemed deaf to all interests except those of big business.

Another crucial factor was the political turmoil erupting simultaneously in a series of countries from the Middle-East to Europe. The trigger was the self-immolation of a young Tunisian street vendor, Mohamed Bouazizi, who, unable to endure municipal officials' never-ending demands for bribes, set fire to himself outside the gates of the governor's office on December 17, 2010. News of his death led to angry demonstrations across the country and by mid-January Tunisia's longtime ruler, Ben Ali, had fled to Saudi Arabia, bringing to an end twenty-seven years of dictatorship. Emboldened by events in Tunisia, the disaffected (often young, educated city-dwellers facing deteriorating economic prospects) began protesting in ever greater numbers against dictatorial regimes in Egypt, Bahrain, Yemen, Libya, Syria, and elsewhere, which up to that point had seemed invincible. Meanwhile in Europe, savage austerity coupled with extraordinarily high rates of unemployment, especially among the young, were provoking fierce resistance in a number of countries. The *Indignados/as*, in Spain, where youth unemployment had reached 47 percent (Castells 2012, 110), were particularly prominent. It would take us too far afield to look in more detail at these movements, or at their ultimate outcomes. This wider environment of erupting social movements, however, is a key element of the ows story. We live in a world in which, in a few short years, as Manuel Castells writes, "large scale communication," has "experienced a deep technological and organizational transformation." Castells terms this transformation "mass self-communication, based on horizontal networks of interactive, multi-directional communication on the Internet and, even more so, in wireless communication networks, the now prevalent platform of communication everywhere" (220). Nowadays, those with access to the Internet—an increasingly large percentage of the world's population, particularly in urban areas—live not only within the boundaries of their particular nation-state, but in a virtual globalized world. The movement that erupted in New York City was both a very American phenomenon and one intimately entwined with other social movements across the globe. This chapter, however, focuses on the emergence of OWS and the specific, local, economic and political contexts that underpinned that emergence.

A Dying Dream

Fundamental to how America defines itself is the notion of the American Dream. America, it is claimed, is the land of opportunity where prosperity awaits anyone willing to work hard, no matter how humble their origins. A degree of economic inequality has tended to be seen as an inherent part of a healthy meritocracy. Former Federal Reserve chairman Ben Bernanke provided this succinct explanation of the benefits of inequality: "Without the possibility of unequal outcomes tied to differences in skill and effort, the economic outcomes tied to differences in behavior would be eliminated, and our market-based economy—which encourages productive activity primarily through the promise of financial reward—would function far less effectively" (quoted in Page and Jacobs 2009, 15). The trouble is that over the last thirty years inequality has grown ever greater, while the promise of upward mobility has come to seem more and more of a mirage. The journalist Michael Tomasky sums up the situation with some telling statistics: "Since 1979, compensation for the top 1 percent has grown 138 percent, while median wages have increased just 6.1 percent. Worker productivity has grown 63.5 percent in this time, and if wages had kept pace with productivity, the annual median wage today, instead of being around $35,300, would be $54,400" (Tomasky 2015, 18). As a result, "in 2008, among the Organization for Economic Cooperation and Development's member countries, the United States ranked higher in income inequality than any country in Europe. . . . Between 1984 and 2008, the share of America's total income (including capital gains and dividends) that went to the top-earning 1 percent of households rose by almost 40 percent. In the United States, the share of the top 0.1% in total pretax income quadrupled during the thirty years up to 2008. Meanwhile the tax rates paid by the richest declined" (Gitlin, 165). As Gitlin points out, "If income were really a reward for hard work, then the superrich must have been beating themselves into the ground mercilessly, while the 99 percent were lollygagging around their swimming pools" (165). It is true that the Great Recession led to the drying up of Wall Street bonuses and the shrinking of capital gains, but for the rich this was no more than a temporary setback; by 2013 they were back. In the words of the economist Paul Krugman, "The rich have come roaring back, to such an extent that 95 percent of the gains from economic recovery since 2009 have gone to the famous 1 percent. In fact, more than 60 percent of the gains went to the top 0.1 percent, people with annual incomes of more than $1.9 million" (Krugman 2013).

Joseph Stiglitz, another Nobel-prize winning economist, has also stressed how extraordinarily unequal the United States has become: "The United States was the most unequal of the advanced industrial countries in the mid-1980s, and it has maintained that position. . . . We are now approaching the level of inequality that marks dysfunctional societies—it is a club that we would distinctly not want to join, including Iran, Jamaica, Uganda and the Philippines" (Stiglitz 2012, 21–22). Such gross inequality, Stiglitz argues in a *New York Times* article published in 2013, "means that those who are born to parents of limited means are likely never to live up to their potential. Children in other rich countries like Canada, France, Germany and Sweden have a better chance of doing better than their parents did than American kids have" (Stiglitz 2013). "The American dream—a good life in exchange for hard work," he laments in the same piece, "is slowly dying."

We should not forget, however, that the imagined lost land of American prosperity, even if this was seldom acknowledged, was always a very white place. Robert Putnam, a Harvard academic but also the author of the bestselling *Bowling Alone*, begins *Our Kids: The American Dream in Crisis* (2015) with a portrait of his home town in Ohio, Port Clinton. Now it is "a split-screen American nightmare, a community in which kids from the wrong side of the tracks that bisect the town can barely imagine the future that awaits the kids from the right side of the tracks." Sixty years ago, when Putnam was growing up, Port Clinton was, he claims, "a passable embodiment of the American Dream," a town "that offered decent opportunities for all the kids in town, whatever their background." This, however, is to ignore the reality that Port Clinton was an overwhelmingly white town, whose white citizens used discriminatory housing and employment practices in their attempts to ensure that it would remain so. As one of the two black students who graduated with Putnam from the local high school explained to him, "Your then was not my then, and your now isn't even my now" (all quotes Putnam 2015, 18).

Americans of color may have long recognized the whiteness of the American Dream. What is new is that many other Americans, even those who previously never doubted its reality, have begun to question its achievability. One response, as we saw in the previous chapter, is the implicitly racialized Tea Party narrative of a country, run by a profligate government, that is slipping away from those with rightful claims and into the hands of freeloaders, happy to depend on welfare handouts. But there are other long-standing strands within American common sense that are more critical of unfettered capitalism, even if they have been suppressed since the Reagan revolution. One such critique is that the decline of the middle class is not due to government handouts to undeserving moochers, but to the wealthiest taking more than their fair share. One of the achievements of ows was to create a space where these alternative strands of common sense were able to emerge with a new power.

We could see this critique as perhaps the embryonic beginnings of a new, more coherent narrative with the potential to challenge the existing hegemony. It remains to be seen whether this narrative will be genuinely revolutionary or more reformist, essentially a Keynesian reining-in of an unfettered capitalism. What is certain is that developing such embryonic, subaltern good sense into a coherent, and politically effective narrative requires intellectuals. Given my stress in this book on the distinction between traditional and organic intellectuals, the reader may well be asking if the intellectuals here are organic intellectuals. The problem is that it is far easier to identify organic intellectuals in the past than in our own time. This is why the case study in chapter 5 is historical rather than contemporary. From a twenty-first-century vantage point, Adam Smith, whose the *Wealth of Nations* explains why market-based societies will lead to greater "opulence" for all, appears as an intellectual organically linked to an emerging bourgeois class in a way that would have been impossible for his contemporaries to see. Thanks to hindsight, our twenty-first-century eyes know what came after Adam Smith. In the case of our own historical moment, it is far more challenging to distinguish between surface flux and real structural change. There may well be new types of intellectuals coming into being, intellectuals organically linked to subaltern classes beginning their emergence from subalternity, but it is hard for us who share their historical moment to identify them. To ask who precisely might qualify as an organic intellectual within the momentary upswelling of discontent that was ows is not a fruitful question. It is still too soon. What ows does provide is an intriguing glimpse of the way a fragment of what we might call subaltern good sense can become the basis of a popular political narrative that challenges traditional beliefs. That fragment is the slogan around which OWS coalesced: "We are the 99 percent!"

The Miracle of Occupy

The story of OWS is very different from that of the Tea Party, but it, too, can be seen as a response to the widespread feeling that America has taken a wrong turn. "Millions of Americans," as Formisano notes in his history of the Tea Party, "share the sense that they are losing control of their lives" (106). But whereas the Tea Party explains the wrong turn by reference to entrenched "traditional beliefs," OWS, although not giving birth to a completely new narrative, did bring to the fore a long submerged concern with inequality. Rather than being the motor of progress that benefits everyone, inequality becomes the worm destroying the apple of prosperity from within. In telling the story of OWS, I approach its configuration of common sense as a moment in which various fragments of subaltern knowledge began perhaps to come together as a coherent political narrative "rooted in the popular consciousness with the same solidity and imperative quality as traditional beliefs" (SPN, 424). A caution is in order here, however. The occupation of Zuccotti Park should be seen as no more than a beginning. It was a long way from an organized, effective movement with the kind of disciplined leadership Gramsci saw as crucial for any sustained change. He was, it is worth noting, deeply skeptical of anarchism: the "anarchist movement is not autonomous, but exists on the margin of other parties, 'to educate them'" (SPN, 149). And, indeed, the often sorry fate of many of the uprisings of the Arab Spring provide a salutary lesson in the limits of anarchist organizing.

It is hard to think of a traditional belief in the United States with greater "solidity and imperative quality" than the achievability of the American Dream. Bernanke's warning that without inequality the whole system "would function far less effectively" resonates with this deep-rooted belief. Anyone who points out the inevitable inequalities of unregulated market systems, or suggests even the most modest redistribution measures, risks being demonized for promoting "class warfare." Simply naming the elephant in the room, inequality, is often taken as tantamount to snatching the ladder to prosperity from those struggling to better themselves. Fox News, for example, on September 18, 2011, just a month before the occupation of Zuccotti Park, had a story on its website quoting Paul Ryan. Ryan, chairman of the House Budget Committee "accused President Obama of appealing to Americans' 'fear, envy and anxiety' by pushing a new tax rate on people making more than $1 million annually: 'Class warfare . . . may make for really good politics, but it makes for rotten economics'. The 'class warfare path' will only hurt the economy."[2]

Obama's own skittishness around this issue is suggested by a story told by David Remnick in his *New Yorker* profile of the president, published in 2014. At the 2011 annual White House dinner for American historians, held the summer before the occupation of Zuccotti Park, the president "asked the group to help him find a language in which he could address the problem of growing inequality without being accused of class warfare" (Remnick 2014, 44–45). The effectiveness of the "We are the 99 percent!" slogan is that, whether or not it represents class warfare, it seems to many to do no more than state an obvious truth. In other words, while it may frame the economic crisis so many are experiencing in their day-to-day lives in terms of a narrative of class, it does so in the form of a commonsense truth—a truth that seems undeniable to those who see the ladder of prosperity receding ever farther beyond their reach.

The widely shared feeling that the America of the twenty-first century was heading in the wrong direction found expression in ows. Evidence of this is Occupy's unprecedented degree of popular support. Gitlin, former president of Students for a Democratic Society, notes how this distinguishes Occupy from earlier progressive movements:

> Unlike any other movement on the American left in at least three-quarters of a century, this movement began with a majority base of support. It was surrounded by sympathy. What it stood for—economic justice and curbs on the wealthy—was popular. People might disagree with Occupy's tactics. They might dislike the occupiers themselves—might disparage them for vagueness, programlessness, leaderlessness, unseriousness, hippiness, disruptiveness, even foulness and smelliness. . . . But, even when the movement was seen darkly, through a media lens that highlighted the melodramatic, the garish, and the conflictual, outsiders had a pretty clear idea of what was at stake. They could grasp by way of a first approximation what the contrast between the 1 percent and the 99 percent referred to. They could see that the point of the movement was to resist the grotesque inequalities that have become normal in American

2. "Republicans Accuse Obama of Waging 'Class Warfare' with Millionaire Tax Plan," FoxNews.com., September 18, 2011. http://www.foxnews.com/politics/2011/09/18/rep-ryan-accuses-obama-waging-class-warfare-with-millionaire-tax-plan/, accessed January 23, 2014.

life, and along the way, to point accusing fingers at a small segment that bore significant responsibility for the economic catastrophe, those who had rigged the game and escaped with impunity. (33)

Gitlin quotes some striking poll numbers. According to one poll taken in November 2011, some two months after ows had exploded onto the scene, "six in ten Americans said they supported government efforts to reduce disparities in wealth." Another poll taken around the same time "showed 60 percent of registered voters 'strongly agreeing' with this statement: 'The current economic structure of the country is out of balance and favors a very small proportion of the rich over the rest of the country. America needs to reduce the power of the major banks and corporations and demand greater accountability and transparency. The government should not provide tax breaks for the rich" (37). This same poll found there were only "33 percent who preferred to cut the national debt, reduce government, deregulate, and oppose new taxes" (37). In other words, close to twice as many people in this poll favored the ows message over that of the Tea Party. And by its third month, in terms of popularity, according to a number of independent polls, "Occupy [had] pulled even with the Tea Party, which was then in its third year" (41).

As Gitlin reminds us, despite the current celebration of the civil rights movement, the women's movement, and gay liberation as triumphant moments in an unstoppable march to America's ever-greater realization of freedom and equality, none of those movements were at all popular in their early days (34–36). In the case of ows, even the organizers seem to have been taken by surprise by the speed with which it took off and the enthusiasm with which it was embraced by those who would probably never define themselves as left-wing. One seasoned labor activist has referred to the "almost magical appearance of the Occupy Wall Street movement" (Master 2014, 17). Gitlin captures the euphoria of ows's upsurge: "It astounded everyone, not least its participants, many of whom had long pined for a world-changing social movement in the interests of equity, some of whom had experienced such things themselves, or hoped against hope that they might do someday, but had not dared think that a major eruption was possible now; never imagined how quickly it might be possible for a movement to take off, turning the homely verb *occupy* into a rallying cry and making 'We are the 99 percent!' a household phrase" (12–13). If in little else, ows resembles the Tea Party in its apparent sudden emergence out of nowhere.

In reality, however "magical" the emergence of ows may have seemed, and however much it may have come as a surprise even to those who had spent much of their lives hoping, even planning, for some such mass movement, it is possible, at least in hindsight, to discern some of the forces behind this up-swelling of political anger. "This movement," as Castells writes, "did not come out of the blue, even if it was spontaneous and leaderless" (168).

The grassroots activists who brought OWS into being represent the coming together of two groups. The first group, relatively small in number, were seasoned progressive activists, the sometimes rather battered bearers of political traditions long marginalized but never extinguished, often veterans of many political defeats. As in the case of the rise of the Tea Party, the weakness of the organized left in America is a significant part of the story of OWS. The second and far more numerous group of OWS activists were political novitiates, not socialized into the standard nostrums of the left, who had yet to learn what was, and what was not, deemed possible.

This second group included many members of what has come to be called the millennial generation. Peter Beinart, an academic and journalist, draws creatively on the work of the sociologist Karl Mannheim to argue that the political attitudes of millennials are quite different from those of their elders (Beinart 2013). For Mannheim, writing in the early to mid-twentieth century, the events that shape people's attitudes are those they experience between their late teens and midtwenties. Beinart's Mannheimian approach provides a persuasive account of why the message of OWS resonated with millennials, and is worth quoting at some length:

> America's youngest adults are called "Millennials" because the 21st century was dawning as they entered their plastic years. . . . Compared to their Reagan-Clinton generation elders, Millennials are entering adulthood in an America where government provides much less economic security. And their economic experience in this newly deregulated America has been horrendous. This experience has not produced a common generational outlook. No such thing ever exists. But it is producing a distinct intragenerational argument, one that does not respect the ideological boundaries to which Americans have become accustomed. The Millennials are unlikely to play out their political conflicts between the yard lines Reagan and Clinton set out. . . . By 2012, data showed how economically bleak the Millennials' first decade of adulthood had been. Between 1989 and 2000, when younger members of the Reagan-Clinton generation were entering the job market, inflation-adjusted wages for recent college graduates rose almost 11 percent, and wages for recent high school graduates rose 12 percent. Between 2000 and 2012, it was the reverse. Inflation-adjusted wages dropped 13 per-

cent among recent high school graduates and 8 percent among recent graduates of college.

But it was worse than that. If Millennials were victims of a 21st-century downward slide in wages, they were also victims of a longer-term downward slide in benefits. The percentage of recent college graduates with employer-provided health care, for instance, dropped by half between 1989 and 2011. . . . in addition to coming of age in a terrible economy, Millennials have come of age at a time when the government safety net is far more threadbare for the young than for the middle-aged and old. . . . Millennials have also borne the brunt of declines in government spending on higher education. In 2012, according to the *New York Times*, state and local spending per college student hit a 25-year low. As government has cut back, universities have passed on the (ever-increasing) costs of college to students. Nationally, the share of households owing student debt doubled between 1989 and 2010, and the average amount of debt per household tripled, to $26,000. (Beinart 2013)

The economic realities faced by the millennials are reflected in OWS. The demonstrators who took over Zuccotti Park were young: "40 percent of the core activists involved taking over the park were under 30 years old." They were educated. "Eighty percent possessed at least a bachelors' degree, more than twice the percentage of New Yorkers overall." And their economic aspirations had been dealt severe setbacks. "More than half the Occupy activists under 30 owed at least $1,000 in student debt. More than one-third had lost a job or been laid off in the previous five years." In sum, as Beinart writes (quoting Graeber), "the Occupy activists were 'forward-looking people who had been stopped dead in their tracks' by bad economic times."

A number of OWS activists have written accounts of the movement, and I have drawn on these for this chapter. David Graeber, an anthropologist and anarchist, and Michael A. Gould-Wartofsky, a graduate student in sociology, have each written book-length studies of OWS that provide detailed accounts of the movement from the perspective of its participants (Gould-Wartofsky 2015; Graeber 2013).

Precursors

The Great Recession of the twenty-first-century's first decade was a brutal reminder of the reality of the growing gap between rich and poor, particularly when it became apparent that those bearing the brunt of the economic downturn were not the bankers whose reckless behavior had led to the recession but "ordinary" people. In the words of the popular ows slogan: "Banks got bailed out, we got sold out!" It was on the Internet that the anger and frustration felt by so many first began to find an outlet. For Castells, "Occupy was born digital. The cry of outrage and the call to occupy came from various blogs (Adbusters, AmpedStatus, and Anonymous, among others), and was posted on Facebook and spread by Twitter" (171).

In the predigital age, for activists outside the political mainstream, getting the word out to those other than fellow activists presented considerable challenges; the explosion of social media and the general accessibility of the Internet has made reaching beyond those narrow circles exponentially easier. If before activists all too often found themselves preaching to the choir, they can now broadcast from loudspeakers audible far beyond even the church. At the same time, whom their broadcasts will resonate with is inherently unpredictable. It is always much easier to provide a plausible explanation of why a particular blog, tweet, or whatever, went viral after the fact than it is to predict in advance what will touch a nerve. There is also the question of what it means when individuals read Internet postings. When does agreeing with a posting translate into political action? While it is undeniable that digital media played an important role in ows, an effective political movement requires something more than individuals, no matter how numerous, interacting with their computers. It is no accident that the term *occupy* is at the heart of ows. Ultimately, it was the physical reality of a mass of actual human beings physically occupying a space identified with the might of finance capital that captured the attention of the national and international media.

A few months prior to ows's occupation of Zuccotti Park, there was an earlier attempt to create an encampment in downtown New York, this one protesting Mayor Michael Bloomberg's austerity budget. The protest was covered by the *New York Times* reporter David Chen, in a blog tucked away on an inside page. Chen recounts how on the night of June 14 "a collection of labor officials, students and social service workers"—termed by Graeber "a broad coalition of New York unions and community groups" (Graeber, 18)—"parked themselves just outside City Hall in sleeping bags and vowed to stay there, nonstop, 'till Bloomberg's budget is defeated!'" Chen's tone is one of amused condescension:

> So it may not be quite on the scale of the so-called Walkerville sit-in in Wisconsin, or the protests in Tahrir Square in Cairo. Nor will it remind anyone of the anti-apartheid shantytowns on college campuses in the

1980s, or even, on a much less serious note, the legions of Duke students who regularly camp out in a makeshift tent city, known as Krzyzewski-ville, before college basketball games.

But at least give the forces behind "Bloombergville" points for being creative for highlighting their anger toward Mayor Michael R. Bloomberg's proposed layoffs and cuts in his $65 billion budget. (Chen 2011)

In the event, the encampment remained small, "with crowds for rallies rarely exceeding 150 and no more than 50 people staying overnight," according to two of its participants (Singsen and Pomar 2011). The fifty or so core activists managed to stick it out for something like three weeks but never succeeded in attracting much media attention.

The summer of 2011 saw other small protests that for the most part went largely unnoticed by the mainstream media. Graeber describes two small "direct action" protests, in which he was involved, that took place in July. The protests, organized by the group US Uncut, were against the austerity measures that were closing school classrooms while at the very same time some of the largest financial giants, such as Bank of America, were getting away with paying little or no tax. One action involved a teach-in in the lobby of Bank of America. "US Uncut's idea of an 'occupation,'" Graeber explains, "was to set up shop in the bank lobby, take advantage of the initial confusion to begin the 'teach-in,' and then leave as soon as the police began to threaten to start making arrests. . . . Our occupation lasted about fifteen minutes" (Graeber 2013, 15–16). The other "occupation" was even briefer. Both actions, however, were filmed by one of the participants and immediately streamed on the Internet—something that marks them as the political actions of a digital age. The significance of protests in the twenty-first century, it seems, is often not so much the actual event but their recording and posting on-line. In hindsight these small US Uncut actions and the other small-scale protests taking place in the summer of 2011 can be seen as precursors of ows, but at the time none of them attracted much notice. Even those participating in them may have wondered quite what they had achieved.

One interesting fact that emerges from Graeber's account is the unusual diversity of those attracted to US Uncut. Marissa Holmes, the anarchist activist and radical filmmaker who introduced Graeber to US Uncut, warned him that he should not expect to find a bunch of committed anarchists. "They were," she explained, "mostly pretty liberal . . . not many anarchists, but in a way that was what was so charming about the group: the New York chapter was made up of all sorts of people of different backgrounds—'real people, not activist types'—middle-aged housewives, postal workers. 'But they're all really enthusiastic about doing direct action'" (Graeber, 12).

It seemed that many "real" people—and not just millennials—were angry in ways they could not express through any of the normal political channels. At this stage, however, no one, not even dedicated activists like Graeber, could imagine that within two months this anger would find a form of expression that would lead to thousands engaging in a single, focused action that the media and politicians could not ignore. As Graeber writes, "Even those who, like Dina [an Egyptian activist] or myself, organized much of our lives, and most of our fantasies and aspirations, around the possibility of such outbreaks of the imagination [as OWS] were startled when such an outbreak actually began to happen" (4).

Focusing the Anger

The Internet undoubtedly played a key role in focusing the anger felt by so many. And yet the story of the genesis of OWS and its slogan "We are the 99 percent!" (my concern in this chapter) is not solely a digital one. The different, and sometimes conflicting, origin stories of OWS and its rallying cry suggest both the importance of the Internet and the complicated way new political narratives emerge.

As early as February 2010, David DeGraw, an independent journalist, posted on his website AmpedStatus a call for a 99 percent movement—a call that, in DeGraw's words, "blew up virally" (quoted in Gitlin, 14). But it seems to have been in 2011, in the context of the Arab Spring, that the idea really began to take hold. In May 2011, *Vanity Fair* published an article by Stiglitz entitled "Of the 1%, by the 1%, for the 1%" that attracted a lot of attention. He began with the Arab Spring, observing that "Americans have been watching protests against oppressive regimes that concentrate massive wealth in the hands of an elite few." At the same time "in our own democracy, 1 percent of the people take nearly a quarter of the nation's income—an inequality even the wealthy will come to regret" (Stiglitz 2011). In *The Price of Inequality*, Stiglitz notes that "We are the 99 percent!" echoed the title of his article (2012, xi). Then, on July 13, the website of the Canadian-based anticorporate magazine *Adbusters* posted a call to action with the hash tag #occupywallstreet: "Are you ready for a Tahrir moment? On September 17, flood into lower Manhattan, set up tents, kitchens, peaceful barricades and occupy Wall Street" (quoted in Castells, 159). Why September 17? Explanations vary but according to the OWS activist and journalist Nathan Schneider, the date was chosen simply because September 17 was "the birthday of *Adbusters* founder Kalle Lasn's mother" (Schneider 2013, 10).

Adbusters may have issued a call to action, but that was the extent of their organizing role, as *Adbusters* editor Micah White explained in an e-mail to Graeber on August 4: "At this point, we decided that given our limited resources and staff, our role at *Adbusters* could only be to get the meme out there and hope that local activists would empower themselves to make the event a reality" (quoted in Graeber, 36). The hash tag #occupywallstreet did indeed hit a nerve, spreading rapidly through the Internet, appearing on blogs, websites, Twitter and Facebook accounts. In mid-August, two activists, Chris, who was anxious not to reveal his last name since his day job was working for a media outlet, and Priscilla Grim, initially identifying themselves only as "the people who will occupy Wall Street," set up a "We are the 99 percent" Tumblr page (Weinstein 2011). The "We are the 99 percent" Tumblr was not an organizing tool: its aim was to provide a platform where the "99 percent" could tell their stories. Castells quotes one commentator, Graham-Felsen, who makes an interesting comparison between the Tumblr page and the documentary work done by the Farm Security Administration photojournalists during the Great Depression: "Tumblr has humanized the [ows] movement. Tumblr is a powerful storytelling medium, and this movement is about stories—about how the nation's economic policies have priced us out of schools, swallowed us in debt, permanently postponed retirements, and torn apart families. 'We are the 99 percent' is the closest thing we've had to the work of Farm Security Administration—which paid photojournalists to document the plight of farmers during the Great Depression—and it may well go down as the definitive social history of this recession." Graham-Felsen goes on to note that for Ezra Klein, a *Washington Post* columnist, it was the "We are the 99 percent" Tumblr that convinced him he needed to cover ows. Writing in a *Washington Post* blog in early October, Klein explained, "It's not the arrests that convinced me that 'Occupy Wall Street' was worth covering seriously. . . . It was a Tumblr called 'We are the 99 percent'" (quoted in Castells 2012, 173–74).

The Tumblr invited people to post their stories explaining how they were part of the 99 percent, addressing them directly and describing their plight in compelling, accessible language. Under the heading "Allow Us to Introduce Ourselves," "the people who will occupy Wall Street" write:

> Who are we? Well, who are you? If you're reading this, there's a 99 percent chance that you're one of us.

You're someone who doesn't know whether there's going to be enough money to make this month's rent. You're someone who gets sick and toughs it out because you'll never afford the hospital bills. You're someone who's trying to move a mountain of debt that never seems to get any smaller no matter how hard you try. You do all the things you're supposed to do. You buy store brands. You get a second job. You take classes to improve your skills. But it's not enough. It's never enough. The anxiety, the frustration, the powerlessness is still there, hovering like a storm crow. Every month you make it is a victory, but a Pyrrhic one—once you're over the hump, all you can do is think about the next one and how much harder it's all going to be.

They say it's because you're lazy. They say it's because you make poor choices. They say it's because you're spoiled. If you'd only apply yourself a little more, worked a little harder, planned a little better, things would go well for you. Why do you need more help? Haven't they helped you enough? They say you have no one to blame but yourself. They say it's all your fault.

They are the 1 percent. They are the banks, the mortgage industry, the insurance industry. They are the important ones. They need help and get bailed out and are praised as job creators. We need help and get nothing and are called entitled. We live in a society made for them, not for us. It's their world, not ours. If we're lucky, they'll let us work in it so long as we don't question the extent of their charity.

We are the 99 percent. We are everyone else. And we will no longer be silent. It's time the 1 percent got to know us a little better. On Sept. 17, 2011, the 99 percent will converge on Wall Street to let the 1 percent know just how frustrated they are with living in a world made for someone else. Let us know why you'll be there. Let us know how you are the 99 percent. (http://wearethe99percent.tumblr.com/, accessed January 11, 2014)

The response was immediate. Hundreds of people told their stories. Figures 7.1, 7.2, and 7.3 provide some examples. If they wished, they were allowed to remain anonymous, hiding their faces behind hand-written sheets detailing their often desperate economic predicament: colossal student debt in an economy that could not provide them with jobs, no access to health care, and so on. There were no specific political demands, just individuals' accounts of their particular experience of the sharp end of the Great Recession—accounts that chime with Beinart's characterization of the specific plight of the millennials.

The rough, handmade quality of the posts was deliberate, as Priscilla Grim, one of the site's organizers, explained to Gould-Wartofsky: "[The site] looked kind of crappy and not polished. And the people who sent in the submissions, their writing was kind of crappy and not polished. I didn't want it to look slick or anything. I wanted it to look like the people who were sending in their stories" (Gould-Wartofsky 2015, 56–57). These Tumblr posts would surely find a place in Gramsci's archive of subaltern conceptions.

The rallying cry "We are the 99 percent," with its open-ended appeal to all those who felt themselves, in whatever way, exploited and oppressed by the 1 percent, provided a powerful, if somewhat vague narrative that spoke to a wide range of people. The term *the 99 percent* named those with degrees that had left them with a mountain of debt but no job; those whose homes had been foreclosed, not because they had borrowed recklessly but because they had lost their jobs thanks to the recession; workers whose hard-won benefits and pensions were being slashed as "unfeasible" in the new economic climate; jobless veterans. In truth, anyone who felt the decent life the American system was supposed to provide was slipping beyond their grasp could feel themselves included within the embrace of the 99 percent.

While there is wide agreement that the slogan "We are the 99 percent!" was at the heart of ows and was crucial to its success, just who coined it is disputed. According to Graeber, who acknowledges the influence of Stiglitz's *Vanity Fair* article, the slogan, in line with the spirit of the movement, "was a collective creation. I threw in the 99% part, Begonia and Luis [two of the Spanish Indignados] added the 'we,' and the verb was ultimately added by Chris, of Food Not Bombs, when he created the 'We are the 99 Percent' tumblr page a month later" (Graeber 2013, 41).

It is interesting that despite stressing the "collective creation" of "We are the 99 percent!," Graeber still manages to omit Priscilla Grim's well-documented role in setting up the Tumblr page. Gould-Wartofsky provides yet another version of the slogan's genesis (Gould-Wartofsky 2015, 53). In truth, the idea that it captured so effectively was so widespread that precursors can be found in all kinds of places. What is important is not so much to identify the one true begetter of "We are the 99 percent!," but to understand the historical moment that conjured it into being. In the years after the financial crash of 2008, the feeling that there was something terribly wrong with an economic system that seemed to reward superrich, reckless risk-takers, while reducing "ordinary" people to penury, came to be so widely shared that all kinds of commentators and activists began articulating it in different ways. "We are the 99 percent!" gave a name to a sentiment that hovered in the air and demanded articulation.

FIGURE 7.1. Submitted by Jessica Gaughan

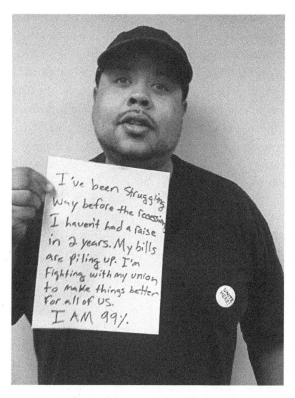

FIGURE 7.2. Submitted by Jeff Hancock.

FIGURE 7.3. Submitted by Dominic Nickens.

The brilliance of the slogan was that it appeared to those who claimed it to do no more than name an obvious, commonsense reality. It did not require explaining or substantiating with evidence. It simply captured the lived experience of inequality. The very fact that "We are the 99 percent!" did not involve any specific political demands, and did not use the language of class or any other political identity, gave it an all-important inclusiveness. The "we" embraced all those outside the tiny little club of the 1 percent, everyone who saw themselves as losing out while a tiny elite enjoyed obscene wealth, a wealth and its associated luxurious lifestyles, which in a digital age that worships celebrity is only too happy to flaunt itself.

From the Realm of the Virtual to Zuccotti Park

Adbusters's call for action certainly hit a nerve, but Graeber and others, concerned that there should be an actual, not simply a virtual, occupation, were worried that the seemingly arbitrarily selected date of September 17 did not allow enough time to organize: "*Adbusters* seemed to think that we could somehow assemble twenty thousand people to camp out with tents in the middle of Wall Street, but even assuming the police would let that happen, which they wouldn't, anyone with experience in practical organizing knew that you couldn't assemble numbers like that in a matter of weeks" (Graeber, 32). Nonetheless Graeber and the others were determined to try.

Graeber is a veteran of the Global Justice Movement and one of the positive outcomes of that movement for him is the transformation of activist culture from what he sees as old style, Stalinist, top-down vertical organizations to more anarchist, horizontal forms: "After the Global Justice Movement, the old days of steering committees and the like were basically over. Pretty much everyone in the activist community had come around to the idea of prefigurative politics: the idea that the organizational form that an activist group takes should embody the kind of society we wish to create" (23).

The organizational form that Graeber and many others in the activist community favored was the people's general assembly, which had been central to the Spanish Indignados. In America, as Andy Kroll, a *Mother Jones* journalist, notes, "the notion of a people's general assembly is a bit foreign," and he provides this explanation of the basic idea and how it worked in ows: "Put simply, it's a leaderless group of people who get together to discuss pressing issues and make decisions by pure consensus. The term 'horizontal' gets tossed around to describe general assemblies, which simply means there is no hierarchy: Everyone stands on equal footing. Occupy Wall Street's daily assemblies shape how the occupation is run, tackling issues such as cleaning the park, public safety, and keeping the kitchen running. Smaller working groups handle media relations, outreach, sanitation, and more" (Kroll 2011, 17–18).

In the eyes of anarchists like Graeber, general assemblies (GAs) represent a total rejection of old-style vertical political organizing. And from OWS's earliest days, this rejection was a powerful strand that helped knit together its many diverse elements. The account Graeber gives of his reaction when he arrived at an early planning event captures the visceral power of that rejection. According to Gitlin, the event had been, "advertised as a 'People's General Assembly on the Budget Cuts' to 'Oppose Cutbacks and Austerity of Any Kind' and to plan a September 17 occupation of Wall Street" (Gitlin, 85). What Graeber encountered on his arrival at this supposed GA was, however, a rally organized (or hijacked) by the Workers World Party on traditional vertical lines:

> For activists dedicated to building directly democratic politics—horizontals as we like to call ourselves—the usual reaction to [a standard rally and march] is despair. . . . Walking into such a rally feels like walking into a trap. The agenda is already set, but it's unclear who set it . . . The very sight of the stage and stacks of preprinted signs and hearing the word "march" evoked memories of a thousand desultory afternoons spent marching along in platoons like some kind of impotent army, along a prearranged route, with protest marshals liaising with police to herd us all into steel-barrier "protest pens." Events in which there was no space for spontaneity, creativity, improvisation—where, in fact, everything seemed designed to make self-organization or real expression impossible. Even the chants and slogans were to be provided from above. (Graeber 2013, 26)

Gitlin's account of the same event, based on what he was told by another participant, a Columbia University undergraduate, bears out Graeber's recollection. According to Gitlin, despite the promise of a people's general assembly, "the gathering seemed set to devolve into a conventional rally organized by the vertically organized Workers World Party, a tiny but vociferous Marxist-Leninist-Maoist sect that dates from the 1950s (when its founder supported the suppression of the Hungarian revolution) that came equipped with prefabricated demands like 'A massive public-private jobs program!' and 'An end to oppression and war!'" (85).

Walking around among the small crowd he estimated at around eighty people, Graeber was struck by the fact that most of them seemed not to be, as he puts it, "verticals—that is, the sort of people who actually like marching around with pre-issued signs and listening to spokesmen from somebody's central committee" but rather "horizontals: people more sympathetic with anarchist principles of organization, non-hierarchical forms of direct democracy" (Graeber, 27). Emboldened by this, he and the friend who had first suggested attending the rally, the charismatic Greek anarchist and performance artist Georgia Sagri, succeeded in taking over the rally and transforming it into what they termed "the real GA." According to established GA procedures, a series of working groups were formed (Outreach, Communications/Internet, Action, and Process/Facilitation). Graeber describes the excitement of the moment: "Despite the provisional nature of all our decisions . . . the mood of the group was one of near complete exhilaration. We felt we had just witnessed a genuine victory for the forces of democracy, one where the exhausted modes of organizing had been definitively brushed aside" (34). This spirit of bringing into being and, as it were, living in a concrete way "genuine democracy" would suffuse the whole OWS movement, infusing its participants with a new and heady sense of excitement and possibility.

A few days later, the outreach group met. As Graeber remembers it, this was the meeting that collectively came up with the slogan "We are the 99 percent!" More meetings using the GA format were held and the idea of occupying Wall Street, circulating on the Internet, began to take concrete form: "Over the next few weeks a plan began to take shape. We decided that what we really wanted to achieve was something like what had already been accomplished in Athens, Barcelona and Madrid, where thousands of ordinary citizens, most of them completely new to political mobilization of any kind, had been willing to occupy public squares in protest against the entire class of their respective countries. The idea would be to occupy a similar public space to create a New York General Assembly, which could, like its European cousins, act as a model of genuine direct democracy to counterpoise the corrupt charade presented to us as 'democracy' by the US government" (42–43).

It was clear that there was huge interest on the Internet in the planned occupation. *Adbusters* assured Graeber "there were ninety thousand people following us on their web page" (Graeber, 43). The question was how many would actually turn up on September 17. And what would happen when they did? A major fear of Graeber and other veteran activists was that the event might, indeed, attract political neophytes but turn out to be a fiasco that would discourage them from ever taking part in this kind of politics again. There was also the continuing tension between the anarchists, with their commitment to horizontalism, and the old-style verticals. This was a battle, however, the horizontals seem to have won, successfully fending off the verticals' attempts to create leadership structures. In terms of the reconfiguring of common sense, we could see what happened as the opening up of a space, free from prefabricated demands, in which a ferment of commonsense understandings of the economic realities could find expression.

The proposal that came out of the planning meetings was that around noon on September 17 people should start assembling at Bowling Green around the statue of the charging bull, so iconic of Wall Street and all it represents. But even as they began making their way to Bowling Green, the organizers still had no idea how many people would actually turn up. At first, there were just a handful of people, but more and more began arriving and soon the crowd numbered close to a thousand. All the while, events were being closely followed on the Internet. Graeber's account of those first few hours suggests the complex intertwining of actual occupation—real bodies in real space—and its exponential amplification via the diverse and sometimes unpredictable spaces of the Internet: "[Arriving early] I spent some time wandering about, snapping pictures on my iPhone of police setting up barricades around the Stock Exchange, and sending the images out on Twitter. This had an unexpected effect. The official #OccupyWallStreet Twitter account (which turned out to have been created and maintained by a small transgender collective from Montreal) immediately sent word that I was on the scene and seemed to have some idea what was going on. Within a couple of hours, my account had about two thousand new followers. About an hour later, I noticed that every time I'd send out an update, ten minutes later someone in Barcelona had translated it and sent it out again in Spanish" (47–48).

By around 2:30 PM, it had been decided that the occupation needed to find a suitable public space where the rapidly growing numbers could camp. The Tactics Committee conferred and the announcement was made that Zuccotti Park had been chosen (Schneider 2013, 25). By the time the crowd reached the park, the numbers had swelled to over two thousand. The occupation that would soon "spread to eight hundred different cities, with outpourings of support from radical opposition groups as far away as China" (Graeber, 53) had begun.

Over the next few weeks, the numbers continued to grow, seeing thousands by day with hundreds remaining overnight. "A community began to emerge, with a library and kitchen and free medical clinic, livestream video teams, arts and entertainment committees, sanitation squads, and so on. Before long there were thirty-two different working groups, ranging from an Alternative Currency group to a Spanish-language caucus" (Graeber, 56).

At the heart of this community were the daily GAs, where, using the People's Microphone, everyone was theoretically free to speak. Familiar to many activists from its use in the Global Justice Movement, the People's Microphone involves the speaker's pausing after each short phrase to allow everyone within earshot to repeat it so it can be heard by those further away. Despite the avowed stress on allowing anyone to speak, in practice, who got to speak remained an issue. However much those "keeping stack," facilitators, noting who wanted to speak and calling on them in order, tried to ensure that those normally marginalized, such as people of color and women, were not shut out, this was difficult to achieve. According to Gould-Wartofsky, from early on, "the college-educated and more affluent occupiers—above all the bearded white-men among them—had already assumed (or been ceded) positions of power, influence, and informal leadership as the 'coordinators'" (Gould-Wartofsky 2015, 73). One underlying tension, particularly intense perhaps in the contemporary United States, is the question of what defines subalternity, and on which of its dimensions the struggle to overcome it should focus. Schneider captures the complexity of contemporary subalternity in a reflection on the debate over the focus of OWS: "Some people [among the OWS participants] would beg for unity and forward momentum: 'Why can't we return to our focus, to the banks, to Wall Street?' Others would call this racist, and classist, and bourgeois. Both were right, I think. In the United States of America, there can be no real revolution against Wall Street or anything else unless people of color, and the homeless, and queer folks, and natives, and so many more of those normally left out are at the front of it" (2013, 66–67).

It was always clear that the occupation of Zuccotti Park could not last indefinitely. Mayor Bloomberg, the NYPD, and other municipal authorities were distinctly unhappy about this burgeoning physical manifestation of direct democracy. At the same time, they were apparently reluctant to come down too hard on the occupiers, who had considerable public sympathy, particularly after some incidents of seemingly unprovoked police brutality. The end came in the early hours of November 15, when, after weeks of indecision and various forms of harassment that stopped short of eviction, the police moved in. In Schneider's words, "At one in the morning, hundreds of police in riot gear . . . stormed the plaza, shining floodlights and tearing down tents." By the morning, "The place had been completely cleared and power-washed" (2013, 101). The occupation of Zuccotti Park was over.

In truth, by mid-November there seems to have been a growing sense among the occupiers that, in Schneider's words, "the movement was starting to outgrow the occupation. The working groups, websites, and other infrastructure were already at such a point that most of the movement's political business had been happening outside the crowded plaza for weeks" (2013, 102–3). Whether or not OWS ended with the eviction of Zuccotti Park, and whether it still continues in different forms, is a matter of debate. For the purposes of this chapter, November 15 provides an appropriate point to move from an account of the events to consider Gitlin's claim, with which this chapter began, that "within a few weeks OWS had succeeded in transforming 'America's political discourse'" (232).

Complexity, Not Chaos

It is noteworthy that even for Gitlin, the veteran of so many struggles, Zuccotti Park was something new. He was, he writes, "astounded" by what he found on his first visit. This, he tells us, was "not because it was wholly new under the sun (although, in sum, it *was* remarkably new) . . . but in no small part because [the participants] were surprising, they made me laugh, they touched me. I was unprepared for their sheer sprawl and inventiveness" (xiv–xv). Gitlin also makes a point that is especially relevant to the argument of this chapter: "These people were not demonstrating—that is, showing authorities that they wanted something in common—*but creating a space where leaders and ideas could emerge*" (4; emphasis mine). Ideas certainly emerged from OWS, whether leaders did is more debatable. I shall come back to this point.

The movement may have frustrated those seeking a focused strategy and a clear set of demands, but what its seemingly chaotic and long GAs did create, as Gitlin suggests, was a space where a multitude of voices could speak of their particular suffering and how they saw that suffering as part of the larger picture of what has gone wrong in America. From the outset, OWS was characterized by spontaneity and a lack of centralized control. Part of what the horizontals found so off-putting about the Bowling Green meeting on August 2, before they took it over, was its rigid predetermined format: "Even the chants and slogans were to be provided from above," while heaped on the speakers' stage were the customary "stacks and stacks of preprinted signs" ready to be handed to marchers (Graeber 2013, 26). The movement that occupied lower Manhattan, by contrast, sprouted a forest of individual, handmade cardboard signs—often making use of the rapidly accumulating, discarded pizza cartons. Figures 7.4, 7.5, and 7.6 show some examples. For the most part, as with the posts of the "We are the 99 percent" Tumblr, the signs were handwritten, their very lack of slick, professional finish giving them an aura of authenticity. "We are not the products of some public relations firm," they seem to declare, but genuine cries from the heart, welling up from the day-to-day experience

FIGURES 7.4–7.6. Occupy Wall Street (OWS) posters
Courtesy of David Shankbone.

FIGURE 7.4.

FIGURE 7.5.

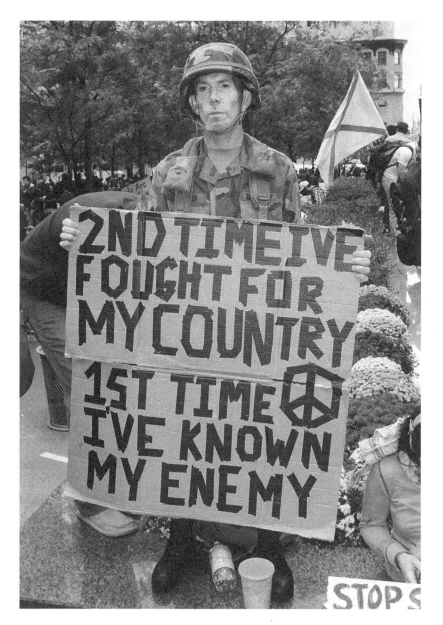

FIGURE 7.6.

of inequality. The rough, handwritten simplicity of the signs is all the more striking given how easy it is nowadays for anyone with even the most minimal computer skills to produce relatively professional-looking signs.

The signs displayed a cacophony of different slogans. There were variants of "WE ARE THE 99%!": "ARREST ONE OF US AND TWO MORE APPEAR, WE ARE LEGION FOR WE ARE MANY / YOU CAN'T ARREST AN IDEA / WE ARE THE 99%; IMMIGRANTS ARE THE 99%; MEMO TO THE 1%: 99% ARE WAKING UP and BE NERVOUS / BE VERY NERVOUS / MARIE ANTOINETTE WASN'T." There were also slogans more directly aimed at banks, corporations, and Wall Street. In addition to "BANKS GOT BAILED OUT, WE GOT SOLD OUT," there were signs like "HUNGRY? EAT A BANKER," "WHEN THE RICH ROB THE POOR IT'S CALLED BU$INE$$, WHEN THE POOR ROB THE RICH IT'S CALLED VIOLENCE," "FACTOID: THE LAST TWO YEARS VERIZON PAID ITS TOP FIVE EXECUTIVES $258 MILLION," and, echoing Ronald Reagan's famous appeal to Gorbachev, "TEAR DOWN THIS WALL STREET." Outrage at the legally protected privilege of corporations was powerfully encapsulated in "I'LL BELIEVE CORPORATIONS ARE PEOPLE WHEN TEXAS EXECUTES ONE." Anger against the power of money in politics was another common theme, as in "I CAN'T AFFORD A LOBBYIST, I'M THE 99%" and "FOR SALE: AMERICA." There were those that were antiwar: "IF ONLY THE WAR ON POVERTY WAS A REAL WAR THEN WE'D BE PUTTING MONEY INTO IT" and a sign held by a man in army fatigues: "2ND TIME I'VE FOUGHT FOR MY COUNTRY, FIRST TIME I'VE KNOWN MY ENEMY." There were also more general signs: "I'M YOUNG EDUCATED AND ANGRY"; "MARX WAS RIGHT"; "ROBIN HOOD WAS RIGHT"; and "YOU HAVE NOTHING TO LOSE BUT YOUR CHANGE." Other signs celebrated OWS itself: "THIS IS THE MOST HOPEFUL I HAVE FELT IN A LONG TIME"; "THIS IS WHAT DEMOCRACY LOOKS LIKE"; and in proud acknowledgment of the signs' home-made nature: "MY CARDBOARD CAN BEAT YOUR BILLBOARD."[3]

The inventiveness and wit of the signs also provided the media with irresistible images, carrying the dialogue taking place among the OWS participants far beyond the confines of Zuccotti Park. Moreover, they transmitted the dia-

---

3. "THIS IS THE MOST HOPEFUL I HAVE FELT IN A LONG TIME" and "IMMI-GRANTS ARE THE 99%," are listed in a 2011 *New Yorker* blog by John Cassidy. "I'LL BELIEVE CORPORATIONS ARE PEOPLE WHEN TEXAS EXECUTES ONE," from a photo reproduced in Gitlin (2012). "FACTOID: THE LAST TWO YEARS VERIZON PAID ITS TOP FIVE EXECUTIVES $258 MILLION," from http://commons.wikimedia.org. All the other signs come from Fjelstad (2011).

logue in simple, commonsense sound bites. Like the posts of the "We are the 99 percent" Tumblr, they seemed to be the direct, immediately graspable responses of individuals to the economic realities of twenty-first-century America. And despite their seeming diversity, there was nonetheless a coherence. As one sign admonished: "Don't mistake the COMPLEXITY of this movement for CHAOS" (quoted in Schneider 2011, 42–43). "Each sign made its own separate demand, but together they had a certain coherence: 'Peaceful Revolution.' 'Bail Out the People.' 'Wall Street Is Our Street.' Those who stopped to read them did so transfixed, as if having a silent conversation with each other over the blaring of drums and the plucking of banjos" (Schneider 2013, 58).

Gitlin, too, argues that it should have been clear what OWS stood for: "Anyone with an ear could figure out the essentials. The loudest, most frequently chanted slogans on the largest marches were 'We are the 99 percent!' and 'Banks got bailed out, we got sold out.' The first meant: the plutocracy that controls the commanding heights of the economy and politics needs to be curbed. The second meant: the federal government under both George W. Bush and Barack Obama caved in to the big banks while failing to relieve household debt or stop foreclosures" (108–9). Might we see Schneider's "coherence" and Gitlin's "essentials" as naming the good sense Gramsci saw as embedded within the confusion of common sense?

OWS's Good Sense

In one note, Gramsci describes good sense as seeing through "fancy quibbles and pseudo-profound, pseudoscientific metaphysical mumbo-jumbo," able to identify "the exact cause, simple and to hand" (*SPN*, 348). In the case of the OWS Tumblr and the placards the protestors held aloft, we might see the "fancy quibbles" and "mumbo-jumbo" they saw through as the rationalizations put out by the right-wing media and think tanks. Within the sprawl and inventiveness of the Tumblr posts and the signs we can discern the good-sense recognition that America is a country divided between a privileged minority getting ever richer and the vast majority whose prospects seem to be getting ever bleaker.

It is true that the slogan "We are the 99 percent!" is not a political program, something that exasperates a number of commentators. As David Runciman notes in his review of a celebratory account of OWS, "It's a brilliant slogan . . . But it's a half-baked idea."[4] "The problem," Runciman continues, "is that 99 per

---

4. This and the subsequent quotations in this paragraph are from Runciman (2012).

cent is far too many. Majorities on that scale sound overwhelming, but they always come apart on closer scrutiny. There is nothing on which so many people will ever be able to agree." But then, as Runciman acknowledges, "Occupy Wall Street is not trying to get 99 per cent of the population to vote for anyone or anything. The movement is simply highlighting an experience that the 99 per cent have in common, which is to have been stiffed by the current system." Writing some twelve months after the Zuccotti Park occupation, Runciman is impatient with some of the exaggerated claims: "Many of the claims being made for Occupy Wall Street are inflated. Its far-reaching effects are available only to the tiny proportion of the population who can be bothered to show up." But perhaps the point is not ows's failure to bring about any lasting change, but its role in bringing to the fore an existing, but suppressed, good-sense understanding of fundamental problems inherent in the current American system. We could say, as many commentators have observed, that ows "changed the conversation." Approached from this perspective, ows can be seen as a particular aspect of the long "war of position" Gramsci saw as an essential element in any struggle for political transformation (see, for instance, *SPN*, 229–38). As such, the ows moment is perhaps more significant than Runciman allows. I shall come back to this point. First, however, I want to look in a little more detail at some examples of the influence of ows within the mainstream political arena.

Changing the Conversation

That ows has given the issue of inequality a new prominence is widely accepted, as Castells writes: "As a result of the [Occupy] movement, and of the debates it has generated on the Internet and in the mainstream media, the issue of social inequality, epitomized by the opposition between the 99% and the 1%, has come to the forefront of public discourse. Politicians (including President Obama), media commentators and comedians have embraced the term, claiming they represent the 99%" (194).

The trajectory of Obama's "embrace" of the rhetoric of ows is a good illustration of how a new commonsense narrative can make its way into public discourse. While some at the White House were slow to acknowledge what was happening in Zuccotti Park, Obama, a master of populist rhetoric, recognized its significance early on. Less attuned to the political winds emanating from downtown Manhattan was White House chief of staff and former investment banker William Daley. Asked on October 5, some two weeks into the occupation, "whether Occupy demonstrations were helpful to the White

House's push for a new jobs bill," the careful Daley responded: "I don't know if it's helpful" (Gitlin, 191). His boss's political antennae were more sensitive; the very next day, "perhaps as a small corrective, Obama ratcheted up his rhetoric, responding to a question about Occupy at the press conference by saying that 'the protestors are giving voice to a more broad-based frustration about how our financial system works'" (Gitlin, 191). As support for OWS continued to grow, so too did Obama's incorporation of its rhetoric. In early December, he delivered a major speech on economic policy in Osawatomie, Kansas, the site a century earlier of a speech by Theodore Roosevelt that has come to be seen as a milestone in the history of progressivism. Any anxiety on Obama's part about using the term *inequality* was gone. Adopting the language of OWS, he spoke about how "in the last few decades, the average income of the top one percent has gone up by more than 250%, to $1.2 million per year. For the top one hundredth of one percent, the average income is now $27 million per year. The typical CEO who used to earn about 30 times more than his or her workers now earns 110 times more. And yet, over the last decade, the incomes of most Americans have actually fallen by about six percent."[5] "This kind of gaping inequality," he argued, "gives the lie to the promise at the very heart of America: that this is the place where you can make it if you try." Such inequality is, he declared, "the defining issue of our time." He also recycled some of the rhetoric from his famous keynote address delivered to the Democratic National Convention in 2004. There he had condemned "the pundits [who] like to slice and dice our country into red states and blue States."[6] In Kansas, he proclaimed: "I believe that this country succeeds when everyone gets a fair shot, when everyone does their fair share, and when everyone plays by the same rules. Those aren't Democratic or Republican values; 1% values or 99% values. They're American values, and we have to reclaim them." One cannot but admire the skilful way Obama here simultaneously embraces "We are the 99 percent!" and defangs its recognition of a fundamental opposition between the 1 percent and the 99 percent.

Then there is Elizabeth Warren, a rising star of the Democratic Party. Beinart has analyzed her powerful appeal to the "young and economically insecure," describing how she "electrified the crowd" at the 2012 Democratic Convention in a way matched only by Bill Clinton and the Obamas. And she did this in part by channeling OWS, attacking Wall Street CEOs, the very

5. This and subsequent quotations from Obama's Osawatomie speech are taken from the transcript published in the *Washington Post*, December 6, 2011.

6. Speech transcript published in the *Washington Post*, July 27, 2004.

people who, in her words, "wrecked our economy and destroyed millions of jobs—[who] still strut around Congress, no shame, demanding favors, and acting like we should thank them." One line in her speech, which received more applause than almost any other delivered at the convention, was a direct echo of ows's commonsense narrative. This was when she declared that "we don't run this country for corporations, we run it for people" (quotations from Warren taken from Beinart).

Even Charles Schumer, veteran New York senator and the Democrats' major Wall Street fundraiser, acknowledged the shift that had taken place and its implications for the 2012 presidential election, declaring in an interview in November 2011: "The whole battleground has changed. There's been a major shift in public opinion. Jobs and income inequality are going to be the number one issue" (quoted in Gitlin, 47). New York's mayoral election in 2013 seemed to bear this out. Bill de Blasio's overwhelming defeat of longtime front-runner and fellow Democrat Christine Quinn was widely interpreted as a rejection of Mayor Michael Bloomberg's New York, which had come to be seen by many as a city of gross inequality run for the benefit of the 1 percent. That this perception is based on reality is borne out by the census data: "According to recent data from the US Census Bureau, if the borough of Manhattan were a country, the income gap between the richest twenty per cent and the poorest twenty per cent would be on par with countries like Sierra Leone, Namibia, and Lesotho."[7]

De Blasio's inauguration struck an unapologetically progressive tone, prompting one *New York Times* op-ed writer to remark that it "featured a concentration of left-wing agitprop unseen since the last time Pete Seeger occupied a stage alone" (Douthat 2014). In his inauguration speech, as he had in his campaign, de Blasio drew on a rhetoric of inequality, proclaiming, "We are called to put an end to economic and social inequalities that threaten to unravel the city we love," and outlining the kind of progressive policies that would allow "New Yorkers [to] see our city not as the exclusive domain of the One percent, but a place where everyday people can afford to live, work, and raise a family" (De Blasio 2014).

In the second decade of the twenty-first century, the reality of profound inequality, an inequality that threatens what Americans understand their country to be, would seem to have become a prominent thread in the multistranded tapestry of common sense. As Bob Master noted of Bill de Blasio's

7. "Idea of the Week: Inequality and New York's Subway," *New Yorker*, April 15, 2013, http://www.newyorker.com/online/blogs/newsdesk/2013/04/idea-of-the-week -inequality-and-new-yorks-subway.html.

election as mayor of New York, "The theme of the 99 percent versus the 1 percent fundamentally reshaped the parameters of dialogue about the US political economy." To a large extent, as Master also notes, this OWS theme has had such a powerful effect "because forty years of neoliberal policies have made it an entirely accurate description of how the economy has been working" (Master 2013). This recognition of the reality, and injustice, of inequality in the United States also explains the unexpected strength of the only self-proclaimed socialist in the Senate, Bernie Sanders's challenge to Hillary Clinton's 2016 presidential campaign. The message at the heart of Sanders's campaign, was the injustice of economic inequality and his stump speeches used the language of OWS. "Now," he would thunder, "is the time to create a government which represents all Americans and not just the 1%."[8] The narrative of a basic and unjust inequality, rooted in the experience of the mass of the population, is one that draws on what Gramsci would surely have termed the "good sense" of the 99 percent.

OWS's War of Position

One of the epigraphs to this chapter (taken from Milkman 2013) quotes an activist's comment that one of the achievements of the movement was to make the reality of "economic inequality and a political system that's rigged to serve the few at the cost of the many . . . the new common sense." But for many of the most dedicated activists this was not their primary aim. "'Changing the conversation' . . . was only the movement's most superficial effect" (Schneider 2013, 171). Indeed, to the puzzlement of many observers—particularly those keen to see OWS as a simple mirror-image of the Tea Party—the movement was seemingly uninterested in engaging in either presidential or congressional elections. Whereas the Tea Party was bent from the outset on shifting the Republican Party to the right, OWS was never a movement about shifting the Democratic Party to the left. "Indeed, establishment figures of any and all kinds made Occupy uneasy" (Gitlin, 146). When mainstream politicians on the left adopted OWS language or tentatively reached out to them, their reaction tended to be one of distrust: "Former House Speaker Nancy Pelosi won little if any praise from movement insiders when she supported them, though at times, sensitive to fluctuations in the esteem in which they were held by public opinion, she did tiptoe gingerly around the name, preferring

8. Quotation posted on "Bernie Quotes for a Better World," accessed March 22, 2016, http://www.betterworld.net/quotes/bernie8.htm.

the locution 'grassroots citizen movements working to hold special interests accountable.' When she told Democrats 'We've got to mobilize the 99 percent,' those who feared co-optation above all else smelled danger" (Gitlin, 146–47). This stance is fundamental to the nature of OWS: "Occupy does not want to be mainstream. It is, at its core, an outsider movement, deeply committed to a radical departure from political norms. That is its identity" (Gitlin, 142).

Nonetheless, however dismissive core activists such as Schneider may be, and whether or not this was an explicit aim of the movement, OWS's effect on mainstream political debate would seem to be its clearest achievement. Crucially, the events in Zuccotti Park got people talking and thinking about class. Castells notes the radical nature of this shift:

> What is relatively new and meaningful is that there are indications that Occupy Wall Street has shaped the awareness of Americans on the reality of what I would dare to call class struggle. Thus, according to a Pew Institute survey on a national and representative sample of adults in the age group 18 to 34, released on January 11, 2012, 66 percent believe there are "very strong" or "strong" conflicts between the rich and poor: *an increase of 19 percentage points since 2009.* . . . 30 percent say there are "very strong conflicts" between poor people and rich people, double the proportion that offered a similar view in July 2009 and *the largest percentage expressing this opinion since the question was first asked in 1987.* . . . All major demographic groups now perceive significantly more class conflict than two years ago. (Castells 2012, 194–95)

The report from which Castells takes his figures reflects on the changes they represent: "These changes in attitude over a relatively short period of time may reflect the income and wealth inequality message conveyed by Occupy Wall Street protesters across the country in late 2011 that led to a spike in media attention to the topic. But the changes may also reflect a growing public awareness of underlying shifts in the distribution of wealth in American society" (quoted in Castells 2012, 196–97).

A key point here is that people never become aware of "objective realities," such as shifts in wealth distribution, in any simple, direct way. Even "realities" we apparently experience directly are always mediated—although not determined—by the narratives we have available to us. And this applies whether we are intellectuals or those Gramsci termed the popular element. Intellectuals and the popular element may draw on different narratives, but we all perceive a world rendered intelligible by the assumptions we bring to it, whether we have unthinkingly absorbed these from our environment, or arrived at them through critical reflection.

When Bloomberg ordered the police to clear Zuccotti Park, he remarked somewhat sneeringly, "Protestors have had two months to occupy the park with tents and sleeping bags. . . . Now they will have to occupy the space with the power of their arguments" (quoted in Schneider 2013, 103). In reality, however, while reasoned argument is certainly crucial, it cannot on its own create persuasive political narratives. Effective political movements need more than this: they need passion. A genuinely progressive and democratic movement needs to combine reason and passion; the intellectuals' knowledge needs to be brought together with the feeling of the popular element. As a slogan, "We are the 99 percent!" achieves this kind of synthesis. On the one hand, it is grounded in the intellectual arguments of progressive Keynesian economists such as Paul Krugman and Joseph Stiglitz. On the other, it captures in a visceral way the anger and pain felt by so many who see their economic future growing ever darker. Political narratives that resonate with common sense are a crucial part of any effective, oppositional political movement. The occupation of Zuccotti Park, and the hundreds of other occupations across the country, may have lacked political coherence, and may, for all their energy and enthusiasm, have soon flamed out, but maybe they nonetheless represent the genuine beginning of such a narrative.

Any political narrative that runs against the grain of the prevailing hegemony faces the problem that hegemony does not just refer to a set of ideas; it is woven into the very fabric of the institutions and practices of everyday life. It is hard for an embryonic conception of the world that genuinely challenges the existing hegemony to find the space to develop. To come back to one of the passages from the notebooks with which I began this chapter, a subaltern group "may indeed have its own conception of the world," but this tends to be "only embryonic; a conception which manifests itself in action, but occasionally and in flashes" (SPN, 327). The occupation of Zuccotti Part and all the other occupations can be thought of as such flashes of political action. Despite their ephemeral nature, such flashes can nonetheless be seen as one of the ways Gramsci's slow, incremental war of position is fought out. A space was opened up by ows in which certain nuggets of good sense embedded within the heterogeneity of American common sense began to coalesce into coherence, a coherence that spoke in a language not of reasoned argument, but of feeling. "We are the 99 percent!" seemed to many to capture the day-to-day reality of their lives in twenty-first-century America.

The creative sprawl of the Zuccotti occupation, as Gitlin observed, created a space where leaders and ideas could emerge, but while ideas and a narrative certainly emerged, the horizontalist, or anarchist, character of the movement militated against the emergence of a clear leadership. In chapter 2, I quoted a note in which Gramsci argues that historical acts depend on "the attainment of a 'cultural-social' unity through which a multiplicity of dispersed wills, with heterogeneous aims, are welded together with a single aim, on the basis of an equal and common conception of the world." Such a conception of the world, the note continues, "[operates] in transitory bursts (in emotional ways) or permanently (where the intellectual base is so well rooted, assimilated and experienced that it becomes passion [that is, active political will])" (*SPN*, 349). The ows movement would seem to represent more of a "transitory burst" than a "well rooted, assimilated and experienced intellectual base." Nonetheless, ows did provide an actual physical space in which the felt, commonsense outrage at the realities of inequality came into dialogue with a wide array of broadly left-intellectual narratives, including Marxism (in many different variants), anarchism, and Keynesianism. It was out of this dialogue that the slogan "We are the 99 percent!" emerged as a condensation of the shared life of twenty-first-century inequality.

Perhaps, as Piketty seems to argue, the best we can hope for in the foreseeable future is a tamed capitalism, one that through fairer taxation regimes and greater regulation reins in the worst excesses. Even this would seem to require new, powerful narratives of economic justice, of "what is just and what is not," but these would not be totally new; within the broad capitalist hegemony there are plenty of strands of good sense, based on notions of economic-justice, available to those concerned to weave narratives that make the case for a more robustly regulated capitalism. Beyond this, there may be intellectuals, organically linked to a subaltern class, beginning its ascent from subalternity, who are indeed laying the foundations of a "solid intellectual base" for the emergence of a new historical bloc that has the potential to supplant capitalism. Such a historical bloc would represent a dialectical unity between the material forces of global, twenty-first-century capitalism, and an understanding of those forces, which views them from the vantage point of the forms of subalternity they produce and traces out a road by which capitalist exploitation and oppression might be overcome. We can recognize Adam Smith as an intellectual organically linked to an emerging bourgeois class, but only because we have the benefit of hindsight. The connection between global capitalism and Smith's critique of feudal oppressions and his vision of "opulence for all" in a world based on free markets only became clear once that global capitalism became hegemonic. For us, who share ows's historical moment, it is not possible to identify with the same certainty which knowledge producers, and which intellectual currents, represent the future.

We can say that while ows did not threaten capitalism in any serious way, it did, perhaps, as the Republican pollster Frank Luntz feared, have "an impact on what American people think of capitalism." The new acknowledgment of the reality of class, that the status quo massively rewards the 1 percent at the expense of the 99 percent, was surely at least a skirmish in the war of position. We can think of it as an incremental step in what Gramsci termed the ongoing "cultural battle to transform the popular 'mentality,'" one small, initial step, perhaps, toward the creation of a popular, alternative narrative of twenty-first-century capitalist reality that has the potential to become "historically true."

Reading Gramsci in the Twenty-First Century

We encounter the *Prison Notebooks* today as a potential "future in the past,"
a neglected moment of the twentieth century that may offer us a possible point of
orientation for the twenty-first. — PETER THOMAS, *The Gramscian Moment*

The world we live in today is very different from the one Gramsci knew. Even so, his approach to the mapping of inequality and oppression still has much to offer those seeking to chart current structural inequalities, and the complex ways those inequalities shape "conceptions of the world."

Like Marx, Gramsci takes it as axiomatic that "the *ultimately* determining factor in history is the production and reproduction of real life" (Marx and Engels 1975, 394), but, again, like the Marxist founding fathers, he stresses that basic economic realities are not experienced directly but are always mediated by a network of "legal, political, religious, artistic or philosophical—in short, ideological forms" (Marx 1970, 21). People become conscious of the contradictions inherent in the underlying economic realities on the terrain of ideological forms, and it is on this terrain that conflicts are fought. To capture the relationship between ideological forms and underlying economic structure, Gramsci uses the concept of the historical bloc. As explained above, in chapter 2, the historical bloc is not a two-tiered entity in which an economic base gives rise to epiphenomenal superstructures, but a complex and dynamic relationship "in which precisely material forces are the content and ideologies are the form" (*SPN*, 377). Radical shifts in the economic relations that "produce and reproduce real life," such as the transition from feudalism to capitalism, occur when an emerging class is able to build a historical bloc, rooted in its specific conditions of existence, capable of bringing into existence a new hegemony. An essential element of such a historical bloc is a popular, commonsense "conception of the world" that while it portrays the world as seen from the vantage point of its dominant class, appears, like Adam Smith's vision of "opulence for all," universal.

The approach to the analysis of inequality we find in the notebooks is one grounded in a Marxist notion of class, but class here bears little resemblance to the economistic caricature so prevalent today. This is a concept of class that recognizes the multifaceted nature of structural inequality, and the complex path between the experience of inequality and the narratives used to explain it. This nuanced understanding of class cannot be reduced to a capsule definition; we need to follow Gramsci carefully as he traces the economic, political, and social realities into which class translates over the course of history, both in Italy and elsewhere. The concepts of subalternity, intellectuals, and common sense, as I have attempted to show, provide us with a useful guide. Taken together, we can see them as delineating a theory of the complex relation between subaltern experience and subaltern narratives.

Subaltern Common Sense and Good Sense

Subalternity, as a concept, gathers together the many different forms in which inequality and oppression can manifest themselves. Its richness lies in this heterogeneity. As we saw in chapter 1, it does not name a specific economic location, such as proletariat, but encompasses all those who are oppressed rather than oppressing, ruled rather than ruling. In the notebook devoted to subaltern groups (Notebook 25), in different notes, slaves, peasants, religious groups, women, different races, and the proletariat are all identified as subaltern social groups (Green 2011b, 69). The common thread is that *subaltern* here refers to a relation of subordination to some other group, or a subordinate location within an overarching institution such as the state. The multitude of shapes subalternity can assume, the many and varied ways in which the experience of subalternity is internalized, and the implications of these protean realities, are central to Gramsci's theoretical reflections in the notebooks, as it was to his work as a political organizer before his imprisonment by Mussolini.

While attentive to relations of inequality in all their diversity, the primary concern of the notebooks is collective experiences of subalternity; individual subalterns feature primarily as exemplars of particular collective understandings. It is "the ensemble of opinions that have become collective and a powerful factor in society" (*PNIII*, 347) that is important. A concern with the collective runs through the notebooks, as in the note that recommends that those interested in the mental worlds of subalterns study the letters to the editor published in newspapers since they represent "one of the most *typical* documents of Italian popular common sense" (*PNI*, 108; emphasis mine). And, for Gramsci, one of the most characteristic forms collective ensembles of subaltern opinion take is *senso comune* (common sense). Subalterns, we might say, inhabit a world rendered intelligible by common sense.

While Gramsci takes common sense seriously, he never romanticizes it. It is this combination that makes the concept of common sense we find in the notebooks so useful for contemporary analysts. Unlike Hannah Arendt, and that strain of philosophical thinking that sees common sense as a reliable touchstone to which intellectual speculation must always return, Gramsci insists on its unreliability. It "takes countless different forms," is "fragmentary, incoherent" (*SPN*, 419). The importance of common sense is not that it represents some "common inherited wisdom" (Arendt 1994, 314)—a formulation that turns common sense into timeless, unchanging verities unmoored from any historical context—but rather that it provides subalterns with the maps they use to navigate the worlds they inhabit. It does contain "wisdom," termed by Gramsci good sense, but this is embryonic and comes encrusted with a mass of beliefs that are anything but good sense. The terrain on which any progressive movement must engage with the existing hegemony is one where good sense exists entangled with common sense that is "crudely neophobe and conservative" (*SPN*, 423).

As we saw in chapters 6 and 7, the reflections on common sense we find in the notebooks can provide a useful guide for those interested in mapping its contemporary contours. The range of media we need to examine to assemble our archive of subaltern conceptions of the world may differ from that of the prebroadcast and pre-Internet world familiar to Gramsci, but his insistence that we take seriously everything that resonates with large numbers of people is as relevant today as when the notebooks were written. Only a political narrative that explains inequality and oppression in a way that connects with subalterns emotionally as well as intellectually can hope to mobilize the kind of movement that might actually bring about significant change. Effective narratives need to describe the reality subalterns confront in an immediate and visceral way, and to offer an alternative in which they can believe. The resonant slogan that emerged together with ows, "We are the 99 percent!," provides an interesting encapsulation of just such a narrative. To the extent that OWS can be seen as a movement, albeit embryonic, that challenged the prevailing capitalist hegemony, we might characterize it as "the expression of profounder contrasts of a social historical order." As a conception of the world, the OWS narrative may often have been incoherent, and the movement itself fleeting, but the widespread recognition and acceptance of its message surely suggests the existence of a social group with "its own conception of the world," distinct from the hegemonic capitalist narrative, even if this conception is "only embryonic; a conception which manifests itself in action, but occasionally and in flashes" (*SPN*, 327).

Gramsci's resolute refusal to romanticize common sense is also useful in that it calls into question the whole concept of political authenticity. Much of the debate around the Tea Party, for instance, has concerned the movement's authenticity: To what extent was it a genuine grassroots movement, to what extent the creation of a right-wing elite? More important than the question of its authenticity, however, as Formisano argues, is the reality that the populist message of the Tea Party resonated with so many. The various Tea Parties are the product both of top-down and bottom-up populism, created "in part by the few—the corporate lobbyists from above—but also from the passionate many expressing real grassroots populism" (Formisano 2012, 8). Rather than arguing about whether or not the Tea Party phenomenon is inauthentic, Astroturf populism, progressives need to trace out, as Formisano, and Skocpol and Williamson do, the common sense that the Tea Party both draws from and helps to create.

As we saw in chapter 3, for Gramsci, the landscapes of common sense, which can vary so widely across time and space, are products of history; their heterogeneous accumulations of different beliefs and taken-for-granted assumptions have emerged in the context of specific historical realities. However timeless commonsense truths may appear, in reality they are inherently in flux, even if certain elements may persist for long periods of time. This makes any given commonsense landscape a terrain that cannot be known in advance. It must be studied; its microlandscapes must be carefully traced out. The notebooks' insistence on locating common sense within history offers a helpful guide for progressives seeking to connect with the good sense embedded in contemporary manifestations of common sense.

Any effective, progressive political movement must speak a language and have a message that is recognized by the mass of those it seeks to reach. And this is certainly one reason why Gramsci saw the mapping of subaltern understandings of the world as so important. There is, however, another more fundamental reason why he pays so much attention to collective subaltern common sense. Subaltern knowledge emerges in fragmented, often chaotic form, but the good sense embedded within it represents the embryonic beginnings of a genuine alternative to the existing hegemony, an alternative that is an indispensable element in the creation of a new economic and political order. This is the epistemological claim traced out in the first four chapters of this book.

Intellectuals and the Creative Spirit of the People

Gramsci devoted his life to the overthrow of capitalism, a change as epochal as that from feudalism to capitalism. Achieving such a transformation entails the creation of a historical bloc that embodies a new conception of the world, one as different from the bourgeois narratives underpinning capitalism as those narratives were from those that underpinned feudalism. In line with this, ideas, for Gramsci, are never simply superstructural epiphenomena. A central "proposition of the philosophy of praxis [Marxism]," he argues, is "that 'popular beliefs' and similar ideas are themselves [or can be] material forces" (*SPN*, 165). And in the notebooks we can see their author continually searching for evidence that a new understanding of the world is indeed emerging in the form of popular beliefs.

The new conception of the world struggling to be born is necessarily still unformed. Even Marxism represents no more than a beginning, groping its way to coherence under the shadow of the existing hegemony (see *SPN*, 396). Philosophies are always entangled in social relations, which they are in part produced by, and in part bring into being. But what gives rise to genuinely new, coherent ways of understanding the world with the potential to become material forces able to inspire radical change? Gramsci's answer is that they are born out of dialogue between the raw knowledge stemming from the experience of a particular subaltern location and the intellectuals created by that particular experience of subalternity. Intellectuals are the conduit that renders experience coherent.

Intellectuals may be crucial if the incoherent common sense of subalterns is to be shaped into coherent, political narratives, but just as important, without the "beginnings of a new world, rough and jagged though they are" that are to be found in subaltern good sense, intellectuals remain locked into the existing hegemony. "Is it possible that a 'formally' new conception can present itself in a guise other than the crude, unsophisticated version of the populace?" (*SPN*, 342). The fundamental epistemological claim here is often missed, in part because of a failure to understand Gramsci's concept of organic intellectuals and its emphasis on the *organic* rather than the *intellectual*. His concern is with knowledge as "conceptions of the world" that represent the lived experience of particular groups, the "historical subjectivity of a social group" rooted in "a concrete social content" (*FSPN*, 348).

The argument here takes us back to Gramsci's original formulation in the letter to Tatiana, written in the first year of his incarceration (quoted in chapter 2), that lays out his study plans. Here he explains that "at the base" of all four topics on which he plans to focus is "the creative spirit of the people in its diverse stages and degrees of development" (*PLI*, 84). In the notebooks he would go on to write, he continually returns to the question of how that "spirit," the expression of a "concrete social content," had in the past, and might in the future, become a "material force" capable of acting in history. As we have seen, the ultimate source of the "creative spirit of the people" is, for Mussolini's prisoner, "the ensemble of social relations" in which subalterns, those who are ruled rather than rule, oppressed rather than oppressors, "move and act." The characteristic form this subaltern creative spirit takes is the good sense that threads through common sense. Intellectuals play a vital role in translating this good sense into narratives powerful enough to become material forces, but they do not create the spirit that lies behind it—the spirit born of a concrete social content. The extent of specific intellectuals' organicity is defined by the degree to which they embody the concrete social content of a given group. The notebooks continually stress the importance of this linkage, as in the note that argues a philosophical movement can only be progressive as long as "it never forgets to remain in contact with the 'simple' [the common people] and indeed finds in this contact the source of the problems it sets out to study and to resolve" (*SPN*, 330).

Even many serious readers of Gramsci fail to recognize the profound epistemological claim at the heart of Gramsci's concept of the organic intellectual, as does Hobsbawm, when he questions the importance of the distinction between organic and traditional intellectuals (Hobsbawm 2011, 325–26). That the epistemological claim is missed by so many of the notebooks' readers is testament to the sheer power of the commonsense image of the intellectual. Even knowledgeable and sophisticated readers of Gramsci, such as Hobsbawm and Said, seem unable to move beyond an understanding of intellectuals as individuals possessed of certain skills who engage in recognizably intellectual activities. Gramsci, however, totally rejects this conventional understanding, insisting that it is the social relations that organize the production of authoritative knowledge on which we should focus. Given the importance of this point, it is worth repeating a passage quoted in chapter 2: "Can one find a unitary criterion to characterise equally all the diverse and disparate activities of intellectuals and to distinguish these at the same time and in an essential way from the activities of other social groupings? The most widespread error of method seems to me that of having looked for this criterion of distinction in the intrinsic nature of intellectual activities, rather than in the ensemble of the system of relations in which these activities (and therefore the intellectual groups who personify them) have their place within the general complex of social relations" (SPN, 8).

Many readers, it seems, read this but continue to operate with a definition of the *intellectual* based on some notion of the "intrinsic nature of intellectual activities." In reality, however, as societies change so does the nature of intellectuals. The individuals who do the work of producing and distributing authoritative knowledge are always linked to the larger society, and as new social groups or classes rise to dominance, they create new kinds of intellectuals. "The capitalist entrepreneur creates alongside himself the industrial technician, the specialist in political economy, the organisers of a new culture, of a new legal system, etc." (SPN, 5). New forms of society bring into being new knowledge-producing institutions: as capitalism develops so too does the modern, secular university, supplanting the old ecclesiastical centers of learning. The point here is that, ultimately for Gramsci, as a Marxist and a materialist, a given social group's conception of the world is rooted in its specific location within the human and the natural world. Over time that group's organic intellectuals translate the group's experience into coherent and plausible narratives, but those narratives have their origin in the experience of living that economic and political location. The knowledge produced by the organic intellectuals of a subaltern group emerging from subalternity is always the product of dialogic engagement. It emerges out of ongoing confrontation between the experience of a social group and the existing explanations available to them within the prevailing hegemony that make sense of their lived reality. It is from that dialogue that new narratives challenging the existing hegemony come into being. These narratives are "the form assumed by a concrete social content." Subaltern knowledge is that social content, the reality they live; it is what subalterns know. This is Gramsci's strong epistemological claim.

This epistemological claim explains why Gramsci would not see the Tea Party movement as creating *new* organic intellectuals. Whereas the Occupy movement can be seen perhaps as the "jagged beginnings" of a political narrative capable of challenging the prevailing narratives underpinning contemporary capitalism, the story told by the Tea Party cannot. That story represents rather a variant of the capitalist narrative that Adam Smith was one of the first to articulate. While not simple Astroturf, top-down populism, the Tea Party phenomenon represents a dialogue between the traditional intellectuals of capitalism (from the lofty heights of a Hayek down to street-level distributors such as Glen Beck) and the fears and anxieties—particularly of older, white Americans—that their America is slipping away from them. This dialogue weaves together strands from a very old capitalist common sense that may claim Smith as an ancestor, but has stripped away his insistence on the need for governments to rein in "the mean rapacity, the monopolizing spirit of merchants and manufacturers" (Smith 1976, 493). This is a common sense that reduces the argument of the *Wealth of Nations* to an *Animal Farm*–like simplicity of government bad/market good. The organic links here are to the economic structures that constitute "the necessary conditions" for capitalism. What was new and challenging to the existing economic order in Smith's day has long been transformed into the received wisdom of capitalism. Its knowledge producers and institutions of knowledge production are now the traditional intellectuals and institutions. It is true that the Tea Partiers have succeeded in fashioning a common sense that appeals not merely to the beneficiaries of the current economic order, but also a self-identified "middle-class" that sees itself as under threat. Ultimately, however, the understanding of reality the Tea Party articulates is one rooted in the same worldview that gave the capitalist class "homogeneity and an awareness of its own function not only in the economic but also in the social and political fields" (*SPN*, 5). We might think here of Gramsci's assertion that "the mass of the [Italian] peasantry . . . does not elaborate its own 'organic' intellectuals" (*SPN*, 6). For this Italian growing up in the early twentieth century, the realities of Italian peasant subalternity with which he was familiar gave rise rather to charismatic millenarian figures such as Davide Lazzaretti—"prophets" who expressed the discontents of their own time through a preexisting religious vocabulary. In somewhat analogous fashion, the Tea Partiers look to charismatic figures who weave together compelling visions of apocalyptic threat draw from a repertory of preexisting capitalist verities. A lavishly-funded, right-wing media plays an important role here in nurturing such prophets of doom, amplifying their message, and enabling them to reach a nationwide audience.

Progressive Intellectuals in the Twenty-First Century

What are the implications of Gramsci's approach to the production of knowledge for twenty-first-century intellectuals and activists interested in changing rather than preserving the status quo? Most usefully, perhaps, it forces us to rethink our understanding of the category *intellectual*. In the place of the universal intellectual, the morally righteous figure who "stands apart" from the grubby world of political struggle, the notebooks offer us organic intellectuals inextricably bound to a specific class or classes—intellectuals who are always, whether directly or indirectly, part of a collective endeavor. To borrow from Marx's terminology, they are the *Träger* (bearers) of a body of knowledge as well as, to a greater or lesser extent, individual knowledge producers.[1] The organic intellectuals of a given class transform the seeds of good sense to be found in the common sense that has emerged from that class's lived experience into coherent and elaborated narratives that explain the world from the vantage point of that class. These elaborated narratives, such as Marxism, then need to be retranslated into a new common sense.

The work done by organic intellectuals, it should be stressed, is very different from some mindless or self-serving adherence to a party line. All intellectuals have an obligation to struggle to be honest, never ceasing to subject their analyses and assumptions to critical scrutiny, and refusing to trim their sails according to the prevailing political winds. At the same time, as individuals and groups, all intellectuals have been shaped by the contending forces of their historical moment; they are never outside politics. Even those apparently safely cocooned within some ivory tower, for instance, depend on the maintenance of that tower and the conditions of knowledge production that allow them to perceive themselves as above the fray. One of the great virtues of Gramsci's insistence that intellectuals never speak from outside their time and place, but always from a particular location within it, is that it moves us beyond the familiar dichotomy of the morally pure, universal intellectual versus hack intellectuals who subordinate themselves to some political master or sell their expertise in the market place.

Said's figure of the intellectual as moral crusader, "a being set apart, someone able to speak truth to power" (discussed in chapter 2), is undeniably seductive, playing into the hubris to which intellectuals as a category are prone.

---

1. In the preface to the first edition of *Capital*, vol. 1, Marx writes, "Individuals are dealt with here [i.e., in *Capital*] only in so far as they are the personifications of economic categories, the bearers [*Träger*] of particular class-relations and interests" (Marx 1976, 92).

In reality, however, all knowledge producers belong to a larger universe of knowledge production. They begin their lives as intellectuals at a certain historical moment in a particular place, confronting a world that has already been named and mapped. They cannot but start from the questions that naming identifies as significant; their initial conceptual tools are all preowned. Over time, they may develop their own questions and their own concepts, and in the case of major thinkers, may even transform the intellectual landscape, but such intellectual innovations are themselves linked, albeit in complex ways, to realities beyond the realm of thought. No intellectual ever completely escapes his or her historical moment. Like so many Gullivers entangled in a thousand Lilliputian threads, intellectuals are bound into larger, collective processes of knowledge production. A careful examination of these bonds is the first task for any critical, self-aware intellectual: "The starting-point of critical elaboration is the consciousness of what one really is, and is 'knowing thyself' as a product of the historical process to date which has deposited in you an infinity of traces, without leaving an inventory. The first thing to do is to make such an inventory" (SPN, 324).[2]

In determining the organicity of intellectuals, more important than their personal political stance are the basic assumptions that constitute the foundation of their "knowledge."[3] In the final analysis, it is not support for the aims or the struggles of a given group, or the fact that they belong to it by birth, that makes intellectuals organic, rather it is the particular economic and political locations in which their practices of knowledge production are rooted, and out of which the questions they seek to answer arise. Adam Smith is organically bound to an emerging bourgeois class not because of his personal biography, or his professed political views, but because he helped give coherent form to a conception of the world grounded in bourgeois experience, even if the political implications Smith drew from his laissez-faire narrative, as Emma Rothschild's study demonstrates, have little in common with the "market always knows best" doctrine of contemporary neoliberals.

2. Curiously, this last sentence is omitted in SPN. See Quaderni del carcere 11 §12 (Gramsci 1975) for the passage in Italian.

3. That colonial anthropology was shaped not by a conscious colonialist project but by the intellectual frameworks that colonial anthropologists embodied is the central argument of Talal Asad's extraordinarily influential, but sometimes misunderstood, volume Anthropology and the Colonial Encounter (1973).

Gramsci's Concept of Class

If we accept that the knowledge produced by organic intellectuals is the product of a dialogue between those intellectuals and the experience of what in the notebooks are often termed "fundamental groups" or "fundamental social groups" (see, for instance, *SPN*, 12, 15, 78, 182, 318), the question arises: What kinds of social groups are we talking about? It seems clear that the notebooks' fundamental social groups are groups that have their origin in the major economic fault lines of capitalism, feudalism, and so on. Gramsci may not always use the terminology of class, but his approach to power is firmly grounded in a Marxist concept of class. This concept of class, as I hope the preceding chapters have shown, has little in common with economistic caricatures that limit class to economic inequality. The major classes may be rooted in "an essential function in the world of economic production" (*SPN*, 5), but the passage from those roots is far from straightforward. Class as it is lived is not confined to economic inequality. Indeed, the value of the approach we find in the notebooks is precisely that it opens up the notion of class to embrace the whole spectrum of ways structural inequalities reproduced across generations manifest themselves in the lives of women and men. This is an approach that recognizes, for instance, that the political entities, such as parties and States, that arise out of the "ensemble of social relations in which real people move and act" (*FSPN*, 347) always include the inequalities of gender, of race and ethnicity, religion, sexual orientation, and on and on. In the notebooks, we see Gramsci mapping out the many different forms inequality can take, and the ways lived inequality and oppression can, in certain times and places, coalesce into self-aware classes that become the bases of historical blocs capable of bringing about radical social transformation. But if class is as central to his thought as I am claiming, why does he seem at times to avoid the term?

Gramsci's sometime avoidance of the word *class* is often explained as a concern not to arouse the suspicions of the prison censors. But why then does he use the word at all? It is true that the degree of surveillance to which Gramsci was subject in prison, and his anxiety about it, varied over the years.[4] Nonetheless, where and when he does, or does not, use the term *class* suggests that something more complex than self-censorship is going on. Two notes that are helpful here, neither of which show any nervousness about the term *class*, are "Agitation and Propaganda" and "'Merits' of the Ruling Classes."

4. Joseph Buttigieg, personal communication with author, April 24, 2015.

In "Agitation and Propaganda," political parties are said to be the expression of economic classes: "parties are only the nomenclature for classes" (*SPN*, 227). Parties are produced by classes but not in any simple or mechanical way; the relationship between classes and parties is complex and dialogic. "The weakness of the Italian political parties," Gramsci argues,

> has consisted in what one might call an imbalance between agitation and propaganda—though it can also be termed lack of principle, opportunism, absence of organic continuity, imbalance between tactics and strategy, etc. The principal reason why the parties are like this is to be sought in the deliquescence of the economic classes, in the gelatinous economic and social structure of the country—but this explanation is somewhat fatalistic. In fact, if it is true that parties are only the nomenclature for classes, it is also true that parties are not simply a mechanical and passive expression of those classes, but react energetically upon them in order to develop, solidify and universalise them. This precisely did not occur in Italy. (*SPN*, 227)

It is important to note here that the term *party* in the notebooks does not simply refer to recognized political parties. It embraces a wide range of both formal and informal organizations. For instance, one note argues that "a newspaper too (or a group of newspapers), a review (or group of reviews), is a 'party' or 'fraction of a party' or 'a function of a particular party'" (*SPN*, 148).

The key point to stress is that, for Gramsci, the various political entities that contend for power are grounded in specific class locations. And this includes states. Marx and Engels, in the *Communist Manifesto*, famously described "the executive of the modern state" as "a committee for managing the common affairs of the whole bourgeoisie" (Marx and Engels 1998, 37). And Gramsci, too, sees states as based on particular classes, writing in the note "'Merits' of the Ruling Class," "the fact that the State/government, conceived as an autonomous force, should reflect back its prestige upon *the class upon which it is based*, is of the greatest practical and theoretical importance, and deserves to be analysed fully if one wants a more realistic concept of the State itself" (*SPN*, 269; emphasis mine). But, as Gramsci stresses in this same note, the relationship between state and class is complex and mediated; indeed, "the identity State/class is not easy to understand" (*SPN*, 269). States may be based on particular classes, but they are not simple reflections of those classes.

One factor complicating the relationship between states and classes is the nature of hegemonic power: an aura of prestige emanates from a state's possession of power. This is part of what hegemony means. Nonhegemonic classes who lack this prestige may, as they advance to power, come to be represented by states in less straightforward ways, through alliances, for example, with other classes. Through such alliances a nonhegemonic class is able to attach to itself the prestige or authority of other classes. This acquired prestige

> is not something exceptional, or characteristic of one kind of State only. It can, it seems, be incorporated into the function of élites or vanguards, i.e. of parties, in relation to the class which they represent. This class, often, *as an economic fact (which is what every class is essentially)* might not enjoy any intellectual or moral prestige, i.e. might be incapable of establishing its hegemony, hence of founding a State. Hence the function of monarchies, even in the modern era; hence, too, in particular, the phenomenon (especially in England and in Germany) whereby the leading personnel of the bourgeois class organised into a State can be constituted by elements of the old feudal classes, who have been dispossessed of their traditional economic predominance (Junkers and Lords), but who have found new forms of economic power in industry and in the banks, and *who have not fused with the bourgeoisie but have remained united to their traditional social group.* (SPN, 269–70; emphasis mine)

Note here that the "Junkers and Lords" are described as remaining united not to their traditional class but their traditional social group. Given the note's frequent use of *class*, this cannot be explained as a simple self-censorship. Rather, Gramsci here seems to be making a distinction between classes, defined by distinct economic locations (the "economic fact" that "every class is essentially") and the social groups with their particular social and political characteristics, who emerge over time on the basis of that economic location. The "old feudal classes" were classes in that their economic predominance derived from specific forms of landownership. Their descendants, the German Junkers and the English Lords are no longer so directly linked to a specific economic location: they "have found new forms of economic power in industry and in the banks." Nonetheless their sense of themselves as a social entity remains tied to their history and what they think of as their traditions. The term *social group* in the notebooks can be seen as in some ways analogous to the concept of subalternity. Just as subalternity embraces many different forms of subordination, there are many different ways people can constitute social groups.

For Gramsci, as for Marx and Engels, the major actors in history are classes rooted in structural economic inequality, but, again like Marx and Engels, he stresses that "the economy is only the mainspring of history 'in the last analysis'" (*SPN*, 162). Epochal change is underpinned by structural economic inequality, but the passage from that inequality to self-aware classes and the constitution of historical blocs is complex and never predetermined. To repeat a metaphor I used in chapter 3, we might think of the basic contours of a society's economic inequality as tectonic plates underlying its varied political and social landscapes. These economic tectonic plates, like their geological counterparts, shape but do not determine those landscapes. And in both cases, the underlying forces are unpredictable; we can never know exactly when, or if, they will erupt. There are limits to the geological metaphor, however. Human landscapes and their political entities are always the result of dialogic engagement; unlike actual tectonic plates, fundamental economic cleavages can be reshaped by collective human action. Such reshaping, however, requires organic intellectuals able to provide the radically new narratives a new epoch, by definition, demands. The identity of these organic intellectuals only becomes clear in hindsight. It is hard for those living through a historical moment in which a new epoch is gestating to identify who among the forest of knowledge producers "personify" the new knowledge organic to the dominant class of the emerging epoch.

One of the great merits of the notebooks' inclusive approach to structural inequality is that, while acknowledging the importance of the economy, in the final analysis it offers a way of thinking about class as a lived reality that does not impose a predetermined hierarchy of inequality. Within and arising from the "ensemble of social relations in which real people move and act" (*FSPN*, 347) there are multiple stands of inequality. To understand just how those strands intertwine in any given time and place, and who the significant political actors might be, requires careful empirical analysis. Gramsci's approach to class, while always locating its empirical manifestations in their historical context, never assumes a predetermined endpoint to which history is inexorably marching. At the same time, his view of history is very far from Henry Ford's "one damn thing after another." There are structural tendencies but these may not be realized. And while there are patterns, these only become fully apparent in retrospect. The notebooks never shy away from the big questions, but equally, they insist that analysts pay attention to the specificities of actual times and places, and never forget that any conclusions as to how the future will unfold are necessarily hypothetical. A caution against intellectual hubris in the face of the contingencies of history is another of the notebooks' leitmotifs.

Taken together, the concepts of subalternity, intellectuals, and common sense we find in the notebooks can help us map the genesis of both the narratives that rationalize, and those that challenge, capitalist forms of inequality.

We can see the three concepts as providing a map, which in broad terms charts the relationship between the condition of subalternity and the knowledge born of subaltern experience first as incoherent and contradictory common sense, but then elaborated and rendered coherent by the organic intellectuals who emerge out of that subaltern experience. Such knowledge—always organically linked to the structural realities of class—is a central element in the reproduction or transformation of any regime of power. Despite being written in the mid-twentieth century, Gramsci's complicated and anything but economistic account of class can provide a helpful guide, although never a simple template, for those trying to imagine the possibilities for radical change in our grossly unequal, twenty-first-century world.

Note on Citations
The English translations of Gramsci's writings are cited in abbreviated form. The full references are listed below with their abbreviations.

1971   *Selections from the Prison Notebooks of Antonio Gramsci.* Edited and translated by Quintin Hoare and Geoffrey Nowell Smith. London: Lawrence and Wishart. (*SPN*)

1975   *Quaderni del carcere*, 4 vols. Edited by Valentino Gerratana. Turin: Einaudi.

1985   *Antonio Gramsci: Selections from Cultural Writings.* Edited by David Forgacs and Geoffrey Nowell-Smith. Translated by William Boelhower. London: Lawrence and Wishart. (*SCW*)

1992   *Antonio Gramsci: Prison Notebooks*, vol. I. Edited by Joseph A. Buttigieg. Translated by Joseph A. Buttigieg and Antonio Callari. New York: Columbia University Press. (*PNI*)

1994   *Letters from Prison: Antonio Gramsci*, 2 vols. Edited by Frank Rosengarten. Translated by Ray Rosenthal. New York: Columbia University Press. (*PLI* and *PLII*)

1995   *Further Selections from the Prison Notebooks/Antonio Gramsci.* Translated and edited by Derek Boothman. Minneapolis: University of Minnesota Press. (*FSPN*)

1996   *Antonio Gramsci: Prison Notebooks*, vol. II. Translated and edited by Joseph A. Buttigieg. New York: Columbia University Press. (*PNII*)

2007   *Antonio Gramsci: Prison Notebooks*, vol. III. Translated and edited by Joseph A. Buttigieg. New York: Columbia University Press. (*PNIII*)

References
Allais, Maurice. 1992. "The General Theory of Surpluses as a Formalization of the Underlying Theoretical Thought of Adam Smith, His Predecessors and His Contemporaries." In *Adam Smith's Legacy: His Place in Modern Economics*, edited by Michael Fry, 29–62. London: Routledge.

Arendt, Hannah. 1982. *Lectures on Kant's Political Philosophy*. Edited by R. Beiner. Chicago: Chicago University Press.

———. 1994. "Understanding and Politics." In *Hannah Arendt: Essays in Understanding 1930–1954*, edited by Jerome Kohn, 307–27. New York: Harcourt Brace.

———. 1998. *The Human Condition*. 2nd ed. Chicago: University of Chicago Press.

Asad, Talal, ed. 1973. *Anthropology and the Colonial Encounter*. Reading, UK: Ithaca Press.

Baumann, Nick. 2013. "Paul Ryan Changes His Story on 'Makers and Takers.'" *Mother Jones*, January 22.

Beinart, Peter. 2013. "The Rise of the New New Left." *Daily Beast*, September 12. Accessed January 22, 2014. http://www.thedailybeast.com/articles/2013/09/12/the-rise-of -the-new-new-left.html#url=/articles/2013/09/12/the-rise-of-the-new-new-left.html.

Benda, Julien. 1927. *La trahison des clercs*. Paris: Grasset.

———. 1969. *The Treason of the Intellectuals*. Translated by Richard Aldington. New York: W. W. Norton.

Beverley, John. 1999. *Subalternity and Representation: Arguments in Cultural Theory*. Durham, NC: Duke University Press.

Boothman, Derek. 2000. "A Note on the Evolution—and Translation—of Some Key Gramscian Terms." *Socialism and Democracy* 14, no. 2: 115–30.

Boswell, James. 1846. *The Life of Samuel Johnson: Including a Journal of His Tour to the Hebrides*. Vol. 5. London: H. G. Bohn.

Bourdieu, Pierre. 1977. *Outline of a Theory of Practice*. Cambridge: Cambridge University Press.

———. 1990. *The Logic of Practice*. Cambridge: Polity.

Broadie, Alexander. 2003. Introduction to *The Cambridge Companion to the Scottish Enlightenment*, edited by Alexander Broadie, 1–7. Cambridge: Cambridge University Press.

Buchan, James. 1995. "Presto!" Review of *The Life of Adam Smith* by Ian Simpson Ross. *London Review of Books* 17, no. 24 (December 14): 13.

———. 2006. *The Authentic Adam Smith: His Life and Ideas*. New York: W. W. Norton.

Buttigieg, Joseph A. 2013. "Subaltern Social Groups in Antonio Gramsci's *Prison Notebooks*." In *The Political Philosophies of Antonio Gramsci and B. R. Ambedkar: Itineraries of Dalits and Subalterns*, edited by Cosimo Zene, 35–42. London: Routledge.

Byrne, Janet, ed. 2012. *The Occupy Handbook*. New York: Back Bay Books.

Campbell, R. H., and A. S. Skinner, eds. 1976. Introduction to *An Inquiry into the Nature and Causes of the Wealth of Nations*, by Adam Smith, 1–60. Oxford: Clarendon.

Cassidy, John. 2011. "Wall Street Protests: Signs of the Times." *New Yorker* blog, October 6. Accessed February 13, 2014. http://www.newyorker.com/online/blogs /johncassidy/2011/10/signs-of-the-times.html.

Castells, Manuel. 2012. *Networks of Outrage and Hope: Social Movements in the Internet Age*. Cambridge: Polity.

Chen, David. 2011. "In 'Bloombergville,' Budget Protesters Sleep In." *New York Times*, June 15.

Coleridge, Samuel Taylor. 1969. *The Friend: The Collected Works of Samuel Taylor Coleridge*. Vol. 4, pt. 1. Princeton, NJ: Princeton University Press.

Crehan, Kate. 1997. *The Fractured Community: Landscapes of Power and Gender in Rural Zambia*. Berkeley: University of California Press.

———. 2002. *Gramsci, Culture and Anthropology*. Berkeley: University of California Press.

———. 2011a. *Community Art: An Anthropological Perspective*. Oxford: Berg.

———. 2011b. "Gramsci's Concept of Common Sense: A Useful Concept for Anthropologists?" *Journal of Modern Italian Studies* 16, no. 2 (March): 273–87.

———. 2014. "Culture." In *Critical Terms for Gender Studies*, edited by Catharine R. Stimpson and Gilbert Herdt, 41–65. Chicago: University of Chicago Press.

Davidson, Alistair. 1977. *Antonio Gramsci: Towards an Intellectual Biography*. London: Merlin.

de Blasio, Bill. 2014. "Bill de Blasio's Inauguration Speech." *New York Times*, January 1. Accessed January 21, 2014. http://www.nytimes.com/2014/01/02/nyregion/complete -text-of-bill-de-blasios-inauguration-speech.html?pagewanted=1&_r=1.

Doherty, Brian. 2007. *Radicals for Capitalism: A Freewheeling History of the Modern American Libertarian Movement*. New York: Public Affairs.

Douthat, Ross. 2014. "De Blasio's Long Odds." *New York Times*, January 4. Accessed January 5, 2014. http://www.nytimes.com/2014/01/05/opinion/sunday/douthat-de -blasios-long-odds.html?hp&rref=opinion.

Emerson, Roger. 2003. "The Contexts of the Scottish Enlightenment." In *The Cambridge Companion to the Scottish Enlightenment*, edited by Alexander Broadie, 9–30. Cambridge: Cambridge University Press.

Engels, Frederick. 1964. Introduction to *Class Struggles in France (1848–1850)*, by Karl Marx, 9–30. New York: International Publishers.

Eribon, Didier. 1991. *Michel Foucault*. Cambridge, MA: Harvard University Press.

Fanon, Frantz. 1967. *Black Skin, White Masks*. Translated by Charles Lam Markmann. New York: Grove Weidenfeld.

Fjelstad, Josh. 2011. "The 50 Best Signs from Occupy Wall Street." BuzzFeed.com., October 7. Accessed January 16, 2014. http://www.buzzfeed.com/fjelstud/the-best -signs-from-occupy-wall-street.

Flanders, Laura. 2010. "Behold the Becchanal!" In *At the Tea Party*, edited by Laura Flanders, 1–12. New York: OR Books.

Forgacs, David, ed. 1988. *An Antonio Gramsci Reader: Selected Writings, 1916–1935*. New York: Schocken.

Forman-Barzilai, Fonna. 2010. *Adam Smith and the Circles of Sympathy: Cosmopolitanism and Moral Theory*. Cambridge: Cambridge University Press.

Formisano, Ronald P. 2012. *The Tea Party: A Brief History*. Baltimore: Johns Hopkins University Press.

Foster, Hal. 2012. "At MoMA." *London Review of Books* 34, no. 9 (May 10): 12.

Foucault, Michel. 1977. "Intellectuals and Power: A Conversation between Michel Foucault and Gilles Deleuze." In *Language, Counter-Memory, Practice: Selected Essays and Interviews*, edited by Donald F. Bouchard, 205–17. Ithaca, NY: Cornell University Press.

Geertz, Clifford. 1973. "Thick Description: Toward an Interpretive Theory of Culture." *The Interpretation of* Cultures, 3–30. New York: Basic Books.

Gitlin, Todd. 2012. *Occupy Nation: The Roots, the Spirit, and the Promise of Occupy Wall Street*. New York: itbooks.

Gould-Wartofsky, Michael A. 2015. *The Occupiers: The Making of the 99 Percent Movement*. New York: Oxford University Press.

Graeber, David. 2013. *The Democracy Project: A History, a Crisis, a Movement*. New York: Spiegel and Grau.

Green, Marcus E. 2009. "Semplici." In *Dizionario gramsciano, 1926–1937*, edited by Guido Liguori and Pasquale Voza, 757–59. Rome: Carocci.

———. 2011a. "Rethinking the Subaltern and the Question of Censorship in Gramsci's *Prison Notebooks*." *Postcolonial Studies* 14, no. 4: 387–404.

———. 2011b. "Gramsci Cannot Speak: Presentations and Interpretations of Gramsci's Concept of the Subaltern." In *Rethinking Gramsci*, edited by Marcus E. Green, 68–89. New York: Routledge.

Greenpeace. 2010. "Koch Industries: Secretly Funding the Climate Denial Machine." March. Accessed September 21, 2013. http://www.greenpeace.org/usa/research /koch-industries-secretly-fund/; http://www.greenpeachorg/usa/global-warming /climate-deniers/koch-industries/.

Gruber, Jacob. 1970. "Ethnographic Salvage and the Shaping of Anthropology." *American Anthropologist* 72, no. 6 (December): 1289–99.

Guha, Ranajit. 1988. "On Some Aspects of the Historiography of Colonial India." In *Selected Subaltern Studies*, edited by Ranajit Guha and Gayatri Chakravorty Spivak, 37–44. New York: Oxford University Press.

Guha, Ranajit, and Gayatri Chakravorty Spivak, eds. 1988. *Selected Subaltern Studies*. New York: Oxford University Press.

Haug, Wolfgang Fritz. 2000. "Gramsci's Philosophy of Praxis." *Socialism and Democracy* 14, no. 1 (spring–summer): 1–19.

Hobsbawm, Eric. 1962. *The Age of Revolution, 1789–1848*. London: Weidenfeld and Nicolson.

———. 2011. "Gramsci." *How to Change the World: Tales of Marx and Marxism*, 314–33. London: Little, Brown.

Ives, Peter. 2004. *Gramsci's Politics of Language: Engaging the Bakhtin Circle and the Frankfurt School*. Toronto: University of Toronto Press.

Jacobellis v. Ohio. 378 U.S. 184. 1964. Accessed June 15, 2012. http://laws.findlaw.com /us/378/184.html.

Kidd, Colin. 2010. "Maiden Aunt." *London Review of Books* 32, no. 19 (October 7): 21–23.

Kroll, Andy. 2011. "How Occupy Wall Street Really Got Started." In *This Changes Everything: Occupy Wall Street and the 99% Movement*, edited by Sarah van Gelder and the staff of *Yes!* magazine, 16–21. San Francisco: Berrett-Khoeler.

Krueger, Alan B. 2003. Introduction to *The Wealth of Nations*, by Adam Smith. Edited by Edwin Cannan, xi–xxv. New York: Bantam Dell.

Krugman, Paul. 2013. "Rich Man's Recovery." *New York Times*, September 12. Accessed January 5, 2014. http://www.nytimes.com/2013/09/13/opinion/krugman-rich-mans -recovery.html.

Lepore, Jill. 2012. "Tax Time: Why We Pay." *New Yorker*, November 26.

Liguori, Guido, and Pasquale Voza, eds. 2009. *Dizionario Gramsciano (1926–1937)*. Rome: Carocci.

Lloyd, David. 1993. *Anomalous States: Irish Writing and the Post-Colonial Moment.* Durham, NC: Duke University Press.

Malinowski, Bronislaw. 1984. *Argonauts of the Western Pacific.* 1922. Long Grove, IL: Waveland.

Maloy, Simon. 2010. "UMD Report: Regular Viewers of Fox News More Likely to Be Misinformed." *Media Matters,* December 17. Accessed February 4, 2013. http:// mediamatters.org/blog/2010/12/17/umd-report-regular-viewers-of-fox-news-more -lik/174484.

Martin, Isaac William. 2010. "Redistributing toward the Rich: Strategic Policy Crafting in the Campaign to Repeal the Sixteenth Amendment, 1938–1958." *American Journal of Sociology* 116, no. 1 (July): 1–52.

Marx, Karl. 1963. *The Poverty of Philosophy.* New York: International.

———. 1970. *A Contribution to the Critique of Political Economy.* London: Lawrence and Wishart.

———. 1973. *Grundrisse: Foundations of the Critique of Political Economy (Rough Draft).* London: Allen Lane.

———. 1976. *Capital: A Critique of Political Economy.* Vol. 1. Harmondsworth, UK: Penguin.

———. 1978. *Capital: A Critique of Political Economy.* Vol. 2. Harmondsworth, UK: Penguin.

———. 1981. *Capital: A Critique of Political Economy.* Vol. 3. Harmondsworth, UK: Penguin.

Marx, Karl, and Frederick Engels. 1975. *Selected Correspondence.* Moscow: Progress.

———. 1998. *The Communist Manifesto.* 1848. New York: Verso.

Master, Bob. 2013. "The Zeitgeist Tracked Down Bill de Blasio: How the Rise of Occupy and Decline of the Neoliberal Narrative Helped Shape the 'de Blasio moment.'" *Nation,* December 27. Accessed February 1, 2014. http://www.thenation.com/article /zeitgeist-tracked-down-bill-de-blasio/.

Mayer, Jane. 2010. "Covert Operations: The Billionaire Brothers Who Are Waging a War against Obama." *New Yorker,* August 30.

Mellon, Andrew W. 1924. *Taxation: The People's Business.* New York: Macmillan.

Mickelmore, Molly C. 2012. *Tax and Spend: The Welfare State, Tax Politics, and the Limits of American Liberalism.* Philadelphia: University of Pennsylvania Press.

Milkman, Ruth, Stephanie Luce, and Penny Lewis. 2013. *Changing the Subject: A Bottom-up Account of Occupy Wall Street in New York City.* New York: Murphy Institute, CUNY.

Morris, Rosalind C., ed. 2010. *Can the Subaltern Speak?: Reflections of the History of an Idea.* New York: Columbia University Press.

Mossner, Ernest Campbell. 1980. *The Life of David Hume.* 2nd ed. Oxford: Oxford University Press.

Nelson, Cary, and Lawrence Grossberg, eds. 1988. *Marxism and the Interpretation of Culture.* Urbana: University of Illinois Press.

Page, Benjamin I., and Lawrence R. Jacobs. 2009. *Class War?: What Americans Really Think about Economic Inequality.* Chicago: University of Chicago Press.

Pasolini, Pier Paolo. 1982. "Gramsci's Language." In *Approaches to Gramsci,* edited by

Anne Showstack Sassoon, 180–85. London: Writers and Readers Publishing Cooperative Society.

PERI [Political Economy Research Institute, University of Massachusetts, Amherst]. 2012. "The Toxic 100 Air Polluters." Accessed January 5, 2013. http://www.peri.umass.edu/toxicair20120/.

Phillips-Fein, Kim. 2009. *Invisible Hands: The Making of the Conservative Movement from the New Deal to Reagan*. New York: W. W. Norton.

Phillipson, Nicholas. 1981. "The Scottish Enlightenment." In *The Enlightenment in National Context*, edited by Roy Porter and Mikuláš Teich, 19–40. Cambridge: Cambridge University Press.

———. 2010. *Adam Smith: An Enlightened Life*. New Haven, CT: Yale University Press.

Piketty, Thomas. 2014. *Capital in the Twenty-First Century*. Cambridge, MA: Belknap Press of Harvard University Press.

Powell, Lewis. n.d. "The Powell Memorandum." Powell Archives. Accessed December 21, 2012. http://law.wlu.edu/powellarchives/page.asp?pageid=1251.

Putnam, Robert D. 2000. *Bowling Alone: The Collapse and Revival of American Community*. New York: Simon and Schuster.

———. 2015. *Our Kids: The American Dream in Crisis*. New York: Simon and Schuster.

Remnick, David. 2014. "Going the Distance: On and Off the Road with Barack Obama." *New Yorker*, January 27.

Rendall, Steve. 2007. "Rough Road to Liberal Talk Success: A Short History of Radio Bias." March 3. FAIR *Fairness and Accuracy in Reporting*. Accessed February 13, 2014. http://fair.org/extra-online-articles/rough-road-to-liberal-talk-success/.

Richardson, Brian. 2001. "Questions of Language." In *The Cambridge Companion to Modern Italian Culture*, edited by Zygmunt G. Barański and Rebecca J. West, 63–79. Cambridge: Cambridge University Press.

Rogall, Neil. 1998. "Subaltern Studies." *London Socialist Historians Group Newsletter* 4 (autumn): 2.

Rosenfeld, Sophia. 2011. *Common Sense: A Political History*. Cambridge, MA: Harvard University Press.

Ross, Ian Simpson. 2010. *The Life of Adam Smith*. 2nd ed. Oxford: Oxford University Press.

Rothschild, Emma. 2001. *Economic Sentiments: Adam Smith, Condorcet, and the Enlightenment*. Cambridge, MA: Harvard University Press.

Runciman, David. 2012. "Stiffed." *London Review of Books* 24, no. 20 (October 25): 7–9.

Said, Edward W. 1994. *Representations of the Intellectual*. New York: Pantheon.

Schneider, Nathan. 2011. "No Leaders, No Violence: What Diversity of Tactics Means for Occupy Wall Street." In *This Changes Everything: Occupy Wall Street and the 99% Movement*, edited by Sarah van Gelder and the staff of *Yes!* magazine, 39–44. San Francisco: Berrett-Khoeler.

———. 2013. *Thank You, Anarchy: Notes from the Occupy Apocalypse*. Berkeley: University of California Press.

Scott, James C. 1990. *Domination and the Arts of Resistance: Hidden Transcripts*. New Haven, CT: Yale University Press.

Shapin, Steven. 2010. "'A Scholar and a Gentleman': The Problematic Identity of the Scientific Practitioner in Seventeenth-century England." *Never Pure: Historical Studies of Science as If It Was Produced by People with Bodies, Situated in Time, Space, Culture, and Society, and Struggling for Credibility and Authority*, 142–81. Baltimore: Johns Hopkins University Press.

Singsen, Doug, and Sarah Polar. 2011. "What Bloombergville Achieved." *Socialist Worker*, July 25. Accessed February 13, 2014. http://socialistworker.org/2011/07/25/what-bloombergville-achieved.

Skocpol, Theda, and Vanessa Williamson. 2012. *The Tea Party and the Remaking of Republican Conservatism*. Oxford: Oxford University Press.

Smith, Adam. 1976. *An Inquiry into the Nature and Causes of the Wealth of Nations*. Edited by R. H. Campbell and A. S. Skinner. Oxford: Clarendon.

Snell, K. D. M. 1996. "The Apprenticeship System in British History: The Fragmentation of a Cultural Institution." *History of Education* 25, no. 4: 303–21.

Spanos, William V. 2011. "Cuvier's Little Bone: Joseph Buttigieg's English edition of Antonio Gramsci's *Prison Notebooks*." In *Rethinking Gramsci*, edited by Marcus E. Green, 288–300. New York: Routledge.

Spivak, Gayatri Chakravorty. 1985. "Can the Subaltern Speak?: Speculations on Widow Sacrifice." *Wedge* 7/8 (winter–spring): 120–30.

———. 1999. *A Critique of Postcolonial Reason: Toward a History of the Vanishing Present*. Cambridge, MA: Harvard University Press

———. 2010a. "Can the Subaltern Speak?" In *Can the Subaltern Speak?: Reflections of the History of an Idea*, edited by Rosalind C. Morris, 237–91. New York: Columbia University Press.

———. 2010b. "In Response: Looking Back, Looking Forward." In *Can the Subaltern Speak?: Reflections of the History of an Idea*, edited by Rosalind C. Morris, 227–36. New York: Columbia University Press.

———. 2012. "The New Subaltern: A Silent Interview." In *Mapping Subaltern Studies and the Postcolonial*, edited by Vinayak Chaturvedi, 324–40. New York: Verso.

Stewart, Dugald. 1980. "Account of the Life and Writings of Adam Smith." In *Adam Smith: Essays on Philosophical Subjects*, edited by W. P. D. Wightman and J. C. Bryce, 269–351. Oxford: Clarendon.

Stiglitz, Joseph E. 2011. "Of the 1%, by the 1%, for the 1%." *Vanity Fair*, May.

———. 2012. *The Price of Inequality: How Today's Divided Society Endangers Our Future*. New York: W. W. Norton.

———. 2013. "Inequality Is Holding Back the Recovery." *New York Times*, January 19.

Street, Paul, and Anthony DiMaggio. 2011. *Crashing the Tea Party: Mass Media and the Campaign to Remake American Politics*. Boulder, CO: Paradigm.

Sydor letters. September 26, October 2, October 3, 1972. Powell Archive. Accessed December 21, 2012. http://law.wlu.edu/deptimages/Powell%20Archives/Powell SCSFChamberofCommerce.pdf.

Theoharis, Jeanne. 2013. *The Rebellious Life of Mrs. Rosa Parks*. Boston: Beacon.

Thomas, Peter D. 2010. *The Gramscian Moment: Philosophy, Hegemony and Marxism*. Chicago: Haymarket.

————. 2015. "We Good Subalterns: Antonio Gramsci's Theory of Political Modernity." Oral presentation at the Department of Political Economy, University of Sydney. June. Accessed July 1, 2015. http://bit.ly/1QPXcNs.

Tindall, George Brown, and David E. Shi. 1999. *America: A Narrative History*. 5th ed. New York: W. W. Norton.

Tomasky, Michael. 2015. "2016: The Republicans Write." *New York Review of Books* 62, no. 5 (March 19): 18–20.

Tosi, Arturo. 2001. *Language and Society in a Changing Italy*. Bristol, UK: Multilingual Matters.

van Gelder, Sarah, and the staff of *Yes!* magazine, eds. 2011. *This Changes Everything: Occupy Wall Street and the 99% Movement*. San Francisco: Berrett-Khoeler.

Vitello, Paul. 2014. "Bob Grant, a Combative Personality on New York Talk Radio, Dies at 84." *New York Times*, January 2.

Vogel, David. 1989. *Fluctuating Fortunes: The Political Power of Business in America*. New York: Basic Books.

Walker, D. M. 1988. *A Legal History of Scotland*. Vol. 5. Edinburgh: W. Green.

Weidenbaum, Murray. 2011. *The Competition of Ideas: The World of the Washington Think Tanks*. New Brunswick, NJ: Transaction.

Weinstein, Adam. 2011. "'We are the 99 Percent' Creators Revealed." *Mother Jones*, October 7. Accessed January 11, 2014. http://www.motherjones.com/politics/2011/10/we-are-the-99-percent-creators.

Williams, Raymond. 1977. *Marxism and Literature*. Oxford: Oxford University Press.

————. 1983. *Keywords: A Vocabulary of Culture and Society*. London: Fontana.

Wilstein, Matt. 2013. "Whole Foods CEO John Mackey Calls Obamacare 'Fascism.'" *Mediaite*, January 16. Accessed March 12, 2016. http://www.mediaite.com/online/whole-foods-ceo-john-mackey-calls-obamacare-fascism/.

Winch, Donald. 1978. *Adam Smith's Politics: An Essay in Historical Revision*. Cambridge: Cambridge University Press.

Wittgenstein, Ludwig. 1968. *Philosophical Investigations*. 3rd ed. Translated by G. E. M. Anscombe. Oxford: Basil Blackwell.

Wolin, Richard. 2010. *The Wind from the East: French Intellectuals, the Cultural Revolution, and the Legacy of the 1960s*. Princeton, NJ: Princeton University Press.

Wood, Paul. 2003. "Science in the Scottish Enlightenment." In *The Cambridge Companion to the Scottish Enlightenment*, edited by Alexander Broadie, 94–116. Cambridge: Cambridge University Press.

Zernike, Kate. 2010. *Boiling Mad: Inside Tea Party America*. New York: Times Books.

economic forces in orthodox Marxism, 4, 20, 22; economic determinism and, 20, 40, 196–97

economics: as distinct discipline, 91, 112–14; Nobel prize in, 95, 151; Adam Smith and, 95, 116

economist, economists, 87, 121–22; as new intellectuals, 86–87, 91

Edinburgh, 84, 88, 96–97, 112

Edinburgh Philosophical Society, 88, 89–90

Edinburgh Society for Encouraging Arts, Sciences, Manufactures, and Agriculture in Scotland, 90

Edinburgh University, 86, 94, 97

Edmond Dantès (in *The Count of Monte Cristo*), 73

education: apprenticeship system and, 104; elite worldview and, 142; millennials and, 157; public, in *Wealth of Nations*, 87, 109–11; Powell memo and, 123–25; in Sardinia, 63; teachers and, 67, 68

Egypt, activists and unrest in, 149, 158, 160

Emerson, Roger, on Scottish Enlightenment, 84, 84n3, 85, 88, 90, 92, 96

emotion, 47, 74–75, 120–21

empirical analysis, 22, 73

Empower America, 130, 133

engagement, 60, 64, 65

Engels, Friedrich, 56, 196; *Communist Manifesto*, 195; on history, 21, 22; letter to Bloch, 20, 35

England, 87, 196; hegemony of, 93–94, 115–16; Scotland and, 85–86, 92

English language, 43–44; translation of Gramsci's writings into, 5, 7; Hume and, 93, 96; educated Scots and, 92–93; Adam Smith and, 96

Enlightenment: *Encyclopédie* (Diderot) and, 89; in Europe, 84; learned societies and, 87, 89; in Scotland, 83–91, 92, 96

equality and equalitarianism, 105

equity, 104, 109, 155

Erasmus, 32

Europe, 89, 93, 103, 149, 150, 168; anthropology in, 54; *The Count of Monte Cristo* in, 71; Enlightenment in, 84, 87, 92; Grand Tour of, 98; language in, 94; patronage in, 96

experts, 34, 91, 113, 129, 131

Facebook, 158, 161

Fanon, Frantz: *Black Skin, White Masks*, 17

Farm Security Administration, 161

fascism, fascists, 4, 50

Federal Reserve, 150

feminism, feminists, 10, 61, 130

Ferguson, Adam, 84

feudalism, 40, 102, 103, 114, 115, 185, 188, 194; dissolution of, 82, 101; Adam Smith on, 106, 182

Fink, Richard, 129–30

folklore, 66, 67–69, 71

folk wisdom, 48

Food Not Bombs, 163

Ford, Edsel, 140

Ford, Henry, 140, 197

Forman-Barzilai, Fonna, 95

Formisano, Ronald, 133, 141; on Tea Party, 119, 120, 121, 136, 138, 153, 187

Foucault, Michel, 11–12, 12n4

Foster, Hal, 61

Fox News, as disseminator of right-wing narratives, 122, 133, 135, 142–44

France, 71, 92, 99, 151. *See also* French Revolution

freedom, 104; of commerce, 108; economic, 113, 114; of press, 112; in *Wealth of Nations*, 101–2, 104, 106–12. *See also* free markets; free trade; liberty

FreedomWorks, 129–30, 133, 134, 137

free markets, 182; invisible hand of, 101; narrative of, 121–22, 135, 148; as right-wing objective, 120, 126, 137

free trade, 112; Adam Smith advocates, 104, 106

French Revolution, 48, 111, 112, 174
Friedman, Milton, 121–22

Gates, Bill, 127
gay liberation movement, 155
Geertz, Clifford, 54
general assemblies (GAs), people's, 166–68, 169–71
Gentile, Giovanni, 50
George Washington University, Mercatus Center, 129, 130, 132
Germany, 122, 151, 196
Ghilarza, Sardinia, Gramsci as native of, 63
Gitlin, Todd, 150–51, 154; on OWS, 148, 154–55, 167, 171, 175, 182
Glasgow, Scotland, 84, 116; learned societies in, 88, 89, 97, 112; as port city, 88–89, 99, 111
Glasgow Literary Society, 89
Glasgow University, 86; Adam Smith and, 96, 97, 102
Global Justice Movement, 166, 170
Global South and Global North, 10, 11–12, 61
good sense (*buon senso*), 47–48, 58, 68, 182; common sense and, 48–49, 51, 55, 68, 76, 145, 186, 187, 192; OWS movement and, 147, 152–53, 175–76; specificity of, 69; subaltern, 152, 188, 189
Gorbachev, Mikhail, 174
Gould-Wartofsky, Michael A., 157, 163, 170
government, American, 155, 156, 168; corporations and, 124, 128, 134, 139, 140–41; fiscal responsibility of, 120, 126; intervention of, 148, 191; limited, 120, 126; regulation of, 124, 143; welfare and, 136–39
government responsibility, 109–10, 116
Graeber, David, 157, 158, 161, 163; general assemblies and, 166–67; on OWS protests, 159, 160; at Zuccotti Park, 167–68
Graham-Felsen, Sam, 161
Gramsci, Antonio, 3; active intellect of,
5–6; bodyguard of, 74–75; committed to overthrow capitalism, 188; education of, 8; father of, 32; health and death of, 5, 8; as journalist, 8, 33; learns Italian, 63; as man of high culture, 70–71, 74; newspaper articles of, 41; as political activist, 8, 32–33, 36, 55, 185; as progressive Marxist intellectual, 32, 36, 57, 64, 190; as materialist, 190; Sardinia homeland of, 8, 28, 32, 52, 63–66; scholarship and, 8, 9, 32; trained in linguistics and philology, 8, 20; at Turin University, 19, 32
Gramsci, Antonio, imprisonment of, 4, 5, 185; access to books during, 6–7, 8, 9; arrest, trial, and sentencing of, 5; authorities and, 5, 6; correspondence during, 7, 16, 18, 19; international protests against, 6; prison library and, 69–70, 71; study project in, 18, 23, 71, 189; surveillance during, 5, 194; visitors to, 6; wife's Moscow residency during, 7
Gramsci, Antonio, thirty-three prison notebooks of, 4, 5; "Agitation and Propaganda" note in, 194, 195; "Analysis of Situations. Relations of Force" note in, 33; anarchism in, 153; antiromanticism in, 49–52, 62; avoidance of word *class* in, 194; Benda on, 26; censorship and, 9, 14, 14n5, 15, 194; coherence vs. incoherence in, 31, 37; complete English translation of, 5; conditions of writing of, 6, 9; culture entangled with common sense in, 53; dialogical character of, 7, 8, 10; form and format of, 6, 10; "The Formation of the Intellectuals," 28; fragmentary, 8, 9; historical blocs in, 184–85; historical moment of, 10; inequality in, 194; as influence on Spivak and Subaltern Studies Group, 11, 14; language used in, 14, 15, 21; mediation of economic realities in, 184; "'Merits' of the Ruling Class" note in, 194, 195–96; nature of, 4, 6;

skepticism of, 97, 98, 102, 103, 107; as Scottish intellectual, 84, 92; Adam Smith and, 97, 99

Hutcheson, Francis, 96, 97

Hutton, James, 84

ideas and beliefs, 7–8, 19, 20–21, 188

ideologies, 16, 38, 184

improvement, as Enlightenment imperative, 87, 89–90, 115

incoherence, 68; of common sense, 31, 46, 77, 181

Independent Women's Forum (IWF), 130–32

India, 11, 12, 14

Indignados (Spanish activists), 149, 163, 166

inequality, 51; American, 178; analysis of, 16; benefits of, 150; class and, 3–4, 194; common sense and, 178–79; Great Recession and, 157–58; of income, 150–51; increasing, 149, 151; injustice of, 179; left dialogues and, 182; meritocracy and, 150; narratives of, 3, 197; Obama and, 177; as oppression, 102; ows and, 148, 153–55, 160, 176, 180; Piketty on, 3; political narratives and experience of, 59, 154, 171; Adam Smith and, 105; structural, 4, 22, 185, 194, 196, 197; as tectonic plates, 57, 197; world conceptions and, 184

inferiority, Scottish sense of, 93

infrastructure, language of, 21

Inquiry into the Nature and Causes of the Wealth of Nations, An. See Wealth of Nations

Institute for Humane Studies, 129

Institute for Justice, 129

intellectuals: dialogue and, 7; in feudal age, 34; French, 99; Gramsci as, 63, 75; hubris of, 192, 197; importance of, 26; as independent of class, 24; as individuals, 24, 26, 27–28; knowledge production and, 26, 83, 90, 122; moral duty of, 28; Mussolini and, 28; narratives

shaped by, 121; nature of, 18; universal, 23–26, 28, 34–35, 82, 192. *See also* intellectuals, Gramsci's; knowledge production and producers; organic intellectuals

intellectuals, Gramsci's, 5–6, 13, 37, 86; centrality of, 36; class and, 4, 17, 33–36; creation of coherent narratives by, 31, 124; creative spirit of the people and, 188–93; embeddedness of, 19, 82–83, 193; "The Formation of the Intellectuals," 28; function of knowledge production of, 27, 47, 131; Italian, 19, 23, 28–29, 36, 42; new types of, 88, 90–91; not defined in prison notebooks, 10, 23; organic, 13, 25–26, 27–33, 40, 41–42, 49, 58, 75–76, 77, 114, 182, 188–89, 190, 192–93, 197; organic vs. traditional, 22–23, 29, 36, 82–83, 122, 152, 189; philosophy and, 46, 147, 188, 189; relationship between common people and, 36–38, 39, 40–41, 180; social role of, 26–27; specificity in time and place of, 35; subalterns and, 55; theorization of role of, 18, 23; traditional, 34, 36, 42, 91, 122, 191. *See also* intellectuals; knowledge production and producers; organic intellectuals

Internet: liberal pressure groups, 134; ows and, 158, 160, 161, 168, 169, 176; Tea Party and, 133, 142; virtual globalized world and, 149–50

"invisible hand," 101

Iran, inequality in, 151

Italian Communist Party, 6, 21; Gramsci and, 5, 33

Italian language, 62, 63, 64–66

Italy: first publication of Gramsci's notebooks in, 5; Left in, 33; peasantry of, 29; political parties of, 195; Popular Universities in, 36, 38; southern, 28; unification of, 62

Ives, Peter, *Gramsci's Politics of Language*, 63

National Empowerment Television, 131
National Public Radio, 135
natural laws, 21
nature of reality, 35
Navigation Acts, 111
neoliberalism, 179
Newfield, Jack: "A Populist Manifesto," 123
newspapers and periodicals, 195; Gramsci and, 7, 41, 69; *Il Grido del Popolo*, 41; *La Giustizia*, 41; letters to the editors of, 66, 75, 186; *L'Ordine Nuovo*, 41; *Mother Jones*, 166; *New Yorker*, 127–28, 132, 139, 154; *New York Times*, 45, 135, 137, 143, 151, 157, 158, 178; traces of subaltern conceptions of reality in, 66, 75; *Quarterly Review*, 88; *Vanity Fair*, 160, 163; *Wall Street Journal*, 135; *Washington Post*, 161
New York City, 158, 170, 178
Nicodemi, Dario, plays of, 70, 70n3
"99 percent," 176, 183; as commonsense term, 148, 153; identity of, 161–62, 163; Obama uses rhetoric of, 177; 1 percent vs., 163, 178–79; protest signs of, 171–73; subalternity of, 162. *See also* "We are the 99 percent!"
Nurra, Pietro: *La Lectura*, 75

Obama, Barack, 154, 175, 176; administration of, 119, 120; Affordable Health Care Act, 135, 144; speeches of, 135, 177; stimulus bill of, 133, 134; suggests taxing rich, 153–54
Occupy Wall Street (ows) movement, 146n1, 155, 160, 168, 171, 176; activists in, 156, 160–61; as challenge to capitalist hegemony, 117, 147, 152, 187; changes the conversation, 176–79; Chris, 161, 163; common sense of, 146–47, 152, 153, 169, 175, 178, 179; as cultural battle, 147–48; general assemblies and, 166–68, 169–70, 171; good sense of, 175–76; #occupywallstreet, 160, 169; historical moment of, 183; on inequality, 148, 153, 180; intellectuals

and, 190–91; marginalized people and, 170; millennials in, 156–57; New York City and, 150, 158, 170, 178; precursors to, 157–60; Sanders's rhetoric and, 179; slogans and signs of, 158, 164–65, 168, 171–75, 186–87; on social media, 159–62; Tea Party vs., 155, 179; youthfulness of, 157; world conception of, 187; Zuccotti Park occupation and, 153, 154, 157, 169–71, 176, 181, 182. *See also* "We are the 99 percent!"
"1 percent," 148, 150–51, 162, 177, 178–79, 183
opera, 73–74
oppression and exploitation, 16, 20
Oreskes, Naomi, 128
organic intellectuals, 13, 25–26, 27–33, 49, 58, 75–76, 77, 114, 182, 188, 190, 197; of bourgeoisie, 81, 82–83; class cohesion and, 40, 198; as collective, 41; creation of, 33; definition of, 20; distinction between conjunctural and, 22; functions of, 30–33, 36, 197; Gramsci as, 33; ows and, 190–91; Said and, 23–24; Adam Smith as, 83, 95; traditional vs., 22–23, 29, 36, 82–83, 122, 152, 189; in twenty-first century, 192, 193
Organization for Economic Cooperation and Development, 150
Osawatomie, Kansas, Obama speech at, 177
Oswald, James, 96, 97
Oxford English Dictionary (oed), 20, 44, 86–87, 88
Oxford University, Adam Smith at, 87, 93, 96, 97

Parks, Rosa, 133, 133n10
parliament: English, 85, 85n5, 93, 97, 103, 113; Italian, 5; Scottish, 85, 93
Pascarella, Cesare: *La scoperta de l'America*, 69, 69n1
Pasolini, Pier Paolo, 63
patronage, 96–97
Paul, Ron, 45

Protestant Reformation, 32, 68
public lectures, 96; by Adam Smith, 97–98, 100
Putnam, Robert, 151–52

Quesnay, François, 91, 99
Quinn, Christine, 178
Quisisana clinic, Gramsci at, 5

race: American Dream and, 151–52; inequalities of, 194
radio, 23, 122, 135, 143
Rakovich, Mary, 134–35
Reagan, Ronald, 147, 174; administration of, 126, 141–43; "revolution" of, 122, 124, 147, 152
reality, 52, 55, 57, 58, 180; common sense and, 44–45; conceptions of, 30, 66, 115; economic, 149, 157, 162, 175; lived, 36, 58, 148, 197; new, 86, 183
reason, 47, 65, 77, 110, 112
reductionism, 4, 38
Reich, Charles, 123, 124n2
Reid, Thomas, 84
Reisman, George, 31
Reith Lectures (Said, 1993), 23–25, 24n2
religion, 73, 86, 194; skepticism of, 97, 98, 102, 107; *Wealth of Nations* and, 107
Remnick, David, 154
Rendall, Steve, 143
Republican Party, 134, 139, 141; Tea Party and, 119, 132, 135, 179. *See also* Tea Party
Right, 175, 187; American, 31, 121–22, 124, 126–32, 137, 139–40, 145; new, 95, 103
Robertson, William, 84
Rockefeller, John D., Jr., 140
romanticism, 70
Romney, Mitt, 136, 138
Roosevelt, Franklin D., 177; New Deal of, 121, 124, 140–41, 147
Rosenfeld, Sophia: on Arendt, 49; *Common Sense*, 43; on common sense, 45, 48
Rosengarten, Frank, 7, 46n3
Ross, Ian Simpson, 95, 107

Rothschild, Emma, 101, 106, 112, 114; *Economic Settlements*, 95, 101; on Adam Smith, 83, 103, 113, 193
Rubieri, Ermolao, 72–73
Runciman, David, 175–76
Ryan, Paul, 137, 138, 139, 153

Sagri, Georgia, 168
Said, Edward, 28; on Gramsci's view of intellectuals, 33, 189; *Representations of the Intellectual*, 23–26; on universal intellectuals, 34–35, 192
Sanders, Bernie, 179
Santa Lussurgiu, Gramsci attends school at, 63
Santelli, Rick, 133–34
Sardinia: Gramsci's childhood among peasants of, 8, 28, 32, 52, 63; language of, 63, 64–66
Schneider, Nathan, 161, 170–71, 180
scholarship, 86, 91, 99; Gramsci and, 8, 9, 32
Schulman, Bruce, 139
Schucht, Tatiana: Gramsci's letters to, 7, 8–9, 18, 19, 23, 36, 42, 69–70, 71, 74–75, 189; prison notebooks and, 7; supports Gramsci in prison, 6
Schumer, Charles, 178
science, scientists, 88, 90–91, 114
Science of Man, 83–91, 85, 97, 100; Act of Union and, 86, 94
Scotland, 90, 92, 100, 101, 112; under English hegemony, 84, 85–86, 92, 94, 115–16; Enlightenment in, 83–91, 92, 96; learned societies in, 87–91, 115; poverty of, 84–85, 86, 92; Scottish accent and, 92–93. *See also* Scottish intellectuals
Scott, James, 29, 59, 60; *Domination and the Arts of Resistance*, 10–11, 13; on hidden transcripts, 13, 30
Scottish intellectuals, 84, 85, 92, 116; emerging bourgeoisie and, 90–91; Adam Smith as, 83, 92, 115; subalternity of, 84, 85–86, 92, 94

Seeger, Pete, 178
Select Society (Edinburgh), 88, 90, 96
semplici, 116. *See also* "simple, the"
senso comune, 3, 8, 31, 42, 118, 186; translation of, 43–44. *See also* common sense
sentimentality, Gramsci and, 74
serial novels: *The Count of Monte Cristo*, 71; Gramsci on, 71–73, 74; as popular literature, 69–70; traces of subaltern conceptions of reality in, 66
settlement law, 105–6
sexual orientation, inequalities of, 194
Shakespeare, William: Gramsci's taste for, 70–71
Shapin, Steven, 91
Sherlock Holmes, 72
Sherman, Cindy: *Untitled Film Stills*, 61
Sierra Leone, 178
"simple, the" (*semplici*): common people as, 8n1, 116, 189
Skinner, A. S., 102, 107, 111
Skocpol, Theda, 135–37, 144, 149, 187; on origin of Tea Party, 119–21, 132, 142; *The Tea Party and the Remaking of Republican Conservatism*, 120; on Tea Party worldview, 138, 141–42
slaves, as subalterns, 185
Smith, Adam, 83, 95, 103, 112, 113, 145; Buccleuch and, 98–99, 100; criticizes Oxford University, 87; death of, 100, 112; on dependency, 102; as economist, 116; Edinburgh lectures of, 97–98, 100; education of, 96; English language skills of, 96; family of, 96; Glasgow and, 89, 116; intellectual formation of, 95–100; as member of learned societies, 88, 89, 97; "opulence for all" of, 114, 152, 182, 185; as organic bourgeois intellectual, 114–17, 152, 182, 193; as professor, 87, 102; religious beliefs of, 107; as Scottish Enlightenment intellectual, 83, 84, 92, 94, 95–100, 115. See also *Theory of Moral Sentiments, The*; *Wealth of Nations*

Smith, Geoffrey Nowell, 46n3; *Selections from the Prison Notebooks*, 5, 70
Snell, K. D. M., 111
social change, fundamental, 36, 40, 55, 58. *See also* social transformation
social classes and groups, 8, 26, 30, 33, 47; subalternity and, 147, 196. *See also* "class" entries
social media, 158, 161, 162–63, 169, 171, 175
social movements, 149, 155, 186
Socialist Party, Gramsci as member of, 33
social relations: ensemble of, 60, 83, 115, 189, 190, 197; knowledge production and, 41–42
social structure, 30, 69
social transformation, 48; as Gramsci's goal, 13, 53; historical blocs and, 76, 194; requires new conception of world, 42, 52–53, 66. *See also* social change, fundamental
Society of Improvers in the Knowledge of Agriculture in Scotland (Edinburgh), 90
Soviet Union, 15
Spain, 149, 168, 169
specificity, Gramsci on, 197
Spivak, Gayatri, 70; "Can the Subaltern Speak?," 11, 11n3, 12; quotes Foucault, 12, 12n4; Scott vs., 59–60; Subaltern Studies Group and, 14; *Subaltern Studies Reader* and, 10; on subaltern voices, 11–12, 13–14, 59
Sraffa, Piero, 6–7
state, 16, 27, 195–96
Statute of Artificers, 103
Stewart, Dugald, 84, 113
Stewart, Potter, 45
Stiglitz, Joseph, 151, 163, 181; *The Price of Inequality*, 160
Street, Paul: *Crashing the Tea Party*, 120
subaltern, subalterns, 52; challenge hegemonic narratives, 40, 76–77; emotional landscapes of, 75; as euphemism for proletariat, 14n6, 14–15; folklore and, 68; hidden transcript of, 13, 30;

subaltern, (*continued*)

    identity of, 14–17; inchoate knowledge of, 42, 75–77, 188; intellectuals and, 39, 49, 55, 71, 76–77; narratives of, 66, 185; rise to hegemony of, 36; Scottish speakers of English as, 94; slow struggle of, 56; study of, 10–11; subordination and, 185; as term, 11, 14; women as, 12, 61; worldviews of, 71, 181

subalternity, 3–17; defining characteristics of, 61; Guha on, 11, 14, 70; of Italian peasants, 191; of Scots, 84, 85–86, 92, 94, 115–16; in United States, 170

subalternity, Gramsci's, 10, 182; archive of conceptions of, 66, 67–75, 163, 186; as articulated by subalterns, 10, 13, 76; collective experiences of, 40, 185–86; common sense and, 58, 62, 71, 75–77, 185–88; conception of class and, 4; culture of subordination and, 55; dominated vs. dominant in, 69; fundamental class emerging from, 33; good sense and, 185–88; hegemony and, 76, 147, 148; incoherence and, 46; internalization of, 16–17; of industrial proletariat, 29; language and, 62–66; mechanical determinism and, 15–16; muting and, 12–13; new political narratives and, 49, 66; overcoming, 55; particularity of, 16, 71–72; popular culture and, 72–73; shared world concepts of, 70; social groups and, 196; subalterns always in plural, 16; Subaltern Studies Group and, 14; as totality, 15; undefined in prison notebooks, 10, 15

Subaltern Studies Group, 11, 14; *Subaltern Studies* journal and, 10, 14

subaltern voices, 10–14, 59–62; as collective, 11, 40, 59–60; individual, 11

subjectivity, 60, 61

subordination, subordinated: agency of, 11; critique of power by, 13; diversity of, 71–72; internalized, 17; types of, 16, 196. *See also* "subaltern" entries

Sue, Eugène, 69, 70

Sweden, 151

Switzerland, 92, 99

Sydnor, Eugene, Jr., Powell memo and, 122, 125–26

Syria, unrest in, 149

talents, in *Wealth of Nations*, 105

Tatiana. *See* Schucht, Tatiana

Tea Party, 45, 118–45; activists of, 134–35, 137; authenticity of, 120, 136, 187; common sense of, 117, 137, 139, 145; corporations and, 120, 134, 139; demographics of, 135–36; feelings of, 120–21, 136, 139, 142; grassroots of, 120, 132, 134–35, 187; intellectuals of, 121–22, 131, 190–91; libertarians and, 132, 136; makers and takers worldview of, 136–39, 141–42; media of, 122, 135, 142–44; objectives of, 120, 126, 137, 142, 145; origins of, 119–35; ows vs., 155, 179; Patriots of, 120, 134, 139, 148; populism of, 120; racism and, 139, 142, 152; worldview of, 138, 139, 141, 145

technology: communication and, 149–50; division of labor and, 107; social media, 158, 161, 162–63, 169, 171, 175. *See also* Internet

Theory of Moral Sentiments, The (Adam Smith), 100, 107, 110; success of, 97, 98, 99

Thomas, Peter, 16, 21n1, 38

Tolstoy, Leo, Gramsci's taste for, 70–71

Tomasky, Michael, 150

totalitarianism, 49, 50

Townsend, Charles, 98

Träger (bearers), of knowledge, 192, 192n1

trauma, of Scottish subalternity, 85, 92, 94

truisms, 51; unexamined, 52

truths: common sense and, 45, 49, 50–51; self-evident, 3, 43, 44, 46, 47

Tumblr, ows and, 161, 162–63, 171, 175

Tunisia, unrest in, 149

Turin, Gramsci as labor organizer in, 33, 41

Turin University, Gramsci at, 8, 19, 32, 63

Wittgenstein, Ludwig, 47

Wolin, Richard, 4

woman, women: common, 71; education and, 110; in folklore, 67; in French Revolution, 48; as grassroot activists, 135–36; imposed roles of, 61; in India, 12; inequality and, 194; as intellectuals, 34; IWF and, 130–32; as marginalized, 170; movement of, 155; as subalterns, 12, 15, 52, 61, 67, 185; as welfare queens, 142

Wordsworth, William, 112

Workers World Party, 167

working class, 33, 41; workers and, 26, 41, 103–4. *See also* proletariat

world conceptions, 21, 22, 40, 73n5, 147, 182; commercial literature and, 73; folklore and, 68; historical blocs and, 184–85, 188; inchoate, 76; knowledge as, 189; new, 42, 66, 188; OWS and, 187; shared subaltern, 70, 181

worldviews, 40, 64, 71, 136, 138, 144; capitalist, 145, 191; class and, 30, 35, 82, 101, 119, 142

World War I, 74, 140

World War II, 121

Zernike, Kate, 134, 139

Zuccotti Park, 174, 176, 180; occupation of, 153, 154, 157, 158, 167–71, 176, 181, 182; stormed by police, 170, 181